CW00546207

Waverley Route

The battle for the Borders Railway

DAVID SPAVEN

ARGYLL ✠ PUBLISHING

First published by Argyll Publishing in 2012.

This edition is published by Argyll Publishing, an imprint of Capercaillie Books Ltd in 2015. Registered Office 1 Rutland Court, Edinburgh EH3 8EY

The moral rights of the author have been asserted.
A catalogue record of this book is available from the British Library

ISBN 978-1-908931-82-5

Printed by Bell & Bain Ltd, Glasgow

ABOUT THE AUTHOR

David Spaven is a rail consultant and author by profession. A railway enthusiast since childhood, and a geographer by training, he has spent his working life in and around the rail industry.

DEDICATIONS

This book is personally dedicated to two individuals who have had a big influence on my life.

My late father Frank Spaven first introduced me to the delights of the Waverley Route in 1961, at magical Riccarton Junction, and in subsequent years – with a strong push from my mother Sheila, a great enthusiast for the rugby 'sevens' – in Melrose. Little did I appreciate at the time just how hard Frank was working behind the scenes in the mid-1960s – in his civil service role at the Scottish Office – to make the planning and economic development case for retaining and developing the threatened railway between Edinburgh and the Borders. He would have been thrilled to know that I was to write a book about this much-loved railway and that a number of his classic railway photos would feature in it.

One of the great ironies of my life is that if the Waverley Route had *not* closed then I would never have met my step-daughter Heide, whose mother – Petra Biberbach – was the driving force and inspirational first Chair of the Campaign for Borders Rail from 1999 to 2002. I have spent most of my adult life missing the Waverley Route, but not half as much as I would have missed Heide.

And also to the stalwarts of the 1968 Borders rail campaign, Madge Elliot and the late Reverend Brydon Maben.

David Spaven
April 2015

'Even a confident community like the Borders was unable to stop London closing down its railway. It was a major Scottish asset, this scenic route south from Edinburgh by Melrose and Hawick, Teviotdale and Liddesdale, past Newcastleton and Hermitage where the roads don't go, across the 'debatable land' to Carlisle. It was called the Waverley route. Where you can see its track it looks like another derelict Roman road, a line of communication withdrawn. It was for a century a unifying force, integrating the community. The decision to shut it down was initiated by experts ignorant of all save the economic consequences of their deeds and often even of these. The rape of the Waverley route is one more argument for taking power out of the hands of the elite and giving it to the people.'

R.F. Mackenzie, *A Search for Scotland* (1989)

'From September 2015, the Borders Railway will re-establish passenger railway services, for the first time since 1969, between Edinburgh, Midlothian and the Scottish Borders.

'On its launch, the line will be transformational in opening up communities as new places to live, work, visit, learn, play and grow. It will be a catalyst for new opportunities – whether for housing developments, businesses or as visitor destinations.

'The project will enhance the Midlothian and Scottish Borders economies and deliver prosperity to those areas by providing opportunities all along the line both for existing and new businesses, ensuring that the economy in the region will thrive.'

Alex Salmond MSP, First Minister,
Borders Railway – Maximising the Impact:
A Blueprint for the Future
November 2014

Contents

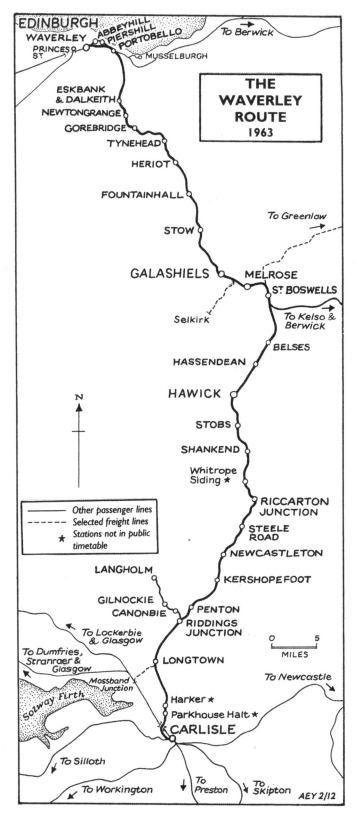

THE
WAVERLEY
ROUTE
1963

EDINBURGH

WAVERLEY
PRINCES ST.
ABBEYHILL
PIERSHILL
PORTOBELLO
MUSSELBURGH
To Berwick

ESKBANK & DALKEITH
NEWTONGRANGE
GOREBRIDGE
TYNEHEAD
HERIOT
FOUNTAINHALL
STOW
GALASHIELS
MELROSE
To Greenlaw
St BOSWELLS
Selkirk
To Kelso & Berwick
BELSES
HASSENDEAN
HAWICK
STOBS
SHANKEND
Whitrope Siding ★
RICCARTON JUNCTION
STEELE ROAD
NEWCASTLETON
KERSHOPEFOOT
LANGHOLM
GILNOCKIE
CANONBIE
PENTON
RIDDINGS JUNCTION
To Lockerbie & Glasgow
LONGTOWN
To Dumfries, Stranraer & Glasgow
Mossband Junction
To Newcastle
Harker ★
Parkhouse Halt ★
Solway Firth
CARLISLE
To Silloth
To Workington
To Preston
To Skipton

N

Other passenger lines
— — — Selected freight lines
★ Stations not in public timetable

0   5
MILES

AEY 2/12

Alan Young

Introduction

KNOWN throughout its history as 'the Waverley Route', the double-track main-line railway from Edinburgh through the Borders to Carlisle – a distance of 98¼ miles – had a working life of 107 years. Its role as an important Anglo-Scottish carrier of passengers and freight came to an abrupt end on 6th January 1969, as probably the most undeserving victim of the infamous 'Beeching Axe'. The untimely demise of the railway subsequently became a source of fascination for railway enthusiasts, historians – and generations of Borderers who rued the area's unwanted status as the only region of Britain without a rail service.

Now, in one of the most remarkable reversals of fortune in British railway history, just over a third of the line re-opens in September 2015 as the Borders Railway, reconnecting Edinburgh, Galashiels and Tweedbank by train. The 30½ miles from Newcraighall in south east Edinburgh through Midlothian to a terminus at the heart of the Central Borders represent the longest new railway

Marking the occasion of the 14th March 2005 announcement of Scottish Executive funding for the new railway, local and national politicians pose with 'heritage' mocked-up station signs – from left, Councillor David Parker, Leader of Scottish Borders Council; Jeremy Purvis MSP; Nicol Stephen MSP, Transport Minister; and Councillor Gordon Edgar of Scottish Borders Council.

Alastair Watson, courtesy of the Southern Reporter

to be built in Scotland since 1901 (the Fort William–Mallaign line), and the longest new domestic railway anywhere in Britain for more than a century. The story of this transformation says much about the politics of Britain's railways in the 1960s, the opportunities created by devolution of power to put right one of the great wrongs of the old model of London-based transport policy – and the power of grassroots campaigning.

This revised and updated edition of the hardback book, originally published in 2012 as *Waverley Route: the life, death and rebirth of the Borders Railway*, incorporates a range of fresh material, notably:

- an update on the construction of the new railway between 2012 and 2015 and the parallel political controversies about the line's infrastructure specification (in Chapters 10 and 11)
- new insider insights into the political tensions – and the stand-off between the railway promoter and campaigners – in the years leading up to the authorisation of the Borders Railway by the Scottish Parliament in 2006 and thereafter (in Chapters 9 and 10)
- newly-unearthed archive material from the late 1960s, shedding further light on the flawed political processes which led to the closure of the Waverley Route in 1969 (in Chapters 3 and 4)
- new research revealing details of the locomotives which have survived from the final days of Waverley Route operation in January 1969 (in Chapter 5)
- a revised and expanded selection of photographs (two thirds of which are new to this edition) and an exclusive map of the Borders Railway infrastructure, to illustrate the contrasting fortunes of the late 1960s' Waverley Route and the new line which puts the Borders and Midlothian back on the railway map in 2015.

Motivation

Having travelled on the line a couple of dozen times as a child in the 1960s, and then being involved in the campaign to re-open the railway since the early 1990s, a key motivation for writing this book was my view that there were two particularly intriguing aspects of the line's history which had not yet been fully written up. The first was the period of the line's demise, from the 1963 Beeching Report through to final closure in 1969, the abortive Border Union Railway Company (BURCo) bid to re-open the railway, and the protracted track-lifting phase concluding in 1972. The subsequent period – with the line essentially forgotten for twenty years, and then a variety of initiatives and campaigns leading up to the re-opening to Galashiels and Tweedbank in 2015 – had also never been critically examined.

Integrated public transport, but not for much longer – the Norman Fox bus replacing the Borders Counties trains, withdrawn in 1956, waits to depart from Steele Road station yard in Spring 1966. In the background what is thought to be the 09.20 Carlisle-Edinburgh stopping train (hauled by an unidentified BR&CW Type 2) climbs the 1 in 75 gradient around the slopes of Arnton Fell. The replacement buses to Kielder and Bellingham ran only twice daily on just two days a week – and as in the case of many rail closures, the loss of trains was eventually followed by the loss of all public transport.

The late Frank Spaven

While I touch on a number of aspects of rail operations (including specific trains and locomotives which played a central role in key episodes in the line's final years), this is firmly in the context of a history written from a business, political and social perspective. My aim has been to understand – not least through extensive research of Government files released under the '30 year rule' – firstly why the line was closed (and what wider lessons can be learnt about the Borders and the politics of the time), and secondly how it came about that the longest stretch of re-opened railway in British history will become a reality in September 2015.

Sources and acknowledgements

My sources over a period of more than two and a half years of research include not only material from the National Records of Scotland (formerly the National Archives of Scotland) in Edinburgh and the National Archives in Kew, but also local and national newspaper coverage surrounding key events, as well as private archives incorporating a unique collection of railway documents which had never before been publically reviewed and quoted. Amongst these are British Rail (BR) management's list of all the jobs to be axed following closure of the line; the final Hawick South signal box train register (courtesy of Ian Bell); and the BR Area Manager's official account of the events of 5th / 6th January 1969 at Hawick and Newcastleton (courtesy of Bruce McCartney). Archive research also revealed that my father, the late Frank Spaven, had played a bigger role in behind-the-scenes debates about the railway's fate than even I or my family realised, during his time as a civil servant at the Scottish Office in the mid-1960s.

During 2014 I was privileged to gain access (courtesy of Alan Bailey, formerly of Borders Transport Futures) to the personal archive of the late Baroness Elliot of Harwood, who led the November 1968 House of Lords debate on the fate of the Waverley Route; I also benefitted from additional thoughts from Lord Steel of Aikwood, who as David Steel MP was one of the key campaigners against closure.

Two former BR managers whose work involved the Waverley Route provided me with particularly valuable insights into the business and management of the line in the 1960s – Rae Montgomery, who in his own words 'was (reluctantly) a member of BR staff obliged to dig out statistical and financial information in 1962 to justify the line's presumed closure'; and Douglas Paul, who spent eight weeks management training with the first Area Manager Hawick in winter 1965–66, and in 1970 undertook an MBA dissertation on *Redundancy and Manpower Policy on British Rail* which included analysis of the impact of closure of the Waverley Route. Rae also assiduously checked the manuscripts of both the 2012 and 2015 editions and provided numerous insightful comments and corrections on both railway history and grammar. Any remaining mistakes and

'Jubilee' No. 45716 *Swiftsure* is about to restart its Carlisle Canal to Niddrie Class 'E' express freight on 18th September 1958, after the obligatory Hawick stop for water and crew changeover. Note the window-level screens on the South signal box (confusingly located at the north end of the station), designed to reduce glare and reflections.
The late Robin Barbour, courtesy of Bruce McCartney

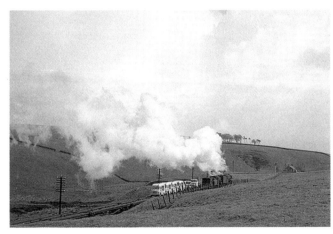

This striking view from 18th May 1963 shows A3 Pacific No.60087 *Blenheim* and Class 4 2–6–0 No. 43011 near Falahill Summit, hauling a southbound 'car train' of new ice cream vans and trucks from the Bathgate BMC plant.
Rae Montgomery

omissions are, of course, my own responsibility, and I will be pleased to be advised of these either via my publisher or my website, www.deltix.co.uk.

During research for the original edition of the book, I discussed the demise of the railway with key players of the time, including the inveterate local campaigner Madge Elliot; the late Professor John Hibbs, who in 1969 produced a well-regarded report for David Steel on the scope to save the condemned line north of Hawick; Roy Perkins, a Director of BURCo (including unlimited access to his extensive personal archive); the late Bob Symes-Schutzmann, another Director of BURCo; and my own contemporaries and colleagues – both in and around the rail industry, and those who have been life-long supporters of the railway. They may have been very young adults or – like me – callow youths at the time of closure, but nevertheless played an important part in the belated campaign against closure or were enthusiastic travellers on the Waverley Route.

A classic location for Waverley Route photography, perhaps particularly associated with the renowned Derek Cross. V2 No. 60933 hauls a southbound goods over the final 1 in 100 towards Falahill Summit on 25th May 1962.
The late Derek Cross, courtesy of David Cross

As 'Black 5' No. 44884 battles towards Falahill Summit with the 3.35 pm Millerhill-Kingmoor freight on 18th May 1963, the classic lines of Tynehead signal box and an interesting optical illusion are well illustrated. Whilst the station siding appears to be steeply inclined, it is in fact almost level, whereas the main line is rising at 1 in 70! *Rae Montgomery*

In this respect I must express my great thanks to Andrew Boyd, Bill Jamieson, the late Neil Macdonald, Bruce McCartney, Allan McLean, Roy Perkins, David Prescott and John Yellowlees for our highly fruitful collective analysis of the demise of the railway. Bill and Bruce had a particularly crucial role in the genesis of the book and both provided invaluable photographic inputs, complementing the work of other fine railway photographers showcased in this volume. Bill and I first met at Edinburgh University less than two years after the Waverley Route closed, and following a gap of more than 25 years our paths then crossed again in the early years of the rail re-opening campaign. It should be recorded that his has been the most consistent, dogged and dedicated presence in the campaign for rail re-opening throughout that long period from the mid-1990s to the present day. More prosaically – but crucially for this book – he also checked the manuscripts of both the 2012 and 2015 editions.

A central aspect of my research was several fruitful discussions with Simon Longland, the inspiration for the Borders Transport Futures rail initiative in the mid-1990s, to refresh my recollections of those heady days. If there is one individual who has been key to the re-opening of the railway, it is Simon.

Special mention has to go to Bernard Lamb, an 'amateur' archive researcher based in London. In 2010 I was getting tantalisingly close to the final explanation of how and why the closure was approved by Government in 1968 when I had the great good fortune to be introduced to Bernard by Bruce McCartney. The National Records of Scotland had revealed much of the debate between the 'doves' of the Scottish Office and the 'hawks' in the Ministry of Transport to within days of the final decision on closure, but it was Bernard's assiduous research at the National Archives at Kew which unearthed the Minutes of the crucial Ministerial Committee meetings in London which sealed the line's fate. These were the critical last pieces in the jigsaw.

On the afternoon of 6th November 1961, Kingmoor-based 'Black 5' No. 45330 drifts into Riccarton Junction with an Up freight conveying only a few wagons (perhaps reflecting the fact that it was a Monday).
The late Frank Spaven

Finally, I have my own recollections of travels on the line – a long time ago now, but never to be forgotten. All the eye witness accounts, and the wealth of archive material I have been able to unearth, have allowed me to write – where it adds to the story – a 'blow-by-blow' description and analysis of events as they unfolded.

My research on the re-opening of the northern third of the railway benefited from lengthy discussions with Douglas Muir of Midlothian Council – who has been a key official throughout the 15-year period since the rail re-opening project secured local authority backing – and with Keith Wallace of consultants Scott Wilson, who played a central role in various studies and designs for the new railway from 1999 onwards. While we continue to disagree about some aspects of the project, I think it is fair to say that if this kind of constructive dialogue with campaigners had been facilitated and encouraged by the Scottish Executive and the Waverley Railway Partnership back in the early 2000s, then we might now be looking forward – to quote the slogan of the Campaign for Borders Rail – to 'the best possible Borders Railway', and at least some of the criticisms the project has attracted would have been avoided.

In early 2015 I was privileged to gain further insight into the politics of the long re-opening saga from Councillor David Parker, Leader of Scottish Borders Council – David has been a doughty proponent of the new railway for more than a decade and has had to steer a delicate path through competing pressures on all sides of the railway debate.

In praise of campaigners

The second part of this book – covering the period from 1992 onwards – has been written unashamedly from the perspective of the great collection of (usually unsung, and always unpaid) groups and individuals campaigning for the reinstatement of the railway. The 'official' perspective – of the Waverley Railway Partnership and its consultants, the local authorities and the Scottish Executive (later, Government) – has received extensive coverage through its own reports, publications, press releases, websites, and (not always sympathetic!) media coverage, reflecting in part the extent to which money and power control how we, the public, receive information.

There is always a danger that the establishment will rewrite history, by design or default, and from the very start I was determined to ensure that posterity records that the official rail re-opening project – led initially by Scottish Borders Council and more recently Transport Scotland – could only have happened with, firstly, the foresight of Simon Longland and Borders Transport Futures in the mid-1990s, and secondly the determination of the grassroots movement led by the Campaign for Borders Rail and its first Chair, Petra Biberbach, in the late 1990s and early 2000s.

The first part of the story of the Waverley Route since 1963 is one of loss and injustice, while the lengthy concluding episode from the early 1990s to the present day has seen inspiration and remarkable perseverance. And like all the best stories, it has a (relatively) happy ending.

David Spaven
Edinburgh, April 2015

CHAPTER 1

The first century

THE 98¼-mile railway from Edinburgh to Carlisle via Galashiels and Hawick had rich historical and romantic associations throughout its 107-year life – and has attracted possibly even fonder affection since its unfortunate end in 1969. While *Waverley Route: the battle for the Borders Railway* focuses overwhelmingly on the period from the 1963 Beeching Report onwards, the story of the railway's closure can best be understood by exploring key events and factors in its earlier life which turned an important Anglo-Scottish passenger trunk route of the Victorian and Edwardian eras into a candidate for complete closure in modern times.

Early years

The origins of the Waverley Route lay, as AJ Mullay records in *Rails Across the Border* (1990), in the North British Railway's 1844 instruction to their engineer, John Miller, 'to make a flying survey of the Country and to report as to the expediency of extending the Dalkeith Line to the South'. The Edinburgh and Dalkeith Railway – one of Scotland's first – had opened throughout from its St Leonard's terminus in Edinburgh in 1831, its primary purpose being movement of coal from Midlothian to the capital.

The North British Railway's double-track line from Edinburgh Waverley to Hawick via Dalhousie (north of the later Newtongrange station), Gorebridge and Galashiels was opened to traffic in 1849, and over the subsequent decade a variety of rival schemes for a line southwards from Hawick to Carlisle were debated. Richard Hodgson, the NBR's Chairman from 1855 (and MP for Northumberland), evidently had ambitions in two directions which would both be served by a route via Liddesdale and Newcastleton – access to the Plashetts coalfield (and to Newcastle via Hexham, thereby largely avoiding use of the tracks of its North Eastern Railway rival) over the Border Counties Railway which was being planned to strike north from Hexham, and to Silloth on the Solway Coast where a packet port for Ireland and Liverpool traffic was envisaged.

The NBR's Liddesdale scheme – entitled the Border Union Railway – succeeded in Parliament in 1859, ahead of a rival Caledonian Railway proposal for a single-track branch line from Carlisle over a somewhat more populous route to Hawick via Langholm. Wild weather in exposed territory delayed the progress

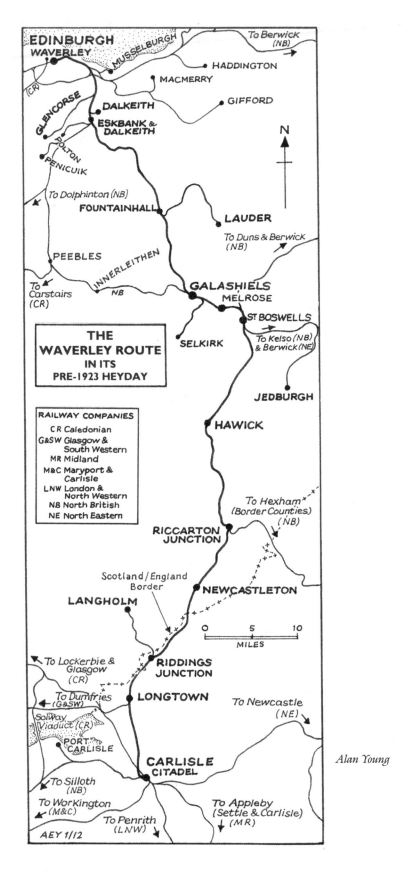

EDINBURGH
WAVERLEY
MUSSELBURGH
To Berwick
(NB)
(CR)
HADDINGTON
MACMERRY
GLENCORSE
DALKEITH
GIFFORD
ESKBANK &
DALKEITH
POLTON
PENICUIK
To Dolphinton (NB)
FOUNTAINHALL
LAUDER
To Duns & Berwick
(NB)
PEEBLES
INNERLEITHEN
GALASHIELS
NB
MELROSE
To
Carstairs
(CR)
St BOSWELLS
SELKIRK
To Kelso (NB)
& Berwick (NE)

**THE
WAVERLEY ROUTE**
IN ITS
PRE-1923 HEYDAY

JEDBURGH

HAWICK

RAILWAY COMPANIES
CR Caledonian
G&SW Glasgow &
     South Western
MR Midland
M&C Maryport &
     Carlisle
LNW London &
     North Western
NB North British
NE North Eastern

To Hexham
(Border Counties)
(NB)

RICCARTON
JUNCTION

N

Scotland/England
Border

NEWCASTLETON

LANGHOLM

0   5   10
MILES

To Lockerbie &
Glasgow
(CR)

RIDDINGS
JUNCTION

To Dumfries
(G&SW)

LONGTOWN

To Newcastle
(NE)

Solway
Viaduct (CR)

PORT.
CARLISLE

CARLISLE
CITADEL

To Silloth
(NB)

To Workington
(M&C)

To Appleby
(Settle & Carlisle)
(MR)

To Penrith
(LNW)

AEY 1/12

Alan Young

of construction, but the line was opened for business in mid-1862 – all double-track apart from the very sparsely trafficked section from Riccarton (the junction for the Border Counties line, opened the same year) to Riddings (the eventual junction for the Langholm branch). The enthusiastic citizens of 1850s' Hawick could not be expected to foresee that the chosen route to Carlisle through the 'Debatable Lands' – which in past times had been the scenes of much cross-border conflict – would ultimately contribute to its demise 110 years later.

Ironically, the Caledonian's Carlisle-Hawick scheme, if it had come to fruition, might have resulted in a completely different outcome, at least for the original line north of Hawick. As a 'spoiler' branch line – with a proposed Hawick terminus located a good half-mile from that of the NBR and a connecting line between the two presumably intended only for the interchange of goods traffic – it is difficult to imagine that the Caledonian proposal would ever have generated more than a modest passenger traffic, readily catered for by a sparse service. In such circumstances, one can easily envisage complete closure between Hawick and Langholm during the 1950s, leaving Hawick-Edinburgh unburdened by any main-line pretensions. However, the best of all worlds might have been realised if the NBR had opted for a Langholm routeing engineered to main-line standards. As Borders rail campaigner Bill Jamieson reflected in 2012:

A Langholm variant Waverley Route would have involved a slightly shorter mileage than via Liddesdale and, far more importantly, much less severe curvature,

NBR 4-4-2 Atlantic No. 906 stands at Carlisle station on 31st July 1912 at the head of a St Pancras-Edinburgh express – the heyday of Anglo-Scottish passenger operations on the Waverley Route
LCGB Ken Nunn Collection

An early postcard showing military activity at Stobs station. From 1903 to 1959 hundreds of thousands of young men trained for war at the camp, which had an extensive network of rail sidings controlled by a main-line signal box (closed in 1963)

Bruce McCartney collection

plus a lower summit level (about 825' at Mosspaul as opposed to over 1,000' at Whitrope). With a journey time perhaps 10–15 minutes shorter than via Liddesdale, it would then have been in a strong position to take over the through Edinburgh-Birmingham/Liverpool/Manchester passenger workings in BR days, allowing these trains to pick up significant passenger numbers intermediately, rather than merely disturbing the Blackface sheep by Beattock Summit.

In the event, such an option never seems to have been considered seriously by the NBR, and as noted by Roy Perkins in 2011 (a Director of the Border Union Railway Company in 1969): 'The NB scheme trying to catch the two major markets of Carlisle and Newcastle well illustrates the problems of compromise: it finished up satisfying neither.' Ex BR-manager Rae Montgomery went further:

> It was only due to inter-company rivalry and the ambitious and financially cavalier nature of Richard Hodgson that the line south of Hawick was ever built. This section of the Waverley Route is the perfect exemplar of the nonsensical Topsy-like basis upon which the British railway network developed, and points very clearly, in my opinion, to the fact that a National Railway (as was indeed posited in the 1840s) should have been set up by Government.

Not long after the Liddesdale line opened in 1862, track doubling throughout was completed, but the railway did not begin its most important role – as a key part of an independent trunk route from Scotland to London – until 1876, when the Midland Railway opened its Settle & Carlisle line over the Pennines. The NBR had already taken on board the Central Borders' strong associations with the life and work of the novelist Sir Walter Scott (1771–1832), whose Abbotsford home stood within sight of the railway south of Galashiels. Not only was Edinburgh's

The Up platform of Newcastleton station is well turned-out in this 1930s' scene, as Station Master Byers (centre) poses for the camera, together with his grand-daughter and railwayman Tom Brown, who later went on to be stationmaster at Grantshouse, Belses and Langholm.
Courtesy of Grace Brown

principal station named – albeit indirectly – after his popular *Waverley Novels*, (the station actually taking its name from Waverley Bridge, often shortened to Waverley until that usage became officially established) but also the NBR's main line to north west England was advertised from the first timetable in 1862 as 'The Waverley Route' (also known as the Waverley Line). The subsequent completion of the second Tay Bridge (1887) and then the Forth Bridge (1890), provided an alternative to the Caledonian routeing via the West Coast Main Line and Stirling, and opened up substantial new markets to the Waverley Route – from the Midlands and North West England to Perth, Dundee, Aberdeen and Inverness.

The operational geography

The operation of the Waverley Route was always difficult, traversing two significant upland barriers – the Moorfoot Hills at Falahill Summit (880') and the Cheviots at Whitrope Summit (1,006') – and being built through countryside which forced a largely sinuous alignment on the route. The combination of steep gradients (1 in 70 climbing to Falahill southbound, and predominantly 1 in 75 in both directions to Whitrope) and sharp curvature made for challenging conditions for both timetable planners and the men at the sharp end, driving and firing the locomotives. The Waverley Route could never match its East Coast and West Coast competitors for speed, but unlike the latter it served a significant intermediate population in Midlothian and the Central Borders, although the lack of potential passengers in the desolate country south of Hawick was always to be a drag on the line's finances.

The Waverley Route may have been slower than competing lines, but the North British and Midland railway companies were quick to emphasise the quality of the railway and its passenger trains compared to its East and West Coast rivals. As Neil Caplan notes in *The Waverley Route* (1985), an NBR advert in an 1877 railway guide read, 'The Waverley is the most interesting and attractive, and is the only Route which enables the Tourist to visit Melrose (for Melrose Abbey and Abbotsford) and St Boswells (for Dryburgh Abbey).' In *Iron Road* (2007) PJG Ransom begins his chapter on the 'golden age' of the railways in Scotland – when there were up to ten trains a day from Edinburgh to Carlisle, with three continuing to London St Pancras – with the unstinting praise that:

> The Midland/North British expresses from St Pancras to Edinburgh were not only among the most luxurious trains in Britain; the manner in which they were worked over the Waverley Route was among the smartest to be found anywhere.

The operation of these luxury trains, from 1906 hauled north of Carlisle by the iconic NBR Atlantic class locomotives, came at a significant price – AJ Mullay noting in *The Railway Race to Scotland 1901* (1987) that, 'between 1903 and 1907 the Midland paid the North British some £11,000 in subsidy for maintaining their share of operating the 13.30 and 19.20 down expresses'. Ultimately, in a later era of intense transport competition, the cost of operating a double-track line through country which did not allow high speeds for through trains was to help seal the fate of the Waverley Route. Even in its halcyon Edwardian years the railway was only relatively successful and by the mid-1920s external forces would be exerting a significant negative impact on its future. As Thomas and Paterson conclude in *A Regional History of the Railways of Great Britain Volume 6, Scotland: The Lowlands and the Borders* (1984):

> It was a millstone round the necks of its successive owners. Its steep gradients called for expensive double-heading of trains. Maintenance was costly. There was difficulty in keeping it open in wintertime. And always there was the spectre of the unproductive miles between Hawick and Carlisle.

The terms of competition change, then nationalisation makes little difference

After the 1914–18 wartime experience of the benefits of unified railway operation, in the 1923 'Grouping' the Government amalgamated 120 railway companies into just four large groups. The Waverley Route (as part of the North British Railway) went to the London & North Eastern Railway (LNER), but its southern Settle & Carlisle connection from Carlisle (and the connecting West Coast Main Line) went to the rival London, Midland & Scottish Railway. This created an anomalous situation for the through traffic on the line, with the LNER inevitably concentrating on its own fast route from Edinburgh to London via the East Coast Main Line – and arguably sowed the seeds of the complete closure of the railway through the Central Borders 46 years later. Roy Perkins traces the eventual closure of the railway to 'the decision to group Scotland's Railways into two London controlled monoliths, geographically polarised between the East Coast and the West. Thereafter the Waverley Route had no raison d'être as a main line.' Rail campaigner Bill Jamieson takes a slightly different view, arguing that the route enjoyed deployment of new locomotives during the LNER period but 'if, as had been mooted, there had been a separate Scottish company at the Grouping, this could well have been to the benefit of the Waverley Route in that a rational decision as to which was the most sensible way to route traffic between north west England and Edinburgh might well have come down in favour of the more populous line through the Borders.'

However, long before this protracted historical process worked through to an unhappy conclusion, the Waverley Route continued to play a bigger national role than might have been expected from a line of essentially regional and local importance. It had played an important part in the World War I effort, not least through carrying troops and equipment to and from the massive Stobs Camp south of Hawick – although the demands of war had also given a fillip to the development of road transport, soon bringing the railway's monopoly position under threat. Like much of the British railway network, the Waverley Route also played a vital role in the exhaustive (and exhausting) war effort in 1939–45.

After peace returned in 1945 it was some years before the quality of the rail service between Edinburgh and Carlisle via the Borders got anywhere close to the standards regularly enjoyed even before World War I. As Neil Caplan notes in *The Waverley Route*, by 1957 the number of through trains from Edinburgh to Carlisle had dropped from nine to six, and the sole remaining daytime train to St Pancras was allowed a painfully long 160 minutes for the 98¼ miles to Carlisle (with four intermediate calls), compared to as little as 131 minutes (non-stop) in 1914.

The railways had of course been nationalised in 1948, but this brought little benefit to the Waverley Route. Ironically, the LNER had converted the Galashiels station area to colour light signalling in 1937 (allowing five signal boxes to be replaced by one), so in a minor way the Waverley Route was ahead of the game in terms of modernisation.

The closures precipitated by the calamitous floods of 1948 – Duns to Greenlaw and the Jedburgh branch – were of ominous character, for Borderers stood idly by while Jedburgh was sacrificed to facilitate temporary diversions of East Coast Main Line trains over the Tweedmouth-Kelso-St Boswells line, and the Duns-Greenlaw gap was simply accepted as a *fait accompli*. Ironically these

On 25th May 1962 – shortly after a substantial proportion of the line's workings had switched from steam to diesel – BRCW Type 2 No. D5312 heads what is thought to be the lunch-time Carlisle-Edinburgh departure past Crookston, just north of Fountainhall. The van behind the loco had presumably been displaced from car-carrying duties by new vehicles, and had simply reverted to being a normal parcels van, but had not yet had the old branding removed.

The late Derek Cross, courtesy of David Cross

1948 diversions were to demonstrate to a wider public the capabilities of the Waverley Route north of St Boswells, handling up to 11 additional Anglo-Scottish trains in each direction daily during the 11 weeks the East Coast Main Line was closed between Berwick and Dunbar. These included on 17 recorded occasions the successful passage – without a stop – of *The Flying Scotsman* non-stop service between Edinburgh and Kings Cross, despite the longer route and the absence of water troughs between Edinburgh and Tweedmouth.

The widespread replacement of steam-hauled services by more economical diesel multiple units (DMUs) began in Scotland in 1957–58, and as Bill Peacock notes in *Border Railway Portfolio* (1982), the Borders was a very early beneficiary: 'on July 11th 1956, what was claimed to be Scotland's first regular diesel service began on the Galashiels-Peebles-Edinburgh route. The two car diesel multiple unit made its inaugural run on the 7.12 a.m. service and proved to be so successful that British Railways later introduced two extra trains a day to cope with the increased traffic.'

Strangely, this faster and cleaner rolling stock introduced as part of BR's 1955

Modernisation Plan would largely bypass the Waverley Route itself over its remaining 12 years of passenger operation. The Peebles line closed in 1962, and although diesel replaced steam on all regular locomotive-hauled passenger services on 'the main line' by early 1966, until the very end on 6th January 1969 – other than a single daily Hawick-Carlisle return working and two return 'short workings' between Edinburgh and Eskbank/Gorebridge – only weekend and seasonal workings were operated by DMUs. In the early 1960s the operation of the Waverley Route remained much as it had for decades. While the NBR had extolled the tourist and leisure interest of the line, and in the 1930s the LNER typically routed the return working of *The Northern Belle* luxury train cruise from Kings Cross to the Highlands via Hawick and the Border Counties line, the Waverley Route's scenic and historic attractions were seriously neglected by BR.

By 1961, BR Scottish Region was operating tail-end observation cars on summer train services to Kyle, Oban and Mallaig, and special 'land cruise' excursions were providing circular tours and other itineraries not possible by normal service trains across many parts of Scotland. But no observation cars would thread their way along the Gala Water, through the rich landscapes around the Eildon Hills, or over the dramatically bleak territory between Hawick and Newcastleton. There is no evidence that this was part of any conscious attempt to 'run down' the line – but more plausible reasons for the promotional neglect of the Waverley Route may have been its relative remoteness from Scottish Region HQ in Glasgow, the limited number of observation cars available, and possibly the line's split control between Scottish Region and London Midland Region (the boundary latterly being at Riddings Junction, 14 miles from Carlisle).

By the late 1950s the primary purpose of the Waverley Route had been reversed from the situation 40 years earlier – it was now predominantly a through route for freight (rather than passenger) traffic. Arguably this role (and its increasing vulnerability to road competition) disguised the importance of the line's function as a passenger link between the Central Borders and Edinburgh – and would contribute to the latter section's ultimate demise.

Having lost its main purpose as a through line as far back as the 1923 Grouping, the Waverley Route was effectively 'out on a limb', and in an era of growing affluence and rising car ownership, a largely neglected main line was particularly vulnerable to changing markets and, crucially, to changing Government views on the role of railways in the British economy and society. As neither a classic branch line or cross-country route, nor a premier trunk route, the railway through the Borders fell between a number of stools – which would prove to be its undoing.

The die would be cast by the 1963 Beeching Report, but not until after BR had considered – and then rejected – an extraordinary opportunity to reshape the rail network south and south west of Edinburgh in a way which would have re-created the Waverley Route as a genuinely viable through route.

Scottish railway history comes close to taking an entirely different course

Of all the fascinating revelations unearthed by more than two and a half years of research for this book, one of the most remarkable came in a typed six-page BR memo, dated July 1962, from the personal archive of ex-BR manager Rae Montgomery ('the Montgomery archive'), now held as part of the North British Railway Study Group archive at the National Records of Scotland in Edinburgh. Produced as part of the two-year period of analysis of the national rail network leading up to the March 1963 publication of the Beeching Report, the memo (and extensive supporting appendices) summarises the financial evaluation undertaken by a Scottish Region team (including Montgomery) to assess route rationalisation options addressing the estimated £113,000 annual loss on the Waverley Route. In 2011 Montgomery recollected his role in this episode which almost changed the course of Scottish railway history:

> There were three of us – all Traffic Apprentices – Hugh Gowans, Robbie Henderson and me, ultimately reporting to the Scottish Region Reshaping Officer, the genial tweed-suited and pipe-smoking CJG Taylor. Our route analysis was to feed into the Beeching team working on what would become the infamous March 1963 report, and we were sent to a room in Scottish Region HQ at 302 Buchanan Street and told to stay there until we'd sorted out the problem!'

The team's report assessed three options for the Waverley Route, namely:

1 Complete closure.
2 Closure of all branches and all but six stations on the 'main line' – Stow, Gala, Melrose, St Boswells, Hawick and Newcastleton.
3 As in (2), but with diversion to the 98¼-mile Waverley Route of the through trains/train portions between Edinburgh and England (Liverpool, Manchester, Birmingham and London) then passing via the 101-mile Carstairs route.

Based on a variety of BR sources of data on revenues and costs, the analysis concluded that the biggest saving would be achieved by Option 3, which would involve complete closure of the 10 double-track miles from Midcalder Junction to Wilsontown Junction (serving the freight branch to Kingshill No. 2 colliery),

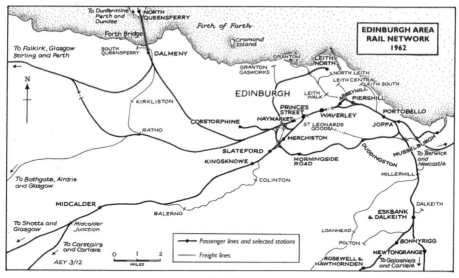

Alan Young

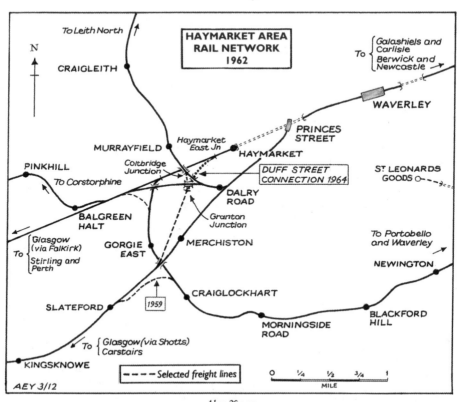

Alan Young

with a single track retained over the next six miles to Carstairs for coal traffic (which in fact ceased in 1963 following closure of the colliery). It was assumed that local services between Edinburgh, Carstairs and Lanark would be discontinued as an independent exercise (as indeed they were in 1966). Seven trains daily would serve the Border towns (three retained, plus four diverted from Carstairs), with the complete package producing a net betterment of £200,000 annually to BR.

The memo also noted that unless through passenger services from England via Carstairs could be diverted to the Waverley Route it would not be possible to close Edinburgh's Princes Street station (the former Caledonian Railway terminus, which served a limited number of routes compared to the through station at Waverley) without either constructing a new chord south-west of Haymarket (the 'Duff Street connection') or 'accepting the material addition to the journey time by routing the trains via Craiglockhart and Portobello [over the South Suburban line].'

The memo concluded that 'the volume of passenger travel between Princes Street and stations in England via Carstairs is, on the average, little short of 5000 journeys per week, and if that revenue is diverted to the Waverley Route *it will transform the financial standing of that line*.' (author's italics) This gem of modern railway history has lain undisclosed since it was written in July 1962. It shows that BR was capable of some very 'blue skies' thinking, but the fascinating (and politically pivotal) question is why a route rationalisation proposal with a seemingly solid financial logic (which would have saved the Waverley Route in its entirety) was turned on its head in just eight months leading up to the publication of the Beeching Report in March 1963?

In practice, the Duff Street connection – which Montgomery described in 2011 as having been 'talked about for ever' – was ultimately built in 1964, allowing Princes Street station to be closed without any need to retain the Waverley Route. But why was the Duff Street project taken forward when the only other passenger services which could use the route (Edinburgh-Shotts-Glasgow, and Edinburgh-Carstairs-Lanark) were both slated for closure? The reason why closure of Midcalder-Carstairs quickly dropped out of the equation may be very simple. As ex-BR manager Allan McLean recalled in 2011:

Some time after ceasing to be BRB Chair, Beeching gave a BBC TV interview in which he ridiculed the idea of having more than one rail line between England and Scotland – he favoured the WCML, which may explain the saving of Carstairs / Midcalder Junction. Asked if he had any regrets, his reply was something to the effect that he regretted not having been able to close the ECML north of Newcastle!

Six months after the report that might have changed history, the Waverley Route experienced one of the biggest challenges of its entire existence when the country suffered sub-zero temperatures continuously from late December 1962 through to early March 1963. The Waverley Route was completely blocked by snow between Stobs and Steele Road stations for 18 days in late January and early February, with two trains and ten locomotives embedded in snowdrifts – and for a further 25 days only single-line working was possible. As Danny Forbes – a fireman at Hawick from 1962 to 1964 and still firing for West Coast Railways in 2012 – told the author:

A southbound train slows to a halt at Whitrope Siding signal box on 15th February 1963. It will now reverse through the crossover opposite the box before proceeding 'wrong line' to Riccarton, the Up line being blocked by snow. Single-line working here lasted for 25 days, following 18 days of complete blockage of the line.
The late Frank Spaven

Trainloads of men on the dole in Edinburgh – many of them ill-dressed for severe weather [Rae Montgomery recollects seeing some of them shod in 'winklepickers'] – were brought to Hawick, given shovels and sent up to Whitrope and set to work digging out the snow to allow the snowploughs to get through!

The line was finally fully re-opened just days before the publication of the report that would effectively seal its long-term fate.

Dynamite having been used to blast down the cornices that had formed at the top of the cutting (on the left hand side), permanent way staff are here seen on the Up line at Whitrope on 9th January 1963, shovelling snow on to wagons sitting on the Down line, which had been cleared. No service trains were running at this time, during the 18 day blockage of the line.
Stuart Sellar

CHAPTER 2

Dr Beeching's lethal prescription 1963–66

*T*HE *Reshaping of British Railways* – 'the Beeching Report' – was published on 27th March 1963. This report – which was to become synonymous in the public mind with drastic contraction of the rail system – was the culmination of nearly two years of intensive analysis by a team led by Dr Richard Beeching, Chairman of the British Railways Board.

Beeching had been appointed by a Conservative Government increasingly alarmed by the mounting financial problems of the rail system, and he came with an enviable reputation for thorough and clinical analysis of business problems at ICI, the leading British chemicals company. Beeching and the Conservative Minister of Transport, Ernest Marples, were to become twin hate figures throughout Britain as soon as the implications of the reshaping report had sunk in. Closure of 'unremunerative' lines had been gathering pace in the early 1960s and there was a widespread expectation that Beeching would propose many service withdrawals. But the sheer scale of the proposals in his 148-page report came as a shock. Passenger services were to be withdrawn from 5,000 route miles and over 2,000 stations would be closed across Britain.

In the Borders, the proposed closure of the Langholm branch came as no surprise, but there was astonishment that the entire Waverley Route from Edinburgh to Carlisle was slated for closure – yet, by contrast, the 'deep rural' lines to Mallaig and Oban were not on Beeching's list for withdrawal. The 29th March edition of the *Hawick News* carried a news item of surprisingly modest length on the planned closure of the Waverley Route under the headline 'All Border Stations to Close – Beeching Recommendation'. One week later the paper ran an editorial which explained its deliberate delay in making a quick judgement on Beeching, by commenting:

> we have found nothing to make us change our first impression that the closure of
> the Border railways is completely unjustifiable under existing circumstances . . .
> What [Provost Henderson of Hawick] said ought to dispel some of the apathy in
> Hawick which undoubtedly exists towards the railway closures. Hawick folk and

Belching a spectacular exhaust, Hawick-based BR Standard Class 4 2-6-0 No. 76050 forges past Bowland signal box on the 1 in 99 gradient towards Falahill Summit, hauling what is believed to be the 12 noon Saturdays-only Hawick-Edinburgh service, during April 1964.
The late Robin Barbour, courtesy of Bruce McCartney

> Borderers generally should face squarely up to the fact that a turning-point has been reached in Border history. The issue is simple; it is one of survival and growth or gradual decay and death . . . it is the duty of every man and woman to make known their total opposition to the Beeching Plan. If they allow the Government to proceed with the present proposals they are signing the death warrant of the Borders.

Strong stuff – and while clearly not a wholly accurate prediction of how the Borders would fare without a railway, it rightly sought to put the onus for action on the people.

The Beeching Report did not hide its light under a bushel, and some critics felt that Dr Beeching was naive in not foreseeing the political storm that such a transparent announcement of drastic surgery would cause. Part of that transparency was a fascinating portfolio of 13 detailed maps showing line traffic densities, station receipts, routes proposed for closure, etc. Map 1 of Density of Passenger Traffic showed that north of Hawick the Waverley Route fell into the same category (5,000 to 10,000 passengers per week) as the Midcalder Junction to Carstairs route which was in part a rival to the line through the Central Borders; south of Hawick, however, density fell into the lowest category of less than 5,000 passengers per week. Map 3 of Passenger Traffic Station Receipts showed that only four Scottish towns with stations in the highest revenue category (£25,000 and over pa) were listed for closure – Galashiels, Hawick, Stranraer and Thurso (but the latter two were soon reprieved). The severity of what was being planned for the Borders was clear, yet a general reaction in the region appears to have been incredulity – 'it'll never happen'.

Wider national opposition to the Waverley Route proposal was however taking shape. A campaigning group, the Scottish Railway Development Association (SRDA), had been formed in 1962 as an advance response to the emerging threat to Scotland's rail network. On 20th July 1962 for example, under the headline 'Cartographic requiem', the *Scotsman* had published a British Transport Commission (BTC) map of passenger traffic densities and a news story which noted, in an interesting juxtaposition which anticipated future debates about strategic route rationalisation, that 'The Waverley line and the connection to the Carlisle route at Carstairs are both dangerously placed in relation to passenger-carryings.' A week earlier the paper had carried a front page story on uneconomic freight routes which was 'openly described by BTC officials as a "softening up" for the master hatchet plan which Dr Beeching will produce at the end of the year.' The need for defensive action was clear far in advance of the 1963 publication of the Beeching Report.

Other regions of Scotland threatened by Beeching were far from complacent. In the Highlands, over 300 miles of line were proposed for closure and an embryonic campaign against the closures emerged rapidly. On 29th March 1963, in an editorial on the Beeching Report, the *Inverness Courier* thundered: 'Today this country is facing the greatest crisis it has ever had to face in peace.'

Just 15 days after Beeching unveiled his report, a conference held in Inverness by the Highland Transport Committee unanimously passed a resolution deploring and opposing the proposed withdrawal of passenger services and calling for the formation of a permanent body 'charged with the examination and co-ordination of all forms of transport in the North, and with the supervision of its development'. This immediate reaction to Beeching soon led on to the formation of the 'MacPuff' campaign which was instrumental in saving more than 230 miles of railway north of Inverness (the Kyle and Far North lines) in 1964.

For reasons of physical geography the Waverley Route as a whole had always been difficult and expensive to operate. BR papers in ex-BR manager Rae Montgomery's archive include a confidential document on 'Trunk Freight Train Haulage' produced by the Traffic Costing Service in Glasgow in May 1963, based on actual operating performance in November 1962. This shows that in the case of diesel-hauled trunk freights, the Waverley Route's average operating cost per train mile, at 12.390 shillings, was the worst in Scotland. Admittedly, in 1962, dieselisation of the Waverley Route was still in its early days and locomotive diagrams were less intensive than they would become once diesel traction became the norm. But the implication was clear – the Waverley Route was essentially a high-cost route for through freight trains, and as this traffic steadily reduced in volume, so the attractions of diversion to the West Coast Main Line would become stronger.

The National Records of Scotland contain a copy letter sent from Tom Hart, SRDA's Honorary Secretary, of 31st December 1963 to the Roxburghshire County Clerk commenting: 'there would appear to be a strong positive case for developing the Waverley Route; the retention of the present pattern of services and number of stations is NOT desirable.' The letter also suggested an improved regular interval service every 90 minutes from Edinburgh to Hawick with every second train extended to Carlisle. Selective development and an overdue focus on tourist potential were also outlined: 'Stations with a positive value would appear to be Galashiels, Melrose, St Boswells, Hawick and Newcastleton. Melrose is included because the station is centrally situated and within easy walking distance of the Abbey.'

The economic and social implications of the Beeching Report were a serious concern for a number of Government ministries, and the Minister of Transport was required to consult other departments and the regional economic planning councils on the strategic impacts of closure proposals, as well as the Transport Users Consultative Committees (TUCCs) on personal hardship to travellers. TUCCs, which had originally been established by the 1947 Transport Act, could make recommendations about the services provided by the British Railways Board – and in the case of closure proposals could consider individual objections by rail users, then reporting their recommendations to the Minister of Transport. These could include enhanced replacement bus services or even a recommendation that the rail service should not be withdrawn. The Minister was not obliged to accept any recommendations, but could choose to make consent to closure subject to certain conditions, or indeed to reprieve the service partially or in its entirety. The Scottish Office clearly took an early interest in the threat to the Waverley Route, an internal Scottish office memo of 28th April 1964 from an RDM Bell noting:

> Ministers will recall that at the meeting of the Committee on the 8th January it was decided that the Minister of Transport should approach Dr Beeching to ask him to postpone publishing notices of the intention to withdraw certain services . . . one was the Edinburgh / Hawick / Carlisle line.

In November 1965 the statutory consultee, the Scottish Economic Planning Council (advised by the Scottish Economic Planning Board (SEPB) of mainly Scottish Office officials) confidentially asked the Minister of Transport to oppose publication 'at this time' of BRB's Waverley Route closure proposal, in view of 'the nature, size and importance of the area served by this line and . . . the need to avoid a move that would be judged inconsistent with the aim of developing the Borders.'

The party politics of the Borders were an important factor in the last years of the Waverley Route. The constituency covering the Central Borders (latterly Roxburgh, Selkirk and Peebles) was represented by the Conservative Party 's Commander Charles Donaldson from 1951 until his death in late 1964. The Liberal Party's young candidate, David Steel, had cut Donaldson's majority in the 1964 General Election, and in the subsequent 1965 by-election he dramatically overturned the Conservative majority – and as Steel reminded the author in 2011: 'Opposition to closure was one of the three main local issues in my 1965 by-election campaign' (the late Donaldson having voted for the 1963 Beeching plan).

Frank Spaven and the Scottish Office / MoT skirmishes

Until his 1966 move to the newly established Highlands & Islands Development Board (HIDB), one of the key Government officials advising the Scottish Economic Planning Council (SEPC) on Beeching closure proposals was Frank Spaven (father of the author), a regional planning specialist at the Scottish Development Department (SDD), which was part of the Scottish Office. In his obituary in the *Scotsman* in February 2003, he was credited with being 'instrumental in saving the bulk of the Highland rail network' through his advice on the 1964 closure proposals for all passenger rail services north of Inverness. His obituary in the *Herald* recorded: 'In his backroom role, Spaven's particular talent lay in marshalling arguments in fluid style, tellingly and without passion, and his many reports forced governments of both colours to re-examine transport priorities . . . Spaven dismissed sentiment, rather highlighting the key role of railways as a green and civilised form of transport,'

The National Records of Scotland contain six internal memoranda written by Frank Spaven between March 1965 and July 1966, shedding light on the developing tensions between the Scottish Office and the Ministry of Transport over the Waverley Route. Spaven had had a lifelong interest in railways, but managed to keep his 'enthusiasm' quite separate from dispassionate analysis of railway development – for example, while still enjoying rail-based family trips to Riccarton Junction in mid-1966, as a civil servant he was commenting that 'if [the Waverley Route's] fairly heavy through freight traffic were transferred to an

'Britannia' No. 70016 *Ariel* approaches Riccarton Junction from the south on 6th November 1961, with the 1.28 pm Carlisle-Edinburgh train. *Ariel* and sister loco *Flying Dutchman* were briefly based at Carlisle Canal engine shed, from September 1961 until May 1962, when they were displaced to the south by dieselisation. The class reappeared on the Waverley Route after 1963, when Kingmoor shed took over responsibility for supplying motive power from the south end of the line, with the last working as late as November 1967.

The late Frank Spaven

A3 Pacific No. 60052 *Prince Palatine* battles up the bank near Stobs with a Millerhill-Kingmoor freight in October 1964.

The late Robin Barbour, courtesy of Bruce McCartney

The 3.46 pm arrival from Edinburgh approaches Melrose behind an unidentified BRCW Type 2 on 13th April 1963. The rugby 'Sevens' – and hundreds of parked cars, symbolising the growing affluence which now threatened the railway – are in evidence in the background.

The late Frank Spaven

The author walks towards the utilitarian Riccarton South signal box on a fine spring evening in 1966. He and his father had trekked cross-country the previous day from Snoot Youth Hostel near Roberton to camp at this lonely railway outpost. The Waverley Route swings away to the right of the signal box, while the surviving stub of the former Border Counties line lies to the left.

The late Frank Spaven

The last passenger train from Berwick-upon-Tweed via Kelso pulls into St Boswells on 13th June 1964, hauled by BR Standard Class 2 2-6-0 No. 78048. This route could have been much more effectively promoted as a tourist railway – and its value as a diversionary route had been tellingly demonstrated after the floods of 1948 severed the East Coast Main Line for 11 weeks. Freight services from St Boswells to Kelso survived until 1968.

Norman Turnbull

The LNER V2 2-6-2 steam locomotives were strongly associated with the Waverley Route from the early 1940s until their demise in 1966 – and memorably captured on Peter Handford's atmospheric recordings of their distinctive exhaust beat on the climb to Riccarton, for the Argo Transacord record label. Handford's ashes were scattered at the site of Steele Road station following his death in 2007. Here the author and his younger brother, Malcolm, admire one of the class pulling away from Riccarton in September 1963 at the head of a trainload of modern 'Presflo' cement wagons – presumably en route from the Blue Circle cement works at Dunbar to Carlisle.

The late Frank Spaven

After reversing at Whitrope, this Edinburgh-Carlisle train is proceeding south 'wrong line' towards Riccarton Junction on 15th February 1963. The Up line beside the wall of snow and ice to the right appears to be largely clear but snow must still have been obstructing operations elsewhere on this two-mile 'block section'.

The late Frank Spaven

Transporting the competition – 'Black 5' No. 45235 and A4 Pacific No. 60027 *Merlin* – hurry a northbound car train through Hassendean in early summer 1965. Trains of motor vehicles were a familiar sight on the Waverley Route in its last eight years, the Up services conveying lorries and vans from the BMC plant in Bathgate to southern markets.

The late Robin Barbour, courtesy of Bruce McCartney

Rarely caught on this side of the camera, the author's father, Frank Spaven, surveys the derelict remains of Comrie station in spring 1966. In his role as a civil servant at the Scottish Office, he was strongly arguing the case against such a fate for the principal stations in the Borders.
David Spaven

electrified Carlisle-Edinburgh line . . . the repercussions of closing it altogether south of Hawick would have to be fully considered.'

Remarkably, in his spare time Frank Spaven was also an active member of the Scottish Railway Development Association, and with hindsight one wonders whether the Scottish Office knew of this. His first recorded commentary as a civil servant on the Waverley Route came in response to Ministry of Transport officials (writing in March 1965) who were unhappy with the wording of the SEPC's opposition to closure, stating that:

> the main investment of resources on Anglo-Scottish services seems likely to be on the Carstairs route' and 'the traffic available will not economically support, in addition to the Carstairs route: (i) the East Coast route, (ii) the Waverley Route, and (iii) the Berwick-St Boswells line.

In an internal Scottish Office memorandum of 23rd March 1965, Spaven responded that 'this is a questionable assumption' in view of a number of points 'which are not answered in the BRB report on major trunk routes':

1   A substantial amount of traffic with a variety of origins and destinations uses all four Anglo-Scottish routes at present [citing 95 passenger trains and 71 'fully fitted' freights] . . . Can all this and other present traffic be diverted to and retained on the Carstairs route?

2   A considerable overall growth in Anglo-Scottish traffic should be in prospect from industrial and population expansion in Central Scotland, from marked improvements in freight and passenger services and from increasing road congestion, at least in urban areas. Indeed a net increase is shown in the BRB

maps for 1964–84. Can all this traffic also be diverted to one route and reliably handled on it?

3 The proposed scale of development at Galashiels-St Boswells [a 25,000 population increase, including a new settlement at Tweedbank] should augment the present appreciable traffic between Edinburgh, Galashiels and Hawick and may well require the provision of more frequent, regular interval trains (to fewer stations).

4 Even if the Borders routes were not in future to be major trunk routes, there should be considerable scope for more economical operation, for example through the use of modern track maintenance and signalling equipment and the possibility of singling sections of track such as the 45 miles between Hawick and Carlisle.

Spaven elaborated on the latter theme in a memo on 28th July 1965 for the next day's meeting of the SEPB:

Whatever the real net [loss] figures are, the costs of operating this route could certainly be reduced (as they now are on the reprieved lines in the north-west Highlands) by eliminating 17 of the small stations south of Gorebridge and retaining only Galashiels, Melrose, St Boswells, Hawick and Newcastleton; by singling long sections of track, especially the 45 miles south of Hawick; by modernising signalling and track maintenance; and by completing dieselisation.

He returned to this issue in an 18th August memo, which noted that 'on the experience of the Inverness/Wick and Kyle lines, savings of at least 50% might be expected to result from more economical methods of operation.' In subsequent years, as National Records of Scotland archive material reveals, the big Scottish Office concern about the Waverley Route closure related to wider economic development issues rather than personal hardship. In part this can be traced back to Frank Spaven's July 1965 comments on the closure proposal process:

It is not a proposal which would benefit from going through the TUCC procedure, because the main considerations are economic, in terms of regional development and railway strategy, and not questions of hardship [the only grounds on which objections could be made to the TUCC] on which local views are already well known. Its publication before a Regional Study which is likely to advocate a New Town in the Borders would obviously be embarrassing and more likely to discourage than attract new enterprises to this relatively isolated area.

In November 1965 – in the lead-up to the SEPC's confidential opposition to publication of the closure proposal – the SEPB briefed the Council on the salient points and planning considerations which justified that recommendation. The MoT was swift to respond the same month:

> The Ministry of Transport wish to report to the Planning Council that they are unable to associate themselves with the recommendation . . . [which] does not in the opinion of the Ministry of Transport appear adequate to override the *prima facie* case for examining in detail this proposal which, if eventually sanctioned, would relieve the tax payer of the very heavy subsidy required by the service.

A key issue highlighted by the MoT was their rejection of the argument (originating in a Spaven memo of 28th July) that a uniquely large population would be left at considerable distance from the nearest railhead – since 'the vast majority. . . do not use the rail service'. The planned growth of population in the Central Borders was also rejected as contributing to the case for the railway, since 'in the five [sic] years between 1960 and 1964 ordinary bookings fell from 196,000 to 123,000 or 37%: season ticket bookings fell from 8,000 to 3,000 or 62%'. Spaven moved quickly, noting in an 11th November internal Scottish Office memo that MoT:

> have now put forward their own story on this which may require a further rejoinder from us at the Council meeting and *as we have diluted our own draft in an unsuccessful effort to accommodate M.O.T.*, the following supplementary points may serve to strengthen our argument. [author's italics]

His points began with criticism of a table – underplaying the importance of rail travel between the Borders and Edinburgh – which he described as 'an incorrect interpretation of an incorrect Ministry of Transport Table'. Spaven highlighted a total of 9,400 Waverley Route journeys per winter week (12,000 in summer), of which 66% were between the Borders and Edinburgh or within the Borders, and just 6% through journeys between Edinburgh and Carlisle and south thereof. Taking up the fact of falling sales of ordinary and season tickets, he pointed out that cheap day, weekend and excursion tickets had 'increased by an average of 40% in Scotland between 1960 and 1964 and may be significant in this area'. On the MoT's commentary on the proportion of the population using the railway, Spaven deployed some more relevant figures:

> In terms of equivalent road/rail personal journeys between the Border towns and Edinburgh, it is estimated by SDD that the average distribution of traffic per day is roughly 30% by train, 25% by bus and 45% by private vehicles; and on Saturdays 40 to 45% by train.

Turning to future prospects for the railway, Spaven noted:

> It is estimated by SDD that if the [25,000] population increase and other transport
> requirements are to be met in ten years' time and in the urban road conditions
> then prevailing . . . depending on assumptions about the car and bus share of
> traffic, rail traffic would increase to between one and a half and three times its
> present level.

This planned population increase in the Borders – and its relationship to wider
plans for the Scottish economy – was to become the core issue as discussions on
the future of the Waverley Route were elevated to the highest political level.

The state of the railway on the eve of the closure proposal

Any observer of the Waverley Route who had emigrated in the early 1950s and
then returned in mid-1966 (just prior to BR's August publication of the detailed
closure proposal) would still have recognised much of the main line railway
operation through the Borders. The few surviving short branch lines were all
freight-only, but no less than 24 intermediate stations survived over the route
between Edinburgh and Carlisle, and most of these were still staffed. Passenger
trains continued to run twice daily from London through the Borders to
Edinburgh (a journey, incidentally, of 8½ hours to Galashiels), although from
September 1964 the day-time service – *The Waverley* – ceased to be a complete
through train during the winter, with just two through coaches running as part
of *The Thames-Clyde Express* from St Pancras to Glasgow. Overall, the casual
observer – perhaps like too many Borderers – might well have found it hard to
believe that this railway really was threatened.

The only big difference on the Waverley Route itself was the replacement of
steam traction by diesel. Following BR's massive 1955 Modernisation Plan, a
diesel-hauled test train had visited the line as early as 1958, and the first of the
new generation of main- line diesel locomotives had begun appearing regularly
in the Borders in 1961. By May 1962 a substantial proportion of the line's trains
(other than 'short workings' from Hawick to Edinburgh and Carlisle) had
switched from steam to diesel. Edinburgh to Carlisle passenger and some freight
trains were in the hands of the medium-powered Birmingham Railway Carriage
& Wagon Company's Type 2 locos, based at Edinburgh's Haymarket locomotive
depot, while the two daily London services (the overnight train and *The Waverley*,
both of which ran via the Settle & Carlisle line) were hauled by the higher-
powered BR-built Type 4 'Peak' locos, based at Leeds.

Initially, while both diesel and steam were being used, the impact on passenger
journey times was modest, but a step change followed a package of measures

introduced by BR in January 1966 – the closure of Hawick loco depot, a major re-organisation and acceleration of through freight workings, and the replacement of the locomotive-hauled Sunday trains between Edinburgh and Hawick by diesel multiple units. As noted in the April 1966 issue of the *Railway Observer*, this meant 'the total elimination of regular steam working over the greater part of the line', the main exceptions being the Carlisle-Langholm branch freight trains and steam substitutions for failed diesels. The very last steam operation on the line was in fact as late as 14th November 1967, when Britannia class No. 70022 *Tornado* substituted for a failed diesel on the 19.44 Carlisle-Edinburgh train.

In mid-1966 most Waverley Route passengers would have taken little or no notice of freight trains, and would be only vaguely aware that increased competition from the operationally and commercially more flexible road haulage industry meant that local and long distance goods traffic had gone into serious decline in the 1950s. This was exacerbated by bigger lorries and improvements to the trunk road network by the mid-1960s (and by a significant minority of road hauliers flouting speed and loading regulations). A comparison of the BR working timetables in summer 1960 and summer 1968 shows that the number of through freight trains over the Waverley Route dropped by more than a third in that period, although the underlying rate of decline was greater as 'car trains' (as they were known on the railway) to and from the new BMC truck plant at Bathgate were normally operated via the Waverley Route. The route's final working timetable shows just eight southbound and eight northbound Anglo-Scottish freights daily on Mondays to Fridays, supplemented by a single Millerhill-Hawick return working daily.

While the Modernisation Plan had almost completely bypassed the Waverley Route itself (other than in the inevitable dieselisation), the opening of the Millerhill (Edinburgh) and Kingmoor (officially Carlisle New) marshalling yards in 1962–63 and 1963 respectively – together with the opening of the BMC plant in 1961 – had temporarily consolidated the role of the Waverley Route as a long-distance through freight corridor. You wouldn't see the ultra-new Freightliner container trains (one of the positive outcomes of the Beeching Report) passing through the Borders, but modern car, cement and chemical wagons were all part of the everyday railway scene between Edinburgh, Hawick and Carlisle. Beginning in 1965 the line also hosted one of Britain's longest-distance freight trains – a thrice weekly trainload of oil from Milford Haven in south west Wales to Thornton in Fife.

By early 1966 most Monday-Friday passenger trains were not well patronised, and subsequent BR data showed an 8% decline in passengers between Border towns and Edinburgh from 1965 to 1966 (and a further 8% drop the following

'Britannia' Class 4-6-2 No. 70020 *Mercury* leaves Millerhill Yard with the 3.25 pm Class 'D' freight to Carlisle on 8th May 1963, whilst J38 Class No. 65914 waits on the main line with a local trip. The marshalling yard was opened in phases in 1962–63, but never realised its planned potential.

Stuart Sellar

year). Part of that decline must have been a reflection of BR's lack of dynamic response to rising car ownership – not least a timetable with irregular departure times quite unlike the 'regular interval' pattern which had been successfully introduced on a number of Central Scotland rail routes since 1960.

Remarkably, across the whole length of the Waverley Route there still lingered a resemblance to the pattern of service shown in the Bradshaw rail timetable for 1922. Costs were also high, with no less than 26 out of 42 staffed signal boxes still surviving in 1966 – one for every four route miles – although this in part reflected the need to split the route into 'block sections' (between signalboxes) sufficiently short to cater for the capacity impact of relatively slow-moving trains (freight in particular) tackling steep ruling gradients.

British Railways' records in the National Records of Scotland include a briefing document compiled for a management 'Waverley Route Tour' (presumably by special train) undertaken on Tuesday 12th July 1966, just five weeks before BR announced the detailed closure proposal for the line. This document reveals some salutary trends in the railway's fortunes. In the case of Hawick:

Knitwear by passenger train provides the most important forwarded [parcels] traffic, but this has decreased by about 76% since 1963 (Lyle & Scott transferred their 'Y-front' manufacture to Gateshead in 1964 because of *shortage of labour and high wages in the area*). [author's italics]

This indirect reference to local prosperity underlines an uncomfortable truth about the railway (not just here but in many parts of Britain) – that rising incomes and car ownership were putting the railways under severe competitive pressure. The BR briefing spelt it out bluntly in the context of the Waverley Route: 'Traditionally a town with strong railway loyalties, Hawick has turned to road for holiday purposes in the last few years.' The town's previous Conservative MP, Commander Donaldson, had alluded in some wonderment to the area's economic providence in the House of Commons on 23rd March 1964:

I have said it myself on more than one occasion in debates on Scottish industry and employment, that we have in South-East Scotland the amazing situation that we have, in Hawick in particular, an average of unemployment of 0.61 of 1 per cent. What that means in numbers of human beings is perhaps three or four unemployables who register each week for their own proper purposes and one person who happens to be changing from one job to another . . . The peculiar thing about the whole of my three counties is that there is relatively no unemployment at all.

Surviving dwelling houses in the railway village at Riccarton Junction in spring 1966.
By the time of this photo – two years after the school closed and a year after the Co-op shut its store on the station platform – just a dozen of the original 33 railway houses remained in occupation. The line closure proposal came in August 1966 and by the following year a further third of the homes had been abandoned. The writing was on the wall for Riccarton.
The late Frank Spaven

The BR briefing painted a picture for local freight by rail which was no more encouraging than the passenger situation. At Hawick 'Freight traffic is of diminishing importance . . . The station is to be retained temporarily for freight.' Unsurprisingly, given its isolated location, no freight had been handled at Riccarton Junction in 1965, yet it was to be 'retained temporarily for freight traffic' for reasons that are not explained – although domestic coal traffic was required for the remaining occupied dwellings and in 1964 Riccarton was still handling trainloads of homing pigeons! The rationale for retention of freight facilities was evidently not any lingering hope that timber-related business from surrounding forests, some planted as far back as the inter-war years, would come to fruition, since the briefing then goes on to comment that nearby Newcastleton 'was suggested for timber traffic from extensive forests in the area to pulp mills at Workington, but this has not developed. To be closed December 1966.'

As will be seen in Chapter 3, this failure to develop timber prospects may have been primarily caused by the business attitude of a single – but important – BR manager. Certainly there does not appear to have been a generally negative BR attitude. Rae Montgomery recollected that in 1965 he and a colleague (Geoff Herbert, who would eventually head up BR's steel marketing team in Scotland) had discussed harvesting figures for the next twenty years with the Forestry Commission's Conservator at Kielder Castle.

The decline of the isolated railway settlement at Riccarton Junction symbolises the wider fate of the railway. It's *raison d'être* was to serve as the junction with the Border Counties line to Hexham, but the latter had closed to passengers in 1956, and to freight in 1958. Only

An unidentified V2 Class 2-6-2 with a freight from Kingmoor to Millerhill takes water at the north end of Hawick station in the summer of 1964. Its opposite number, a 'Black 5' 4-6-0 hauling a freight from Millerhill to Kingmoor, is standing in the Up loop to allow a passenger working to overtake. Up and Down through freight workings were timetabled to pass at Hawick, thereby allowing the Edinburgh and Carlisle crews to swap over and return to their home depots.
The late Frank Spaven

accessible by train until the Forestry Commission built a Land Rover track in 1963, Riccarton lost its school in 1964 and its Co-op store on the station platform in 1965 – the writing was on the wall, almost irrespective of the ultimate fate of the Waverley Route. The Roxburghshire Valuation Roll shows that all 33 railway houses and the School House were still occupied in 1949–50, but there followed an almost continuous decline in occupation. The number of occupied houses fell from 12 in 1965–66 to 8 in 1966–67 – following the announcement of the closure proposal, and doubtless hastened by BR's January 1966 conversion of the 06.30 mixed (freight and passenger) train from Carlisle to Craiginches (Aberdeen) to freight-only. Towards the end, in 1968–69, just two dwellings at Riccarton were occupied by a total of four residents – No1 (the Station Master's house occupied by William McGregor), and the School House. After 6th January 1969, all but one person moved out.

Life at Riccarton – virtually unique in its lack of road access – had its ups and downs. In 2014, looking back on his stint as Station Master from 1959 to 1964, Buckie-born Alastair Farquhar commented: 'The great thing was the peace and quiet – you walked out of your front door and you were on the hillside.' The tribulations of snow-bound winters on the railway brought out the best in railway people, and the *Sunday Post* of 17th February 1963 recorded how Farquhar's wife Eleanor welcomed two stranded passengers to their home for three nights, and that 'they kept each other's spirits up by chatting and joking, and playing with six-year old Colin, the Farquhars' boy. There were no newspapers to while away the time, so Mrs Kennedy asked Mrs Farquhar for some mending to do – and she ended up by patching Colin's breeks!' Alastair Farquhar also recalled the quirky side of the railway village's dependence on water supply from a well on the hill behind the village: 'I remember the chemist would come from BR HQ in Glasgow periodically. We would walk up the hill together, and on one occasion when we lifted the lid from the well and stuck our heads over the edge, I spotted movement in the water and said "But there's fish in there!" – and the chemist replied "Aye, that's what keeps the water clean."

Returning to the July 1966 BR briefing document, the financial prognosis for the Waverley Route as a whole was not good, as had been made clear to a wider audience earlier that year, in the February issue of *Modern Railways* magazine. Geoffrey Freeman Allen's report of a wide-ranging interview with Willie Thorpe, General Manager of BR Scottish Region, referred to the line having 'long been one of the most serious lossmakers in the Region, bleeding the system of about £0.5m a year, mainly in track and signalling costs.'

Yet the rest of the interview demonstrated that closure of the Waverley Route would be far from a panacea for the solution of Scottish Region's financial ills.

Compared to retrenchment, 'much bigger gains were realised from increased productivity and efficiency in 1963–65'. A classic example of cost saving had been the re-organisation and rationalisation of freight working in the Glasgow conurbation: '1.5m tons more originating freight than in 1963 are being worked at a cost of 1m fewer freight train-miles a year, with 169 fewer locomotives and with 12 fewer marshalling yards. The financial saving is in the region of £1.5m a year.' Compared to this, the Waverley Route's losses were small beer, but unfortunately the line through the Borders had become a symbolic scalp for some (but not all) railway managers.

The debate between Government Ministers

So, despite superficial appearances, the Waverley Route was not in good shape. The publication of BR's closure proposal was long awaited but much delayed by high-level wrangling between the Secretary of State for Scotland, Willie Ross, and the Minister of Transport, Barbara Castle, about timing. Ross was well aware of the political sensitivity of Borders development plans in the wider context of the Scottish economy. The National Records of Scotland hold briefing notes for his discussion with Castle on 3rd February 1966, which comment 'the Edinburgh-Hawick-Carlisle line is the only Scottish service closure proposal in the Beeching Report which has not yet been advertised, principally because of the Scottish Planning Board's and Council's opposition to the closure.'

In her letter of 16th March 1966 Castle indicated to Ross that she was concerned about the impact of delay on costs to the taxpayer and had concluded that the right course was to agree publication of the proposal in April. Replying on 28th March, Ross firmly spelt out his priorities:

I am still entirely clear that it would be politically most unwise to follow the White Paper on the Scottish Economy so quickly with the advertisement of the proposal to withdraw the passenger services on this line; and to take this step immediately after the Election would invite really damaging criticism.

In a draft memo on 27th April, Ross disputed the projected timescale of nearly 12 months for the statutory processes to be completed; but presumably received that same day Castle's firm rejection of his plea to protect the Labour administration's image in Scotland:

> I am afraid I cannot agree to ask the Railways Board to postpone the publication of Edinburgh-Hawick-Carlisle as I don't think your proposed timetable is realistic . . . I do not consider therefore that I should be justified in asking the Board to stay their hand any longer on this very costly service; every week that passes may be costing the Board, and hence the taxpayer £12,000.

By the time of a memo of 3rd May 1966 to Castle, Ross had accepted the inevitable and procedures had been agreed which met his clear priority of political protection for the Scottish Office's plans for national economic development:

> I expect to be able to announce the composition of the local consultative group for the Borders sufficiently in advance of the Railway's Board's notice to ensure that our continued determination to carry on with the development of the Borders is fully in the public mind before the threat of closure becomes public knowledge.

Although the option of retaining only the northern half of the Waverley Route seems not to have been countenanced by campaigners until the consent to closure of the whole route was given in July 1968 – by which time it was too late – the Scottish Office had been considering this possibility for some time. On 7th July 1966 an HHA Whitworth noted in an internal memo, referring to the forthcoming Central Borders Plan, that:

> we should I think even at this stage make the point that the industrial use of the line is very small and we might quote the idea that the possibility of retaining the railway from Edinburgh to Hawick only will need to be investigated.

This was indirectly echoed in Frank Spaven's final Scottish Office railway memo – just days before he moved to the HIDB – on 19th July 1966 (on BR/MoT's planned 'basic railway network' for development, which was ultimately published in March 1967), in which he commented:

> The case for the retention of the Waverley Route through the Western Borders has already been set out several times. It is unique in Britain in the large and otherwise isolated population served (70,000) and the large new development

[around Galashiels / Tweedbank] now starting on the fringe of the Central Belt within commuting distance of Edinburgh . . . If its fairly heavy through freight traffic were transferred to an electrified Carlisle-Edinburgh line, it would become possible to single the line, at least south of Hawick; and the repercussions of closing it altogether south of Hawick would have to be fully considered.

As it transpired, the Waverley Route's loss of this consistent civil service advocate was to be very much the Kyle line's gain, in its subsequent second reprieve from closure in 1974. Meantime, in the Borders, the full drama of the threatened loss of its main-line railway was about to enter a more public and hotly-debated phase.

CHAPTER 3

Closure proposed
and two years in limbo
1966–68

O N 17th August 1966, nearly three and a half years after publication of the
Beeching Report, British Rail (as it was now known) finally issued its
closure proposal for the entire Waverley Route and its 24 stations. The last line
of the public notice advised that 'if no objections are lodged to the proposal the
service will be discontinued on 2nd January, 1967'. The notice referred to the
proposed replacement bus services, which in the case of Eastern Scottish's
Hawick-Selkirk-Edinburgh service involved an increase in winter frequency from
seven to 16 buses each weekday. It did not clarify that the bus would take a
minimum of 55 minutes longer than the train from Hawick to Edinburgh.

The closure notice invited individuals who felt they would suffer personal
hardship – in the case of stations from Eskbank to Newcastleton – to write to
the Transport Users Consultative Committee for Scotland (TUCC). TUCC
papers in the National Archives of Scotland (NAS) recorded that closure notices
had been posted in the *Scotsman* and nine local newspapers, and at 26 stations in
Scottish Region, 13 in London Midland Region, two in Eastern Region and one
in North Eastern Region – in other words, not many more than those stations
directly served by trains which operated over the Waverley Route.

The BR 'Heads of Information' cited estimated route receipts of £101,800
and direct expenses of £357,800, potentially implying an annual loss of
£256,000 – but subsequent clarification, based on an assumed retention of just
a third of the line's additional £64,690 contributory gross revenue to the rest of
the network, would produce an estimated net financial saving of £232,000 from
withdrawing all passenger services.

In the immediate aftermath of the closure proposal there was a surge of
popular support to save the railway, articulated predominantly by a few key
individuals as well as the main local newspapers, who were quick to react, and
overwhelmingly in uncompromising terms. On 18th August, in a front page

editorial under the headline 'Fight to Save the Railway ', the *Southern Reporter* commented:

> The statement made by the chairman of the BRB that there was nothing inconsistent with the closure of the line and the designation of the Borders as a development area just doesn't make sense. Too many people however appear to be unaware of the seriousness of the threat, or have been lulled into a sense of false security by the long lapse of time, and believe that the axe will never fall. This attitude is wrong and decidedly dangerous; let there be no mistake, the threat is very real. The fight to retain the Waverley Route must go on with renewed vigour and in complete unity.

On 19th August the *Hawick News* reported that as closure notices were being posted at local stations: '5000 protest questionnaires calling for public support went out to shops, offices, factories and hotels in the Borders'. 1,000 public notices also went up on behalf of 14 local authorities, including eight in the Borders. Two weeks later, under the headline 'Good Response in Rail Closure Protest' the paper's report quoted the Deputy County Clerk of Roxburgh as finding the return of more than 1,650 questionnaires 'very gratifying'. The *Southern Reporter* of 25th August carried a long article headlined 'Battle to Retain the Border Rail Line is on', in which the issue of apathy – a recurring theme throughout the campaign against closure – was well illustrated:

> Borders Provosts have been strongly critical of the proposal to close the Edinburgh to Carlisle line, especially in view of the newly planned development which is scheduled to take place in the Eastern and Western areas. Several expressed some fear that the attempt to present objections to the public enquiry held by the TUCC may be prejudiced by apathy among Borderers, who do not realise the serious nature of the situation. Provost William Pate of Galashiels said that there was always the danger of apathy, particularly from car owners. 'It is not that they don't want the railway but having got a car they assume an independence. What they must remember is that women and elderly people, possibly less well off, and youngsters under 17, do not drive cars . . .' Provost Tom Plenderleith of Kelso felt sure that there would be a degree of apathy. 'Apathy is common in the Borders and unless people in the street are really aware about it, we are going to be without a railway line . . .' Provost James Henderson of Hawick was rather gloomy in his forecast of the eventual result. 'I do not know where people get the idea that the line might stay. All the way to Edinburgh stations are deteriorating and everything points to a close down."

The proposed closure was attracting interest nationwide, and in a news report for the *Guardian* of 30th August 1966, its Planning Correspondent, Terence Bendixson – later to be the acclaimed author of the prescient book *Instead of Cars* (1974), and recently a Senior Visiting Research Fellow at the University of Southampton – highlighted the inconsistency between rail closure plans and the proposed 25,000 increase in population in a new town (Tweedbank) just east of Gala:

> Doubts have also been expressed as to whether any employers will want to settle in a place that is fairly remote from the national motorway network and in imminent danger of having its railway links with Edinburgh and Carlisle closed.

> Roxburgh County Council is campaigning against this closure and one of its protest forms was filled in by your correspondent following the earnest entreaties of a commuter travelling home on the 17 56 from Edinburgh. The railways say that the line costs £500,000 a year but with double track working, lots of signalmen and a porter at every station, it can hardly be said that they have tried to economise.

On 22nd September, under the headline 'Border Burghs Deplore Threat to Railway', the *Southern Reporter* noted:

> The proposed closure of the Waverley Route was described as a 'severe body-blow to the economy of the Borders' at the AGM of the Border Burghs Convention at Coldstream on Tuesday. Provost W. Pate of Galashiels stated that the Waverley Route may not be paying its way but there were many things in this country which did not pay yet were extremely necessary. 'There is considerable development in the area where the railway runs,' said the Provost. 'There must be a strong fight to keep the railway open.' . . . Police Judge Smith, Peebles, said it was little use getting people to sign a petition. The only way to try to keep the line open was by putting forward a key argument.

As we shall see in Chapter 4, the Provost's enthusiasm for the railway had waned by 1968, and petitions did prove to be insufficient to save the Waverley Route. But we now find an early mention of the man who (together with David Steel MP) was to be the most consistent public campaigner over the next two and a half years, and whose name will always be associated with the most dramatic incident in the last rites of the railway. On 29th September, the *Southern Reporter's* news story about a protest meeting in Hawick, attended by almost 350 people, recorded that: 'The Reverend Brydon Maben of Newcastleton called the proposal to close the Edinburgh-Carlisle railway line a "low blow" to the Borders and attacked the British Railways Board for systematically running down the line since 1962.'

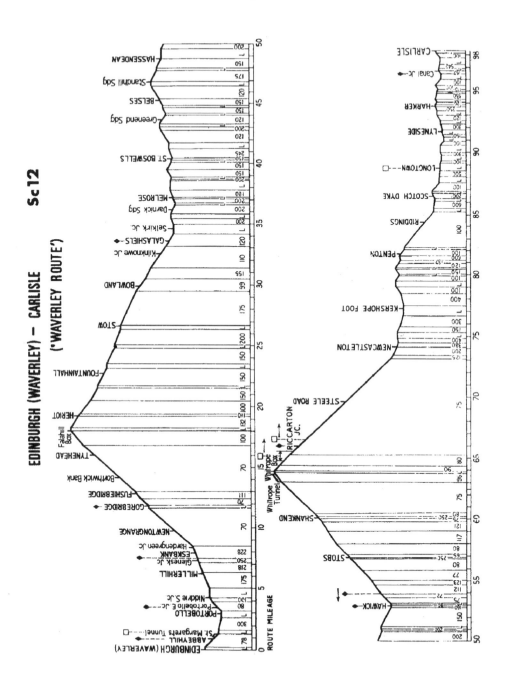

The operational challenge posed by the Waverley Route is all too clear in this gradient profile, showing mileage along the bottom horizontal axis and, above that, gradients – eg '75' = 1 in 75.
Ian Allan Publishing Ltd

While the closure proposal was generating plenty of headlines in the public domain, the case for the railway was also being pursued behind the scenes. The Montgomery archive contains an internal memo by BR Scottish Region Assistant General Manager Gordon Stewart – evidently written in October 1966 – in which he reports on a 21st October meeting with the Earl of Dalkeith (later the ninth Duke of Buccleuch), Conservative MP for Edinburgh North, who would work closely with David Steel on the campaign against closure right through to the last days of the Waverley Route. In response to a query as to whether any planned 'major maintenance' might be inflating the annual maintenance figures supplied in the closure proposal, Stewart had explained to him, 'that so far as I was aware there was no major work to be done but, in any case, the figures for maintenance were the annual maintenance figures and had nothing to do with capital expenditure.' Pressed by Dalkeith as to how he could know that maintenance figures really were not inflated by exceptional circumstances, Stewart had indicated:

> he would have to take my word for it. On the other hand, if he had not had the opportunity to speak to me he was at liberty, as was anyone else, to raise this direct with the Minister who was responsible to ensure that our figures were correctly presented.

Outside observers might have taken a less sanguine view of the Minister of Transport's presentational motivation, and Stewart's choice of words – 'so far as I was aware' – looks an odd way for an Assistant General Manager to describe his level of knowledge of major works in his own territory. However, this was evidently not pursued further at the time and Dalkeith then raised an issue which had been privately flagged up within the Scottish Office by civil servant Frank Spaven just six weeks before the publication of the closure proposal. Interestingly, Spaven lived in Dalkeith's Edinburgh North constituency until his July 1966 departure to Inverness, and it is possible that he had been briefing Dalkeith off-the-record about the Waverley Route. The author certainly recollects correspondence – encouraged by his father – between the MP and the Spaven household at 25a Inverleith Terrace, when as a teenage enthusiast for the railway he wrote to advocate re-opening of the Edinburgh suburban lines. The Stewart memo continued:

> Lord Dalkeith floated the possibility that we might retain the Edinburgh-Hawick section and asked whether we had considered this. I indicated that this naturally was a factor which had been in our minds, but we were satisfied that there was a greater pay-off in the complete withdrawal than a partial withdrawal as the retention of the

Due to its combination of gradients and curvature, the Waverley Route was one of the most challenging main lines to operate in Britain. This January 1966 shot of the gradient post on the 'Up' (to Carlisle) side of the line at Stobs records the single steepest gradient on the entire 98¼ mile route – a short section of 1 in 65 through Stobs station. *Roy Perkins*

Edinburgh-Hawick lines [sic] would still give us a loss. It was our duty in accordance with the Act to go for the greater pay off between Edinburgh and Carlisle.

Dalkeith had also asked whether singling of the line (another point raised by Frank Spaven within the Scottish Office) had been considered. Stewart had responded that the conversion from double line to single line 'did not mean halving of our maintenance costs, and that we would indeed incur considerable capital costs in altered layout and the introduction of a new type of signalling.' This reads like a particularly negative interpretation of the outcome of singling.

The objectors and the public hearing

Despite the extensive publicity about the closure proposal, just 508 individuals and organisations lodged official objections with the TUCC in Edinburgh within the allotted six weeks – less than one third of those who had gone to the trouble of completing protest questionnaires only a few weeks earlier. One wonders if there was confusion about the function of the local authority questionnaire and the need to make a formal objection as well?

The number of objections also compared very poorly with the response from users of another threatened line which had some parallels with the northern half of Waverley Route – the 49-mile East Suffolk line (of which, more in Chapter 4). The 1965 proposed closure of this double-track rural route from Ipswich to Lowestoft, serving small market towns and villages, attracted no less than 1,916 written objections, as reported by John Brodribb in *An Illustrated History of the East Suffolk Railway* (2004). Yet passenger numbers on this East Anglian line were not much greater than on the Waverley Route – 2,222 on a winter Tuesday sampled for the closure process (compared to 1,771 on the Waverley Route) and 2,683 on a sample winter Saturday (compared to 2,767). A route with around 20% more passengers had generated 277% more objections to closure.

Closer to home, the North Berwick branch whose patronage was some 300,000 passengers per annum (compared to around 500,000 on the Waverley

Route) managed to generate almost as many objections to proposed closure (450) as its near neighbour. In fairness, a higher proportion of users of the North Berwick commuter service were 'movers and shakers' who were able to bring their professional skills and networking contacts to bear in the ultimately successful campaign against closure.

An (incomplete) set of copies of the Waverley Route closure objections is held by the National Records of Scotland in Edinburgh. Reflecting the technology of the times and the breadth of objections, most were handwritten – unsurprisingly in the case of nine-year old Ralph Coleman from Galashiels, who (not perhaps unprompted!) was astute enough to comment that 'Galashiels has been named as a growth area in the new Border development plan, and the absence of a railway will be [sic] nonsense of this proposal'.

A Colonel Smiley of Branxholm near Hawick lodged an exotic objection, albeit of dubious social import, noting that his two sons travelled to school at Eton by train, and that 'as military adviser to King Feisal of Saudi Arabia, I am on call whenever he sends for me'. A private jet might have been more appropriate, and the esteemed Colonel certainly did not appear in the list of passengers regularly using the overnight sleeper to St Pancras, compiled by BR in a briefing for its Liaison Officer attending the Public Hearing in Hawick later in 1966. The list did include eight Lords and Ladies, David Steel MP (a weekly user), Baroness Elliot (the most frequent user, at twice weekly, who later led the November 1968 House of Lords' debate on the railway), and representatives from five Borders' knitwear firms.

An objection from Mr H Kerrod, Managing Director of the cutting-edge knitwear design firm Bernat Klein, based in Galashiels, illustrates how significantly business expected to be affected when he commented, 'we have a great many customers travelling from England by train via Carlisle and there would be considerable inconvenience to such personnel if the Waverley / Carlisle service were to be closed.' This was not just a concern about passenger transport – and evidence cited in the TUCC Report suggested that 50% of the knitwear and tweed industries' products were sent to market by rail, in particular to London.

Most objections came of course from individuals who faced personal hardship, typified by Madge Elliot of Hawick (later to become one of the key campaigners against closure), whose typed 1st October 1966 letter to the TUCC described a Sunday journey to visit her son in hospital which had to be undertaken by bus because of the lack of suitably-timed trains. She wrote: 'the homeward journey of 2½ hours was most unpleasant. I never undertook the bus journey again.' Sadly, of course, she had to undertake the bus journey many times after 5th January 1969 – and was still a regular bus user more than 40 years later.

Other noteworthy objections included a collective letter from no less than 47 Glasgow 'overspill' families who had shifted some years earlier to Hawick, and faced a much-extended journey time back to family and friends if the railway closed.

The Reverend Brydon Maben made a more political point: 'We have had to stand by and watch while British Rail have systematically run down the Waverley Route.' Many other objectors deplored the lack of a strategic vision for the railway, including the County Councillor for Melrose North, Marguerite F Douglas, who wrote on 3rd October 1966:

> I have been brought up mostly in Switzerland where the railways are run differently, where stations are clean and attractive and where people do use them in great numbers. If our railways were run half as well the same would happen here. I am appalled at the short sightedness of a Government which cannot organise its transport system to make full use of all its potential instead of cutting down. At this rate the sooner Scotland gets home rule the better.

This was an insightful comment – roads policy in Scotland (including trunk roads and grants to Local Authority roads) had been controlled by the Scottish Office since 1956, but rail policy was entirely a matter for the distant Ministry of Transport in London.

The lack of understanding of local circumstances by southern decision makers is well illustrated by David Steel, who recalled in his 1989 autobiography *Against Goliath* the words of the Labour Transport Minister who condemned the route to closure, Richard Marsh: 'who never showed any sympathy for our case, asking me at one interview, "How do you pronounce Hawick?" – the largest town on the route.'

Other objectors didn't just bemoan the lack of vision for the railway, but came up with some very positive ideas to rejuvenate the Waverley Route. A Mr JM Melling of Edinburgh submitted four pages to the TUCC entitled 'Towards a more efficent railway service for the Scottish Borders', suggesting that just two staffed stations be retained at Galashiels and Hawick, with ticket issuing on trains, and lower cost diesel multiple units operating a 2-hourly frequency between Edinburgh and Hawick.

The volume and diversity of objections to closure of the Waverley Route ensured that the arguments for and against closure would get a full airing, and on 16th and 17th November a Public Hearing was held in Hawick Town Hall, where every objector was given the opportunity to speak in support of written objections. AJ Mullay notes in *Scottish Region A History 1948–73* (2007):

> the Scottish Borderers turned out in impressive force and even more impressive unity. Ranged against closure were the County Councils of Berwickshire,

Roxburghshire and Selkirkshire, along with the Town Councils of Galashiels, Jedburgh, Innerleithen, Hawick, Kelso, Selkirk and Peebles. All but two of these towns had already lost their own railway stations, but clearly believed in the importance of having access to a railhead.

The Waverley Route hearing was in fact the last of the Beeching Report's Scottish closure proposals to come before the TUCC, reflecting the difficulty of assembling a credible bus alternative, as well as political concerns over the impact of timing on the Labour administration's plans for the Scottish economy.

The Committee's subsequent report was long and comprehensive, and contained some striking comments, such as 'the evidence presented by the objectors emphasised that the fabric of community life in the Borders would be entirely disrupted by the withdrawal of the passenger train services.' It also included many sobering facts, not least that for 850 'regular' travellers from the main Borders stations to Edinburgh (travelling at least once a month, as identified by the Roxburgh County Council survey) 'the withdrawal of the train service to Edinburgh would result in the journey times by alternative bus services of all these passengers being practically doubled.'

The numbers game was however effectively deployed by BR where it suited them. Assistant General Manager Gordon Stewart commented to the Public Hearing:

> In a representative week the total number of passengers using comparable train services in 1964 was 5,354 as opposed to 4,342 in 1966, a reduction of 1,012. Over the same 10 year period, in which this drastic reduction in rail patronage has taken place, the number of motor cars registered in the counties of Berwick, Peebles, Roxburgh and Selkirk has increased from 8,700 to 18,600, a ratio of one car for every 5 persons residing in the area, which is higher than the national average of 5.9 per head of population. The effect of this high percentage of private car ownership on public transport services, particularly so far as railways are concerned, is that they are regarded merely as stand-by services to be used only when the family car is not available or when adverse Winter road conditions and traffic congestion difficulties may be prevalent.

This latter point was an uncomfortable truth for campaigners (albeit that BR had done little to stem the tide of decline), but Stewart was skewing the level of car ownership by incorporating data from Berwickshire, south-east Roxburghshire and Peeblesshire – all areas devoid of railway stations since 1964 or earlier, and with much more thinly spread populations, notably the lack of any town even approaching half the size of Galashiels or Hawick.

Car ownership in Galashiels and Hawick was almost certainly well under 50%

of households at the time, and considering that these two towns constituted around 90% of the population along the railway within the Central Borders it becomes harder to argue that the Waverley Route was necessarily that much more severely affected by rising car ownership than any other part of the country.

The adequacy (or inadequacy) of the replacement bus service was naturally the main focus of the TUCC report – not just in terms of journey times and reliability (particularly in winter weather), but also qualitative issues such as lack of toilets, non-smoking accommodation and luggage space, plus the 'less favourable travel conditions for the elderly, handicapped and people who suffer from bus sickness.' The bus replacement issue was a key concern for the SRDA, which was represented at the Hearing (as noted in its December 1966 Development Report) by a Mr JG Ramsay, whose report included some interesting commentary:

> The local authorities' case (among them our corporate member Roxburgh County had nearly 4,000 completed questionnaires) was an extensive one. It turned out that in examining the alternative service for Castleton [sic, perhaps describing the parish as a whole] the TUCC's bus had followed the wrong road. The correct road rises to 1,100 ft. To nowhere in Liddelsdale [sic] will it be possible to make a return journey from Edinburgh within a single day.

Responding to Gordon Stewart's comment that the Borders had one car for every five people and that rail passenger traffic had declined by 55% from 1955 to 1965, the SRDA noted that: 'In Mr Ramsay's judgement, however, this results from BR not doing its best' – a very widely held view at the time and thereafter.

After considering all the written and oral objections, the TUCC unanimously concluded that in the event of closure:

> Substantial hardship would be experienced by the existing users of Galashiels, Melrose, St Boswells and Hawick Stations. There was sufficient evidence to indicate that a considerable number of passengers rely on the train service when travelling regularly to Edinburgh for business, educational and social/recreational purposes, and to a lesser but equally important degree, those who use the through trains and sleeping car facilities for business journeys to the Midlands and London in connection with the textile industry.

> Although the proposed alternative bus services are adequate quantitatively to cater for displaced rail passengers, these could not be regarded as a reasonable alternative for journeys of from 30–50 miles, particularly during Winter months when extreme difficulty may be experienced in maintaining time-table working.

The TUCC Report concluded that the proposed introduction of a daily bus service to Carlisle 'would alleviate hardship to the majority of passengers using Newcastleton Station', but that the proposed use of workers' bus services between Newcastleton and Hawick 'would not remove the hardship which would be caused to the small number of passengers who travel intermittently between these points.' While the TUCC's sole remit was 'hardship', it did report objectors' views on the regional development issue, flagging up an indirect impact which was to become a repeated theme later in the campaign against closure:

> Without a rail service the area would be less attractive to industrialists, and difficulty would also be experienced in arresting the flow of people leaving the four Border counties which, in the period 1951–1961, lost 20% of the working population in the 20–45 age group. The *psychological impact* [author's italics] would, in all probability, exacerbate the problem of depopulation in this area.

With regard to all other stations on the line, the Committee agreed that the proposed bus alternatives would be adequate to deal with displaced passengers – providing further support for the view that the railway had not been focusing on what it could do best in an era of increasing car and bus competition. BR's closure proposal figures had showed that a majority of the intermediate stations saw less than 20 passengers a day – station staff at these locations were clearly superfluous (and BR would soon address this) but every stop for few, if any, passengers still added time and operating cost to the longer and more rail-suited transits to the main traffic-generating stations at Melrose, Galashiels, St Boswells and Hawick.

The TUCC's report (15 pages plus nine appendices) was sent to Barbara Castle on 22nd December 1966, but it was to be no less than 19 months until her successor as Minister of Transport sealed the fate of the Waverley Route.

19 months in limbo

In his 1968 rail report to David Steel MP (see Chapter 4), John Hibbs said that railway management had been 'unable' to make alterations to services while their line was under review. Looking back in 2010, Hibbs did not attach particular criticism to BR Scottish Region managers, since the pattern of no timetable changes being introduced until such time as the Minister refused consent to closure 'was BRB policy [ie throughout Britain], rarely if ever questioned'. Within Scotland, no less than four routes in the Glasgow area had had an irregular service but became hourly-interval in 1966 after reprieve – to Barrhead, East Kilbride, Kilmacolm and Shotts. In apparent defence of the policy of having left the Waverley Route service preserved in aspic, Gordon Stewart, by now BR's

General Manager Scottish Region, wrote in a 20th January 1969 letter to the *Glasgow Herald*:

> How foolish it would have been to spend large sums on new signalling and the singling of track and then receive the Minister's permission to withdraw the services. All schemes of this nature had to be put in cold storage pending the Minister's decision.

On the face of it, a logical argument, but what Stewart failed to address was the available low-cost option of introducing the long-overdue regular-interval service on the *existing* (double-track) infrastructure, in order to boost revenue and reduce the deficit. Services could have been operated by diesel multiple units rather than the more expensive locomotive-hauled trains used for all-year Monday-Friday services north of Hawick until the very end. Given that freight and parcels/mail service changes were entirely a matter for BR's commercial judgement (and therefore did not need Ministerial consent), the eight or so through freight trains (and one parcels/mail service) in each direction could have been re- routed via Carstairs – as they would be on 6th January 1969 – enabling the cost of perhaps three signal boxes (those not controlling road level crossings) out of eight south of Hawick to be eliminated and many of the remaining boxes on the entire route to be brought down to two-shift working. Of course, the policy of not changing the timetable once a closure proposal was published may also have been based on the reasonable logic (if closure is the corporate objective) that improving the timetable would generate more passengers which would therefore generate more hardship in the event of closure, thereby making closure more difficult!

British Rail did make important economies between 1963 and 1968. Within the Rae Montgomery archive now held by the National Records of Scotland is an undated late 1968 internal BR memo which records that 12 stations were destaffed (all but one in 1967) and 19 signalboxes closed (the majority prior to 1966 – presumably reflecting dieselisation as well as traffic losses). The same memo records that staff numbers on the line (London Midland plus Scottish) were reduced from 439 in 1963 to 274 in 1968, a 38% reduction.

Only seven intermediate stations remained staffed – Galashiels, Melrose, St Boswells, Hawick, Newcastleton, Penton and Longtown. 15 signal boxes survived between Port Carlisle Junction and Millerhill on the edge of Edinburgh, and the number of freight depots had fallen from 21 in 1963 to just three in 1968 – Gala, St Boswells and Hawick.

BR Scottish Region management's October 1968 memorandum to staff on redundancies arising from closure nevertheless reveals – certainly by today's standards – an incredible level of staffing along the overwhelmingly Scottish portion of the route. No less than 209 posts were identified, including 92 at Hawick alone – from the Area Manager through platform and clerical staff, engineers and train crew to two plumbers! In fairness, this reflected management-union agreements of that era – and the inevitably labour-intensive nature of operating and maintaining a double-track and almost entirely (except at Galashiels) semaphore-signalled railway, over a long and in places difficult rail corridor. However, at least one important observer of the local scene disapproved of the heavy cost burden on the railway. In her 2nd December 1970 letter to the Secretary of State for Scotland, anticipating the disposal of the formation of the Waverley Route, Madge Elliot commented:

> Young railway enthusiasts who frequented the station were given minor duties to do by railway personnel who preferred to sit around playing cards, dominoes or spend their working days sleeping in a bothy. One even got the impression when queuing up at the ticket office that they would have preferred to do without our custom. Many economies could have been made by British Rail themselves.

A contrary view of staff attitudes was given by BR manager, Bill Kent, in a filmed interview on one of the final special trains to traverse the line on 4th January 1969. Kent, who had worked on the Waverley Route early in his career and went on to be a 'high flier' in posts as Divisional Manager Bristol, Deputy General Manager Western Region and at the British Railways Board in London, commented on the imminent closure:

> My own feelings – it's a matter of great regret to me personally, because I enjoyed my days in the Borders more than almost anywhere else in my railway career because of the quality of the staff, the railway staff in the Borders. They were wonderful people to work with, and I had a great admiration and respect for them.

Whatever the qualities of BR employees in the Borders, it is clear that a heavily rationalised and modernised single-track railway from Hawick to Edinburgh would have required only a fraction of the prevailing staffing levels 43 years ago. As we have seen, alternative approaches to the function and operation of the Waverley Route had been mooted as early as 1963 by the Scottish Railway Development Association (SRDA), and on 13th February 1967 a draft report 'The Waverley Route – the case for retention and development' by its Honorary Secretary, Tom Hart, was circulated within the Scottish Office. Hart's report cited the scope for more cost-effective operations, with an hourly Edinburgh-Hawick service (every third train continuing to Carlisle) operated by

'Inter-City' diesel multiple units (DMUs) which were due to be replaced on front-line duty on the Edinburgh-Glasgow service.

Interestingly, the SRDA report mooted in one option – as well as a radical restructuring of fares, closure of smaller stations and provision of additional car parking at the remaining stations – rerouting all through passenger and freight trains via Carstairs, with track then able to be singled south of Stobs, and between Hawick and St Boswells, Galashiels and Heriot, and Tynehead and Millerhill. It was also suggested that the remaining Hawick-Carlisle passenger trains be diverted south of Longtown via the single-track freight chord to Mossband Junction on the West Coast Main Line opened in 1963 for southbound traffic only (see map on page 60), thus further reducing track and signalling overheads. Unbeknown to campaigners – and only discovered in searches at the National Archives at Kew in 2012 – just two months later that proposition got official, but off-the-record, backing. The Minutes of BR's Regional Rationalisation Committee of 11th April 1967 record that the line:

> would be retained on the basis of being a passenger and freight route so as to enable Carlisle-Edinburgh Waverley services to be diverted away from the direct route between Longtown and Carlisle if the Minister refuses to consent to the full withdrawal of the passenger service.

This decision implies that freight traffic on both the Waverley Route and the West Coast Main Line had declined sufficiently by 1967 to overcome the capacity problems on the latter which had prevented northbound freights being diverted over the Mossband-Longtown chord when Kingmoor Yard opened in 1963.

The SRDA quoted two key examples of rail routes where there had been substantial reductions in losses after services had been reprieved – the Far North line from Inverness to Wick and Thurso, and the Central Wales line from Swansea to Shrewsbury (both of which served much smaller intermediate towns than the Waverley Route). SRDA also suggested that an improved service between Edinburgh and Hawick could by 1970 generate annual receipts of £190,000 – a considerably more optimistic view than BR's 1967 estimate of just £90,000 from such a service. Disagreements about cost and revenue figures were a recurring feature of the closure process, and we return to examine this issue in some detail in Chapter 4.

Tom Hart in 2010 recalled 1967–68 meetings with a BR Scottish Region manager who had contingency plans, if closure was refused, to introduce an hourly limited-stop service between Edinburgh and Hawick operated by diesel multiple units (DMUs). The BR manager anticipated this could fully cover operational (but not track and signalling) costs, and stimulate a rise in usage, reversing many years of decline – and potentially showing a better business performance than some other Scottish services. Unfortunately the SRDA could not push this as hard as it would have liked due to lack of resources and limited membership in the Borders. Hart also recollected that with high employment and increasing car ownership 'a lot of people were either not bothered about the railway closing, or thought it could never happen'. Some may simply have felt closure was a *fait accompli*, for good or ill.

A further nail in the coffin of the Waverley Route came in BR's May 1967 publication of its *Network for Development* plans, which confirmed that the line qualified neither as a main trunk route to be developed nor as a rural route justifying subsidy on social grounds. Formal acknowledgement of the social role of the rail network finally came with Barbara Castle's ground-breaking 1968 Transport Act, which as Christian Wolmar says in *Fire & Steam* (2007), his history of Britain's railways:

> relieved the railways of the impossible target set by Marples of breaking even or making a profit. She recognised, for the first time, that the railways needed financial support from the government, creating a distinction between commercial services which should pay for themselves and 'social' ones which needed subsidy.

The future direction of the rail network was of course primarily determined by politicians and rail management, but BR was also a heavily unionised industry where the workforce was potentially very influential. The attitude of the railway trade unions to the Beeching cuts is a moot point in consideration of the Waverley Route. There was less opposition nationally to the BR closure progr-amme than one might have expected, and it has been suggested that the unions' priority was above all to protect the terms and condition of established grades and the heavy concentration of jobs in the major conurbations. Employment losses from rural branch lines were modest relative to the unions' urban strongholds, and there is anecdotal evidence that at least some rail employees in the Borders welcomed the prospect of redundancy payment at a time of relative prosperity and high employment in parts of the region. Madge Elliot in 2010 recollected receiving an anonymous letter (post-marked Stow) from a railwayman warning her off the campaign against closure.

The calibre and attitude of local railway management during the interregnum between announcement of the closure proposal in mid-1966 and the closure consent in mid-1968 were arguably of some importance for the fate of the line. In late 1965, BR Scottish Region had made its first appointments in a new Area Management structure, designed to give stronger power locally by grouping a number of stations under one local manager and abolishing individual Station

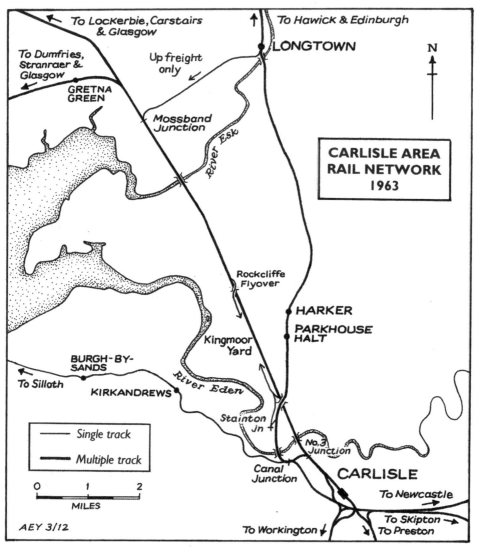

The new connection created at Mossband Junction in 1963 – extending part of the
former NBR Longtown-Gretna branch (also serving the Ministry of Defence sites at
Longtown and Smalmstown) to create a south-facing link to the WCML – allowed freight trains
from Millerhill Yard (Edinburgh) to run directly into Kingmoor Yard. Arguably, the junction
could have been enhanced to enable both southbound and northbound freight and passenger trains
on the Waverley Route to use this chord – eliminating the cost of maintaining the
Longtown-Harker section of the railway.

Alan Young

Masters. Scotland was divided into more than 30 geographical areas, and the new Hawick Area, set up on 8th November 1965 covered the Waverley Route and its branches within Scotland south of Millerhill.

Just a few weeks later, a BR graduate management trainee, Douglas Paul, was told to report to the new Area Manager at Hawick for eight weeks management training. As Paul recollected in 2011, to local railway staff 'the fact that Hawick was chosen as the first candidate for Area Management was seen as a positive sign and raised their hopes that they would now have a champion for their cause', but these hopes were not to be realised:

> Unfortunately, the reality was to fall well short of these expectations as it became all too apparent that the new Area Manager did not share their belief in the line's future. [Name expurgated to save his family any embarrassment] had come up from the south to take charge and, in a community with close knit family ties, he was very much an outsider showing no empathy with them or their concerns . . .
> I recall in particular one of his assistants, a former station master at St Boswells, inviting me for dinner with him and his wife and seeing at first hand the visible strain that his management style was putting them under.

Douglas Paul himself had an early direct experience of the new Area Manager's bizarre management style, reflecting the development of a bunker mentality, 'with communication by written edict rather than face to face, and a sense that he was alienating himself from his staff.' At the end of his earlier training period in Dundee, Paul was told to report to the Area Manager at Hawick the following Monday, and to hand in his report on the Dundee training to the Divisional Manager in Edinburgh en route to Hawick. This he did, arriving in Hawick around 10am on the Monday. The Area Manager was away having a driving lesson, so:

> I waited . . . and waited. He did not appear all day so I left a note on his desk saying sorry I had missed him and that I would see him the next day. The following morning I introduced myself to him and he said 'you're 24 hours late, why is that?' I asked if he had received my note and he told me he had sent it to the Divisional Manager. I was to get on the next train to Edinburgh to see him. Somewhat in shock, I did so and explained the situation to the Divisional Manager's secretary. She made enquiries but no one had any knowledge of the note or the Divisional Manager's request to see me. By now totally bemused, I returned to Hawick and asked the A.M. what that was all about. His reply floored me. "That's just to teach you a lesson," he said!

While Paul was able to develop a degree of rapport with his boss during eight weeks at Hawick, it became increasingly evident to him that there was no prospect of that happening with his colleagues. He remembers staff representatives making proposals for efficiency savings and increasing business on the line, including the possibility of gaining timber traffic from Kielder Forest, but 'to my knowledge all of these were rejected, the attitude being that every penny spent trying to regenerate the line was wasted.' One may also note that in the late 1960s plans were being discussed for creation of the largest reservoir in Britain at Kielder Water, just seven miles down the old Border Counties line from Riccarton. Given the scale of the project, and rail's strengths in the emerging full trainload transport of aggregates and cement – and the major timber potential – the re-opening of this rail link should have been a priority for BR.

In July 1967, Osmond ('Ossie') Simpson replaced the first Area Manager incumbent, who transferred to Darlington after 20 months at Hawick. Simpson, who had moved from a post in Kirkcaldy, had a different attitude to the job and to his staff – Douglas Paul noting that when the line eventually closed he 'did his utmost to alleviate the pain of redundancy' – and it is arguable that had he been appointed say a year earlier then the rate of decline in Waverley Route traffic might have been stemmed. Interestingly, as recalled by ex-BR manager Allan McLean in 2011, that would have involved a longer overlap with the period when the BR Edinburgh Division Commercial Manager, Ron Cotton – later to become renowned for his BR role in generating new business on the Settle & Carlisle line while it was still under threat – was organising a variety of excursion trains that featured the Waverley Route in their itinerary.

Rae Montgomery – who went on to have a long career on the railway, culminating as Project Manager in Glasgow – recollected in 2011 that he had been interviewed in late 1965 or early 1966 for the post of Operating Assistant at Hawick. Had the opportunity arisen for Cotton, Simpson and Montgomery to work together for a decent length of time, perhaps there would have been a different outcome for the Waverley Route, at least north of Hawick? But it was not to be – Montgomery's application was unsuccessful, and by the time Simpson arrived in Hawick, the die was nearly cast.

Arguments behind the scenes

In *Scottish Region: A History 1948–1973*, AJ Mullay comments:

> Considering the size of this closure – the UK's biggest until the Great Central was broken up – there is remarkably little about the Waverley Route in BR management files (nor Board Minutes . . .) in Scotland's National Archives. Indeed, there is far more about recovery of assets in the event of closure than in discussing how costs could have been reduced by the singling, unstaffed stations and so on . . .

Fortunately the National Records of Scotland (NRS) do contain a wealth of Scottish Office archive material which sheds light on much of the political discussion, and indeed argument, which was going on behind the scenes from as early as 1964 through to closure, and beyond. A Scottish Development Department (SDD) memorandum of 24th January 1967, setting out 'Consolidated Planning Observations' on the Waverley Route closure proposal, invited the civil servants on the circulation list to refer to papers of the 18th and 19th August 1965 by Frank Spaven and in particular his observation that closure would:

make this region by far the largest population grouping in Britain with no accessible railway services' and his calculation that the population in this area who will be more than 25 miles by road from the nearest railway station will amount to 70,000 persons.

The SDD memo concluded:

this line cannot be closed and all efforts should now be directed towards developing a co-ordinated transport service which will be integrated with the development proposals [to increase the population between Galashiels and St Boswells by 25,000 by 1980, as proposed by the White Paper on the Scottish Economy].

It was suggested that 'the present substantial losses could be reduced considerably in the short term', and perhaps surprisingly retention of the entire route was recommended, with stations retained at Galashiels, Melrose, St Boswells, Hawick and Newcastleton, and possibly also Eskbank, Newtongrange and Gorebridge ('which would depend on proposals for Edinburgh.')

As seen in Chapter 2, the Minister of Transport was required to consult regional economic planning councils on the strategic impacts of closure proposals. The Scottish Economic Planning Council (SEPC) received considerable input to the Waverley Route deliberations from the Borders Consultative Group, chaired by Ernest Tait, a local industrialist. In March 1967, after a number of discussions with the Scottish Office and associated redrafts, the Group reported to the SEPC to the effect that they 'are of the opinion that the proposed withdrawal of services would have a detrimental effect, both materially and *psychologically*, on the economic development planned for the Western Borders.' [author's italics]

The Borders Consultative Group report had evidently taken on board at least part of the SRDA's analysis, arguing that 'there is scope for a considerable reduction in costs and for an increase in earnings', the Group citing the opportunity to close or de-staff most stations, single the track and modernise the signalling, and operate all services with lower-cost diesel multiple units. There was equally forthright criticism of BR's revenue failings:

> Passenger earnings (including passenger freight) [ie parcels] could be improved by better services, more suitable to the needs of travellers and users in the region. British Railways have lost a great deal of trade because they have provided a poor service on this line, eg trains at inconvenient times, dirty carriages, unreliable and slow freight services, etc . . . [We] understand that in several cases of lines proposed for closure, on the grounds that they were running at a loss, much improved financial results have been obtained when the lines were reprieved.

The Group's core conclusion was simple, advising SEPC that they 'consider the rail closure proposal to be quite inconsistent with the development plans for the Borders.' The line should be retained, 'and every effort made to run it as efficiently and economically as possible'. Looking to the future the Group 'envisage the railway as a vital and more remunerative line servicing the new communities and expanded towns of a revitalised region.'

That position could of course have been consistent with retention of the line only north of Hawick. As seen in Chapter 2, even before BR published its closure proposal the Scottish Office had confidentially mooted the possibility of retaining only part of the route, and on 3rd April 1967 civil servant GF Hendry wrote to GW Stewart, Assistant General Manager, BR Scottish Region, requesting estimates of cost savings from operating economies over the whole line, together with estimates of costs and revenue if the line were operated on this revised basis only as far south as (a) Galashiels, (b) St Boswells, or (c) Hawick. BR estimated that the best (or strictly speaking, least worst) revenue-to-cost ratio (1:4.1) was for a single-track Hawick-Edinburgh passenger-only option requiring an annual subsidy of £276,000.

In the same month as the Scottish Office had asked BR for these figures for a rationalised Waverley Route, the Economics Department of Edinburgh University (which had been engaged by the Scottish Office to report on the closure case, as well as a wider remit to produce a Central Borders Plan) submitted its rail report. This is neither the easiest nor the most convincing of reads, but its key conclusions were relatively straightforward. The likely actual costs of operation appeared to be lower than what BR had advised and there was room for operating economies. The deficit would be partly eliminated by the planned increase in population in the Galashiels / Tweedbank area, and:

> the railway has a considerable value which is not reflected in the commercial account. It is difficult to quantify all but time savings of these social benefits, but

this limited attempt at quantification suggests that the magnitude of these benefits would justify the line.

An interesting aspect of the decline in rail usage was unearthed in the report; evidence given by the Scottish Bus Group suggested that bus usage on the Edinburgh-Hawick-Carlisle route had declined by 66% between 1955 and 1965, compared to a rail decline of around 55%, showing that 'the railways have fared better than their rival'.

The Borders Consultative Group and Edinburgh University reports were both considered by committees of the SEPC before the closure proposal, along with various alternatives to complete closure, was considered by the full Council at its meeting on 9th June 1967. This meeting in St Andrew's House, Edinburgh was attended by 16 members and 21 officials (including an MoT representative), and was chaired by Willie Ross MP, the Secretary of State for Scotland. In general discussion it was agreed that 'closure of the line at this stage would have an adverse *psychological* impact on the prospects for the Borders and would make attraction of new industry to the area very much more difficult'. [author's italics] Several members also drew attention to BR accounting methods which 'made it very difficult to reach an objective assessment of the real costs of keeping the line open'. The Minutes then noted that in summing up:

> the Chairman said that the discussion had clearly shown that the decision on the line would be of the greatest importance as regards its effect on the success of the plan for the Borders.

It was agreed that retention of the whole line was desirable until the development of the area was completed and its needs could be assessed. If that was not possible then the Edinburgh-Hawick section should be retained and particular attention given to the problem of communications between Hawick and the Langholm/Newcastleton area and the provision of overnight sleeper facilities between Hawick and London.

Borders' complacency ignores the bigger economic picture?

With hindsight, it is clear that the fate of the Waverley Route cannot be seen in isolation from the wider UK economic situation and the associated pressures on public spending. Chris Harvie (who as a then office bearer of SRDA had campaigned against closure) commented in 2010:

> The Labour government was deep in financial mire after devaluation in November 1967 . . . My hunch is that investment in West Coast electrification could only be

chiselled out of government in exchange for considerable rationalisation, particularly of "duplicate main lines".

As Terry Gourvish notes in *British Railways 1948–73: A Business History* (1986), 'there is no doubt at all that the government was responsible for constraining the level of investment resources available to the railways after 1960.' He shows that aggregate disinvestment in 1963–73 was such as to cancel out the net investment of 1948–62, with 1967 clearly the worst year, when the disinvestment amounted to £55 million in 1948 prices.

Within that wider picture, Scottish unanimity against closure was nevertheless impressive – by mid-1968, retention of some or all of the route was supported publically by the Transport Users' Consultative Committee for Scotland, the Scottish Economic Planning Council, and (as the *Hawick News* reported on 5th July) by thirty local governmental, business, union and non-governmental organisations; also privately by the Scottish Office. But where was the mass mobilisation of public opinion, setting the heather on fire like Highlanders had done in the face of threatened closures? As the indomitable campaigner Madge Elliot put it in a January 1969 talk to Hawick Round Table:

> We were all told for quite a long time that the Waverley line would be closed. Unfortunately, because the majority of us did not believe that any Government would actually take the final step to axe this mainline, we remained completely apathetic to the situation, apart from prominent individuals who, for a long time, fought a lone battle.

Roy Perkins (a director of the Border Union Railway Company) had many relatives who worked on the railway in and around Newcastleton. When asked in 2010 why there was never a serious protest movement until closure consent was announced, his answer – without hesitation – was 'because, right to the very last week, they thought that the line would be reprieved.'

Bruce McCartney recollected that when he travelled in 1967 on the last Langholm freight train, which also served Newcastleton and Penton, at the latter station one of the BR employees said to him, 'Liddesdale without the railway would be like hell without the fire.' This was misplaced confidence, not least since Beeching himself had talked of the Waverley Route being the biggest money loser in the British railway system – and by 1967 there was ample evidence across Scotland that the Ministry of Transport could force through some pretty drastic closures, including:

- the 1965 withdrawal of services from Fraserburgh and Peterhead, two towns broadly the same size as Galashiels and Hawick, and almost as far away from the rest of the rail network – just over 40 miles in the case of Fraserburgh, and some 30 from Peterhead

- the complete closure the same year of the 66-mile cross-country line from Dumfries to the ferry port of Stranraer – despite the National Union of Railwaymen having offered to operate the 'Port Road' for free (with staff working rest days for nothing)
- the 1967 loss of the central 'Strathmore' section of the Glasgow-Aberdeen double-track main line through Forfar – the fastest stretch of railway in Scotland at the time.

This failure to learn lessons from elsewhere, and the consequent absence of powerful popular evidence that the Borders really cared about its railway, was to prove one of the decisive factors in the fate of the Waverley Route.

The focus shifts to London – for the final decision

After protracted internal debate within Government – in particular between the Scottish Office and the MoT – the final phase of the decision-making process came with Barbara Castle's 2nd April 1968 memorandum to the 8th April meeting of the Cabinet Ministerial Committee on Environmental Planning. Over subsequent years, a number of sources have suggested that Castle was ready to sign a document refusing closure north of Hawick and requiring BR to economise, but that civil servants placed a different document in front of her successor Richard Marsh – however, the meeting Minutes in the National Archives at Kew reveal that this was not so.

Castle began the memo by noting that the Waverley Route closure proposal was of 'special importance' and that, unlike the normal closure process, the Government Departments involved had been unable to make a unanimous recommendation to her following the usual Inter-Departmental Working Party. She observed: 'it is common ground that retention of the whole line cannot be contemplated' since this would involve a grant of around £700,000 pa. Retention north of Hawick only [over double track] would require an initial grant of £390,000 annually – a deficit of 16.8d per passenger mile, which was 'much higher than any other possible grant to which we are likely to agree.'

Castle continued:

Even if during a [three year] trial period it proved worthwhile to invest the necessary money to eliminate surplus track capacity over this section, the grant would amount to about £250,000 a year (over 11d. a passenger mile) and this is still excessively high.

Harold Wilson MP –
Prime Minister 1964–70
and 1974–76.

Richard Marsh MP –
Minister of Transport
1968–69.

The grants referred to were those calculated by the 'Cooper Brothers' formula – as part of the powers provided by the 1968 Transport Act to support loss-making but socially-necessary railways – and identified the deficit which would be required to be met in continuing a passenger service. These included an allowance for the interest liability of the British Railways Board and provision for the replacement of assets at current costs. In contrast the data presented to the TUCC was based on the 'Carrington' formula which outlined the net financial effect of withdrawing the passenger service, with amortisation and depreciation charges based on historic costs, and interest excluded. As a later (1968) BR memo would accurately comment: 'The use of these different methods undoubtedly causes confusion to the layman, and this has been especially so in the Waverley Route case.'

This is a complex topic, but the impact of the Cooper Brothers' formula should be seen – as set out in *Modern Railways* in January 1969 – to have created the difference between an annual saving from complete closure of £536,000 and a grant requirement of £700,000 to keep the whole line open.

Castle's reference to elimination of "surplus track capacity" is an interesting reminder that the 1968 Act included provision for a surplus capacity grant payable to BR – which has prompted the suggestion that this may have been another incentive to close the Waverley Route. In practice, the grant was payable to cover BR's temporary maintenance costs pending removal of track within five years. So, if a single-track Edinburgh-Hawick 'basic railway' had been the chosen long-term outcome – eliminating some 75% of the Waverley Route's 1968 track capacity – BR could have been grant funded to maintain the second track until singled, thus reducing the operational costs during the transitional years.

In addition to the sheer cost of grant aid, Barbara Castle's other main argument was around the steady decline in patronage over a number of years, in the face of growing car ownership. The annex to the memorandum cited a 1966–67 decline of 20% over the whole route on Monday-Friday southbound services, and 14% north-bound, with somewhat less decline over the Hawick-Edinburgh section (15% and 3% respectively). 'Known regular daily users of the Border Towns stations' were said to be 18 at Galashiels, 12 at Hawick, 8 at St Boswells and 3 at Melrose, including just '30 regular commuters to Edinburgh'.

Of course, during the 1960s there was nationally much less travel as a whole, most towns were far more self-contained in terms of employment and services than nowadays, and the acceptable length of daily commute was much shorter. Still, as the Local Authorities' survey in 1966 had shown, there were many more regular travellers on the Waverley Route on a less-than-daily basis.

Barbara Castle MP – Minister of Transport 1965–68.

The various different official figures quoted at different times for the line's financial performance were a growing bone of contention amongst those organisations and individuals opposed to closure. Their confidence in the validity of the numbers would not have been strengthened had they been able to scrutinise Castle's annex at the time, rather than waiting 30 years for the papers to be released from the 'restricted' category. In a column setting out the projected finances of a 'reduced basic service' (five trains southbound and six northbound) between Edinburgh and Hawick, two arithmetical errors are made, and the net annual loss based on direct expenses is shown as £241,000 rather than £272,000. In any event, Castle indicated that any grant for Edinburgh-Hawick would be in addition to the £55m estimated for social grants in the Transport Bill, and would therefore:

Willie Ross MP – Secretary of State for Scotland 1964–70 and 1974–76.

> inevitably, jeopardise the chances of grant approval for unremunerative services elsewhere in Great Britain. I am forced to the conclusion that to admit the services on any part of this line for social grant would be quite inconsistent with the general policy which we have to adopt in relation to grants for railway passenger services . . . I accordingly seek my colleagues' agreement to giving my consent to the discontinuance of rail passenger services from Edinburgh to Hawick as part of the closure of the entire Waverley line from Edinburgh to Carlisle.

Castle was well aware of the political difficulties that this would create for Willie Ross, recognising that 'a closure announcement will give rise to a great deal of resentment and public outcry – this emphasises the importance of the public relations angle in handling any such announcement.'

But Ross was not ready to throw in the towel, and his 4th April memorandum in response was a damning indictment:

> I am convinced, and my views are shared by the President of the Board of Trade

[Anthony Crosland], that a withdrawal of these services and the consequent complete closure of the line would seriously affect the prospects of economic development of the Central Borders to which we are, as a Government, committed . . . Any announcement of a decision to close this railway line at this point of time will call into question the whole of these plans and intentions, and will be regarded as casting serious doubt on the Government's good faith. By ignoring the findings of the Scottish Transport Users Consultative Committee and rejecting the recommendations of the Scottish Economic Planning Council, the Minister will go far to destroy her own consultative arrangements and undermine the credibility of the whole economic planning machine.

By the time the Ministerial Committee on Environmental Planning (MCEP) took its seats in a House of Commons conference room on 8th April, Barbara Castle had been reshuffled (on 6th April) and Richard Marsh – a then rising political star – had taken her place as Minister of Transport. In his 1978 autobiography *Off the Rails*, Marsh recalls that he was extremely unhappy about being switched from his post as Minister of Power: 'I could not see the slightest reason why I should be shifted into a Ministry about which I knew nothing and cared less.' At the Ministerial Committee meeting, the initial presentations covered much the same ground as the two opposing memos, Marsh adding that patronage between Edinburgh and Hawick had dropped by 30% between 1964 and 1967, compared with a population decrease of 9.5% and a rise of 120% in the number of cars – and it has to be said in hindsight that these were all (if correct) pretty dramatic statistics, illustrating some very major changes within the Borders. In discussion, the 'pro-closure camp' (comments are not attributed to individuals in the Minutes) stated:

> The heavy cost of keeping open the Edinburgh-Hawick section and the low passenger traffic on it made this an ideal candidate for closure. There was no evidence to suggest that closing this part of the line and making more intensive use of roads would harm the area economically. If the case for closure of the whole line was rejected it was difficult to see how rail closures could be justified anywhere else.

The 'anti-closure camp' responded that 'it would be *bad psychology* [author's italics] to withdraw rail facilities at a time when we were encouraging industry to move into the area'. The meeting then concluded with general agreement that it would be wrong to reach a final decision before the Central Borders Plan was received on 19th April. The stage was therefore set for this long-awaited and hefty document to become arguably the key factor in the failure of even the Edinburgh-Hawick section to survive.

'Black 5' No. 44767 approaching Kelso Junction northbound on 11th April 1967, hauling 1955-built Class 05 Hunslet diesel shunters No's D2608, D2617 and D2593, from overhaul at Bradford Hammerton Street to Haymarket engine shed. *Bruce McCartney*

The Central Borders: A Plan for Expansion was duly delivered to Ross by the University of Edinburgh consultants, led by Professor Percy Johnson-Marshall and by Professor JN Wolfe whose cost-benefit work on the Waverley Route a year earlier had singularly failed to impress the Scottish Office and MoT. As long anticipated (and used in evidence by rail campaigners two years earlier), it projected a 25,000 population increase by 1980, concentrated along the corridor between Galashiels and Newtown St Boswells served by the railway. The plan noted that the economic future of the area was largely dependent on the development of transport links to Edinburgh, yet it was equivocal in its assessment of the impact of loss of the Waverley Route – an assessment which was to prove critical to the 21st May collective Ministerial decision for closure. The closure of the railway to Edinburgh would 'reduce the economic interchange' and associated benefit to the Central Borders, and particularly north of Galashiels would have an 'unfortunate effect' on planning targets. It sensibly suggested the idea of modifying bus services to concentrate on 'feeding into the railway rather than running in competition with it to Edinburgh', but overall this was not exactly a call to the barricades. Of the report's 21 recommendations, four concerned roads but none rail. Not one out of 577 numbered paragraphs was devoted wholly to the rail issue.

With hindsight, this half-hearted support for the railway can be seen as a reflection of the prevailing patterns of urban expansion typified by the 1950s and 60s 'New Towns' – and of the underlying attitudes of some (but not all) regional planners to their transport needs. The new / expanded settlements at Cumbernauld, East Kilbride, Glenrothes and Livingston were conspicuously designed around the car, with the nearest rail routes far from central – geographically or psychologically – to their existence.

As Christian Wolmar reflects in *Fire & Steam*, both Conservative and Labour administrations at Westminster through the 1950s and 60s were strongly influenced by 'the feeling within government that cheap fuel for motoring was a permanent fixture and therefore the demand for travel by railway would inevitably fall over time.'

So the general culture of the time did not help the chances of a run-down loss-making railway being seen as key to Borders redevelopment – yet the Central Borders Plan was actually one of the few urban expansion schemes of that period which had zoned housing and industrial development around and along a rail corridor. It is a supreme irony that this railway was lost, yet the railways skirting the Scottish New Towns either survived and prospered or were reopened (as in the case of Livingston) to serve expanding populations for which the car did not prove to be a transport panacea.

The plan was clearly not the hoped-for life saver, but Ross put a brave face on its relevance to the railway in his 8th May memorandum for the 21st May MCEP meeting at the House of Commons. In this he asked his colleagues to agree 'in principle to retain rail passenger services between Edinburgh and Hawick for a period of three years and invite British Rail to submit an application

Following a derailment on the East Coast Main Line in Northumberland on the evening of Saturday 15th July 1967, Anglo-Scottish traffic was diverted between Newcastle and Edinburgh via Carlisle and the Waverley Route until the situation reverted to normal on the Monday. 'Deltic' No. D9018 *Ballymoss* crosses Shankend Viaduct on the evening of Sunday the 16th, with the 10.00 Kings Cross to Aberdeen train.
Bruce McCartney

for grant in respect of this section of the line' while also making it clear that this 'special dispensation' was to give time to allow the importance of the rail service to the new Borders development to be properly assessed. Addressing the issue of the level of subsidy required to maintain an Edinburgh-Hawick service, Ross rightly (as we shall see) queried figures provided by BR for a minimalist 'Basic Railway' service – 'I have never myself been satisfied with these estimates'.

Unfortunately, the Scottish Office had no railway advisers, and Frank Spaven's knowledge of the subject had been lost to the HIDB two years previously – so any re-examination of the estimates would be done by MoT civil servants who were intent on closure!

While the author has found no evidence that the arguments placed in front of Marsh were any different from those given to Castle (other than the weight added to the case for closure by the contents of the Central Borders Plan), it is nevertheless important to bear in mind the role played by MoT civil servants, given that Marsh had only been in post for a matter of days and had come with no great knowledge of, or indeed at that stage any interest in, transport. Although there appears to be no record of Marsh ever commenting publically on this episode in his political career, a chance encounter with a retired BR senior manager many years later sheds some fascinating light on what happened in 1968.

In June 2006, Mike Chorley – who had retired as Area Civil Engineer at Perth in 1993, after a 37-year railway career – was invited to a prestigious birthday celebration dinner at a stately house in the Home Counties. Knowing of Chorley's railway background, the hostess sat him beside the only other ex-railwayman in the party – Marsh, who of course had become BRB Chairman some years after his time as Minister of Transport. In 2011 Chorley recalled – with great clarity – how this encounter went:

B1 Class No. 61029 *Chamois* thunders through Penton with the 11.15 Kingmoor-Millerhill freight on 16th September 1967. Leaning out of the cab window is Fireman David Hay of St Margaret's engine shed in Edinburgh.
Rae Montgomery

A classic location for railway photography was just north of Falahill Summit. Seen here on Sunday 8th October 1967, an engineering train returns towards Edinburgh, working 'wrong line'.
Norman Turnbull

I had met Richard Marsh a couple of times years before, and introduced myself. Initially he was rather preoccupied and replied to my opening gambits with well-rehearsed social pleasantries. I decided to stimulate the conversation with a few humorous tales of railway history and trivia. Slowly Marsh thawed and began to respond. Whether it was my stories or the mellowing effect of the Burgundy I have no idea, but when I turned the discussion towards larger policy decisions, he seemed to switch his memory and emotions to a higher and more factual level. Amongst other matters (including unflattering comments on his contemporary politicians, civil servants and others) he said that looking back on his life his biggest mistake was to authorise closure of the Waverley Route. Noting my intense interest in that remark, he then commented, "It was not really my fault – I was badly briefed. I should have looked more closely at what I had been told to say."

Whether Marsh's enlightenment came in general through his experience of managing the railway as BRB Chairman, or more specifically through observing how the Waverley Route could have acted as a highly effective diversionary route during the 1970–74 electrification work on the West Coast Main Line, we can only speculate now. Marsh died in July 2011 (aged 83) and had been in poor health for a number of years, previously declining or being unable to respond to requests for comment. Chorley's encounter does beg one question – if Marsh subsequently felt he had been badly advised in his early weeks as Transport Minister, how does that fit with Barbara Castle's backing for closure after more than two years in post, a period during which she must have become very familiar with the arguments for and against?

In any event, back in 1968, Marsh's 14th May memo retort to Willie Ross's plea to save the northern half of the line was an effective demolition job, opening with the comment that 'I cannot agree that the Central Borders report lends any

On an unidentified date in the mid to late 1960s, a pair of 'Clayton' Type 1s pass through Fountainhall on a passenger working. This is almost certainly the summer-season Saturdays-only 09.15 service from Dundee to Blackpool North – the only regular passenger duty for Claytons on the Waverley Route, and a train which made just four intermediate calls between Edinburgh and Carlisle (Galashiels, Melrose, St Boswells and Hawick). *The late Robin Barbour, courtesy of Bruce McCartney*

support to the argument that rail passenger services between Edinburgh and Harwick [sic] should continue to be subsidised'.

Ross had less than a week to pull together a final argument for Edinburgh-Hawick that would convince a majority of the Ministers at the 21st May meeting. A paper submitted to him by the Regional Development Division of SDD on 20th May echoed many of the arguments made by grassroots campaigners over the years, not least the much extended journey times by bus compared to train.

The Scottish Office was gearing up for the retention of a rationalised Edinburgh-Hawick service, to be announced in around four months' time as part of a co-ordinated message on the railway and Borders development. But it had reckoned without Richard Marsh's powers of persuasion – utilising the arguments of his civil servants – following the Central Borders Plan's lukewarm support for the railway.

At 7pm on Tuesday 21st May, seven Ministers gathered in the Large Ministerial Conference Room in the House of Commons to decide the fate of the Waverley Route. The seventh meeting of the Ministerial Committee on Environmental Planning that year was chaired by Peter Shore, Secretary of State for Economic Affairs; the other Committee members around the table being Willie Ross, Richard Marsh, Tom Urwin (Minister of State, Department of Economic Affairs), Ray Gunter (Minister of Power), Dick Taverne (Minister of State, Treasury) and Ernest Fernyhough (Joint Parliamentary Secretary, Department of Employment and Productivity). Notable absentees were Anthony Crosland (President of the Board of Trade) and Lord Brown of Machrihanish

(Minister of State, Board of Trade), both of whom Willie Ross had previously prayed in aid as supporters of retaining the Edinburgh-Hawick section. Their absence may well have been crucial.

As recorded in the Minutes, Ross opened the discussion by restating the key arguments against closure north of Hawick. By now familiar arguments were restated on both sides, the anti-closure camp suggesting an *'unfortunate psychological impact'* [author's italics] on any firm contemplating development in the Borders, and noting that 'the very low figure of 30 or so regular passengers between Edinburgh and the Border Towns covered season ticket holders only and particularly during the summer hundreds of people used the line daily.' The pro-closure camp's final gambit was to remind the meeting, within the context of the wider economic situation, that the estimated £55m required for social grants to railways was already likely to be exceeded by some £7m.

The Minutes then record the Chair (Peter Shore) summing up the discussion:

> the main question was whether the retention of these passenger services was crucial to the development of the Galashiels area. The Central Borders report was perhaps rather ambiguous on this point but it was clear enough that it did not make the case for retaining the line. Closure was likely to have little effect on the transport of freight and although it would cause some inconvenience to passengers, this was the inevitable result of any closure. The balance of opinion in the Committee favoured the closure of the passenger services on the whole of the Edinburgh/ Hawick / Carlisle line as quickly as possible.

Willie Ross must have left the meeting in sombre mood, sent on his way with Shore's monumental understatement about 'some inconvenience to passengers' ringing in his ears. But even after this seemingly terminal defeat, Ross did not give up, and indeed escalated the issue to the highest possible political level with his 23rd May memorandum to the Prime Minister, Harold Wilson. He strongly emphasised the possible consequences of closing the line to the Government's standing in the Borders 'and indeed throughout Scotland as a whole', and then made some highly revealing comments on a potential campaign tactic, which, had it been deployed some months earlier, might arguably have swung the decision the other way:

> You will have seen from this morning's press – and may already have been told by Dick Marsh that David Steele [sic], whose constituency would be most vitally affected by the proposal to close the line, has said that he would have no alternative but to resign his seat so that the issue involved could be put to the electorate. I do not think that this is in any way an idle threat and, while you may feel that Steele's

decision should not cause us to lose any sleep, I think it must be seen as a measure of the serious feeling which is likely to be created. If we are to face a by-election on the credibility of our intentions in regard to the Borders at this juncture I would have no illusions about the outcome . . . I am prepared to argue my case on the outstanding issues on their own merits; but this apart, *I would beg you to look at the cumulative consequences of our course of action on our standing in Scotland*. I very much hope that you will be prepared to consider with the Ministers what can be done. [author's italics]

Interestingly, new light has now been shed on the perceived by-election threat by Steel, who, in a letter to the author in early 2014, commented:

If I had carried out my threat to resign it would have gathered more publicity, that is all. My local party was not keen on the idea having financed three elections in 64, 65 and 66, and not liking the thought of 68 as well! But more important, various Tories indicated they would not take part as the fight was between me and Labour, and the latter having lost their deposit before, likewise would have avoided participation and humiliation. So it would have been pointless.

Steel added that, 'Your own research and judgement is much more revealing and we were at fault in not trying to enlist Ross, while support for the Hawick-only compromise came too late.'

In any event, back in May 1968, Ross copied his memo to Marsh, Gunter, Roy Jenkins (Chancellor of the Exchequer), Richard Crossman (Lord President), and Sir Burke Trend (Cabinet Secretary). Marsh responded swiftly to the Prime Minister with a memo incorporating a summary of the personal hardship impact which was verging on the dishonest – 'Only about 200 regular travellers are affected, of whom all but 30 would be adequately catered for by alternative bus services' – and concluded with the wider financial argument:

If we were to change our minds on this case, then it would be extremely difficult to persuade the country to accept the closure of many other services, where the loss per passenger mile would be smaller, and the hardship very much higher. Thus a decision to retain this service would make it inevitable that the total amount available for these rail grants would <u>have</u> to be increased – probably by several million pounds per annum.

Peter Shore sent a memo to the PM on 27th May defending the Committee's decision, principally on the grounds that the Central Borders report 'did not . . . provide sufficient support for the view that the economic viability of the area depended upon the retention of either the passenger or freight services.'

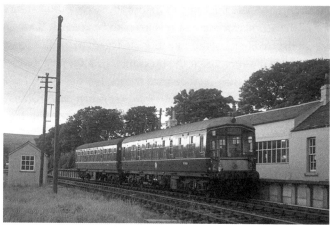

In the last years of the Waverley Route, other than 'short workings' between Edinburgh and Eskbank / Gorebridge, the only all-year Monday-Friday services operated by light-weight diesel multiple units – more economical to operate than locomotive-hauled trains, and better for tourists with their views to the front and rear – were the 06.41 Hawick-Carlisle and 18.13 Carlisle-Hawick commuter trains. Named locally as 'the Scud' – thought to derive from the Norse / Northumbrian word meaning 'haste' or 'hurry', as in 'scudding clouds' – it is seen here at Riccarton's northbound platform in 1966, on the 18.13 working.
The late Robin Barbour, courtesy of Bruce McCartney

Ross's last hope for retention of the Edinburgh-Hawick section was dashed in the Prime Minister's 5th June letter which stated:

I have considered carefully whether there ought to be an appeal to either Cabinet or S.E.P. on the two specific cases discussed by the Ministerial Committee on Environmental Planning which you have mentioned – the Edinburgh/ Hawick line and the Fauldhead colliery. I appreciate, and sympathise with, the political difficulties which these decisions involve; nevertheless I do not think it would be right to reopen the decisions reached by the Committee.

The fate of the whole Waverley Route had finally been sealed by the highest political authority in the land. All that remained for the Government was to come up with the best possible presentational gloss on what would be a highly unpalatable decision in the Borders and beyond.

CHAPTER 4

Execution pronounced

1968

THE prolonged public agony finally came to an end on 15th July 1968, with a statement by the Minister of Transport, Richard Marsh, to the House of Commons. The battle between the Ministry of Transport and the Scottish Office had been won by the bigger London-based Ministry, with its statutory powers over rail policy. The official closure notice confirmed that 'ALL passenger services will be discontinued between Portobello East Junction and Carlisle no. 3 Junction' and 24 stations would be closed. The closure of the Waverley Route was also to lead to the loss of a train service between Edinburgh and the East Midlands which had been in existence since the Settle & Carlisle line opened in 1876.

To the frustration of campaigners, the statement advised that: 'The Minister has considered the report of the Transport Users' Consultative Committee for Scotland, the advice of the Scottish Economic Planning Council and other relevant factors.' Yes, he had considered their views and recommendations, but had then dismissed them. Marsh did however place a two-year moratorium on disposal of the route formation north of Hawick.

There had been a few enhancements to the original alternative bus arrangements. Instead of an additional nine journeys on the Eastern Scottish service from Hawick to Edinburgh, there would now be an additional 11 – a marginal improvement unlikely to placate rail users faced with the loss of their faster and more comfortable train service to the capital.

At the foot of the notice's narrative was the traditional sign-off. 'I am, Sir, Your obedient Servant, D.G.Fagan, Assistant Secretary, Ministry of Transport.' John Yellowlees (latterly First ScotRail's External Relations Manager) was a fellow civil servant when Fagan retired from the International Transport Division in 1978, and recollects him commenting on his last day at work, 'of course we'd never do it now, but it seemed the right thing then.'

Marsh's closure consent announcement provoked widespread dismay. On 16th July the *Scottish Daily Mail* led its front page with the banner headlines 'It's the end of Border line' and 'Heavy losses cannot be allowed to continue says Marsh' and an editorial on the same page condemned this 'crazy' decision:

> In a properly integrated transport system it is likely that no one would have dreamed of closing the Edinburgh-Hawick-Carlisle line. But we do not have transport based on anything remotely resembling a unified road-rail system, and in that somewhat muddled context this line was a natural for the axe-wielders of Whitehall.

David Steel told the *Mail* that it was 'by far the most serious blow' to campaigners for Border development, and asked, 'How much longer is Mr Ross prepared to stay and swallow these rebuffs and watch Scotland's assets being dismembered?' Ernest Tait of the Borders Consultative group said 'it will certainly be a hefty obstacle' to Borders development, while Provost David Atkinson of Hawick described the decision as 'dreadful'. But not everyone was dismayed. The *Mail* reported that Steel's fears were not shared by Provost William Pate of Galashiels (an enthusiastic supporter of the railway back in 1966), who commented:

> We have become reconciled to the closure. Not enough people were using the line. We regret its going very much, but we feel that the money should be spent positively on road development rather than negatively keep this line going after it has outlived its usefulness.

Hawick, of course, stood to lose more than Galashiels from closure, being significantly further away from the nearest railheads, in particular Edinburgh. But the contrast in the Provosts' reactions said much about the lack of a strong united front in the Borders; and Pate's evident lack of appreciation of the scope for rationalisation, modernisation and a reversal of the fortunes of the railway north of Hawick must have been profoundly depressing for local campaigners. An alternative view is that he now felt, faced with the *fait accompli* of closure consent, that it was best to psychologically adjust to the reality of having to take the development of the area forward without the railway.

The *Southern Reporter*'s 18th July front page headline announced 'The Axe falls on the Waverley Line' and included extensive comments by David Steel. The editorial on the same page was mostly concerned with the Central Borders Plan (which appears to have been the big issue of the time) but at the very end commented:

> In conclusion – the Waverley Line – every point that could possibly be made has been aired. We believe this is politics gone mad. Here we have the Government

speaking with two voices, one proclaiming a Development Plan, the other retarding it. We deplore this decision and even at this late stage refuse to accept that it is final.

In the *Hawick News* the next day David Steel revealed that he had considered resigning over the issue in order to contest a by-election, but had decided 'to stay and fight for development, whatever obstacles are placed in the way.' Steel indicated that he had tabled nine questions about 'road improvements which will be needed immediately to compensate for the loss of the railway', a theme that rapidly gathered momentum in the Borders.

All six letters to the editor in the *Hawick News* of 2nd August concerned the railway. Arthur D Bethune of Newcastleton (the local doctor) drew attention to the plight of his village, where 32 men – around 10% of the male working population – would be thrown out of work.

By 9th August, local unease within the governing party was evident, the *Hawick News* reporting that 'fifteen leading members of the Labour Party in Edinburgh have signed a memorandum asking the Government to reconsider the Minister of Transport's decision to close the Edinburgh-Hawick-Carlisle railway line.' The signatories, who included the MP for East Edinburgh and the Chairman of Edinburgh City Labour Party, commented:

> We are given to understand that £50,000,000 per annum will be made available to pay 'social grants' for such services after the Transport Bill becomes law. We think it quite inexplicable that the Minister is not prepared to release one-half of one per cent of this to safeguard a vital Scottish link . . . If this line [Edinburgh-Hawick] does not qualify as one to be kept open for social reasons, we are at a loss to understand what line would ever qualify.

Following the closure announcement which they had fought so hard to prevent, the Borders Economic Planning Consultative Group had to restrategise. The *Southern Reporter* of 29th August carried a long front-page story headlined 'No Delay for Tweedbank Scheme Urged – Railway Closure not Death Blow', reporting that the Group was:

> deeply disappointed by the announcement that the line is to be closed and feel that this decision is a mistake at the present time, when economic development in the Borders is in hand. While the Group recognises the heavy cost of maintaining the line according to the figures issued by the Minister of Transport and while they acknowledge that use of the line has been declining, they feel that closure may have a *psychological effect* [author's italics] on hopes for expansion out of all proportion to the actual use of the rail service that might have been made. This makes it all the more important for roads in the area to be improved . . .

There then followed a long list of strong recommendations for road improvement, including the A7, A1, A68, A698, A72, A699, A6105 and B6355. In early September a lead letter in the *Scotsman* from Chris Harvie, Edinburgh Group Secretary of the SRDA, bemoaned the Borders Consultative Group throwing in the towel:

> What is needed in the Borders is the realisation that a 'modern transport infrastructure' is going to be a long time coming, and that meanwhile in Central Scotland public transport is going to become faster and more efficient principally through the medium of the railways . . . If Mr Tait thinks he can make the Borders a more viable unit when it will be faster to travel from Edinburgh to Ayr or Aberdeen by train than to Hawick by bus, he's kidding himself.

The 'Hibbs Report'

The date on which closure would take place was not announced in the official notice – but clearly, urgent action was needed to salvage anything from the imminent wrecking of the entire Waverley Route. In his 1989 autobiography *Against Goliath*, David Steel recalls that: 'In desperation, recognising that the tunnel on the southern section [Whitrope] was a major cost problem, I persuaded the local authorities to hire a consultant who produced an excellent report'. Interestingly, the Montgomery archive contains an internal BR briefing paper produced in November or December of 1968 which notes that Whitrope Tunnel 'is a factor, but not a singularly decisive factor, in the costs of operating the line.'

Steel – backed financially by councils in the Borders and Midlothian, and by the South of Scotland Chamber of Commerce – turned to a transport expert who had previously been Market Research Officer at BR's Eastern Region Head-quarters and was now branching out into teaching and consultancy. John Hibbs – who subsequently became an internationally recognised authority on transport regulation – was called in from his East Anglian base to produce a report on *Transport in the Borders*, reviewing the justification for closure and seeking to identify a viable way of retaining some kind of rail service.

Time was not on Hibbs' side, and he was evidently frustrated by lack of access to the detail and assumptions behind official rail costing figures – a recurring theme of the whole closure saga. Hibbs reported to Steel on 1st December 1968 – unfortunately just five weeks before the entire Waverley Route was due to close. Hibbs' report was certainly even-handed – neither hesitating to criticise the 'establishment' (notably the secretive approach of BR and the Ministry of Transport to closure, and the lack of connection between regional economic development policy and rail policy in the Borders), nor glossing over some of the more ill-considered and emotive arguments against closure.

Tellingly, the report's introductory remarks noted the lack of general outcry in the Borders when the Beeching Report was published in 1963, with Hibbs concluding that no-one really believed the closure of the Waverley Route would be enforced and/or 'that not enough people depended upon the line for an effective opposition to closure to emerge.' This hard-nosed analysis was based in part on acknowledgement that passenger (and freight) traffic on the line had long been in decline. It is worth quoting in full Hibbs' wider reflections on this issue, as it sets the scene for an analysis which might well have convinced the relevant authorities – if it had been commissioned at least a year earlier, *before* definitive decisions had been reached by government:

> It is this decline which lies at the heart of the problem, both in the Borders and every-where else in the Kingdom. We are living in an age of transition, and the accepted means of travel and transport are losing their traditional importance. No amount of nostalgia for the past can do anything but worsen the problem of adaptation, and this Report is contributed in the hope that an objective analysis of the course of events, with some forecast of their future, may clarify a situation that has been obscured by not a little emotion and a great many pre-conceived ideas.

The specification for the study took for granted – given the major railway strategy decisions over the years – that there was no case for retaining the southern half of the railway. An estimated 94% of the line's passenger traffic was between the Borders towns and Edinburgh, and official BR data showed a Monday-Friday summer average of just 27 passengers per Carlisle-bound train south of Hawick (excluding the London trains overwhelmingly made up of through long-distance travellers). Although this represented less than half the seating capacity of a single BR Mark 1 coach, it was far from moral justification for Richard Marsh's throwaway comment that it would be cheaper for the taxpayer to provide taxis for all the local passengers between Hawick and Carlisle. They are still waiting for those taxis.

Hibbs took the view that rail traffic growth projections from the Scottish Railway Development Association were far too optimistic, but did criticise BR – principally for its historic failure to re-assess the role of the railway and close the smaller intermediate stations; its neglect of tourist potential; secrecy over cost and revenue figures; and the crucial failure to address the revenue potential of an Edinburgh-Hawick service better geared to local needs.

The latter concept was the key development recommendation of the study, based on a fast hourly regular-interval service operating over a single-track railway, backed by a vigorous tourist sales policy. Trains would call only at the principal locations – Hawick, St Boswells, Melrose and Galashiels – where improved park-and-ride facilities would be provided, but all station staff withdrawn. Hibbs' suggested hourly service (requiring four diesel units) was – bearing in mind that the Borders economy, like most parts of Scotland, was much more self-contained at that time – probably a case of over-provision in the off-peak. A two-hourly frequency (with strengthening in the peaks and at weekends) would have been significantly cheaper to provide, and would still have been attractive, with a consistent, fast journey time of 75 minutes to Hawick.

With tickets issued only on the trains, and costly infrastructure severely rationalised, Hibbs was taking on board the lessons learned over the previous couple of years on branch lines in his home territory of East Anglia. Unstaffed stations had been rare in Britain until the innovations pioneered in the mid-1960s by the charismatic and controversial General Manager of BR Eastern Region, Gerry Fiennes, who demonstrated one of the key omissions of the Beeching Report by showing that 'Paytrains' and 'Basic Railways' could cut costs dramatically on loss-making lines, while still retaining and even increasing patronage.

The Basic Railway approach could and should have worked between Hawick and Edinburgh, but like so many aspects of the campaign against closure of the Waverley Route, the Hibbs report came too late – not least when a central recommendation was the untried concept of the railway being taken over by a consortium of the local authorities, *which had not been consulted on this issue by Hibbs*, due to lack of time.

With hindsight – an attribute which is of course critical to this analysis – it can be concluded that the local authority funding proposal was not the most productive approach. Particularly if Hibbs' report had been commissioned earlier, it would have been appropriate not just to query BR's cost, revenue and grant aid projections, but also to model some alternative (and more optimistic) scenarios based on experience elsewhere (including his own in East Anglia), rather than labouring arguments against the new Cooper Brothers' formula – which was being introduced nationally to calculate the long-run cost of subsidising individual rail routes and which the Government was never going to change for the benefit of a single route.

Run down, or just a lack of vision?

Many of the Beeching closure proposals across Britain prompted local allegations that BR had deliberately run down services to justify withdrawal. The Waverley Route was no exception. John Hibbs noted that:

. . . the Scottish Region of British Railways did little, apart from some cutting of cost, to show that they had any interest in the line. The railway management is widely accused in the area of running it down, and this is an accusation very hard to rebut even when one knows perfectly that such a policy would never have been acceptable to railwaymen. It is the lack of a policy for development that inevitably leaves this impression; 'Thou shalt not kill, but needst not strive, Officiously to keep alive' is an apt quotation in this context.

Scrutiny of the 1947–48 timetable shows that in the 'Down' (ie to Edinburgh) direction from Hawick – other than three local trains which had been withdrawn by 1963 due to very poor patronage – timetabled train departure times were virtually all within a few minutes of what applied twenty years later. Given the major changes in individual prosperity, car ownership and travel patterns which had taken place over that period of time, this does not say much for BR's responsiveness to market circumstances along the route.

What is striking for services north of Hawick in 1968 is how irregular the pattern was compared to broadly comparable rail corridors from Edinburgh to Kirkcaldy, Dunfermline and Glasgow Central via Shotts, all of which enjoyed a largely regular-interval pattern. In the last Waverley Route timetable before closure, there was a spread of eight northbound Monday-Friday trains over a 15 hour period but with no consistency in departure times from Hawick to Edinburgh (all trains leaving at different minutes past the hour) The gap between trains varied from 64 minutes to 3 hours 38 minutes, and the trains which did operate failed to meet the needs of some important markets. Madge Elliot noted in a February 1969 letter to the Border Union Railway Company that 'a Borderer could not even go up to the city by rail to see a cinema-scope film or show without having to miss a part either at the beginning or end'.

The pattern of service was even worse from Edinburgh to Hawick – just seven trains a day, with intervals between trains varying from 1 hour 17 minutes to the dreadful 5 hours 25 minutes gap between the 09.30 and 14.55 departures from Waverley station. While this aspect of service was poor, rail journey times from Edinburgh to the Borders were generally significantly faster than the competition, and the bus (though much slower) typically offered a fare saving of only 5%–10% over the train.

However, the competitive picture in Midlothian was markedly different. From Eskbank, for example, there were just five (albeit fast) trains to Edinburgh daily, while the bus user enjoyed *over 80* services a day, with fares typically 15%–20% cheaper. Significant settlements somewhat remote from the railway, but which from the 1980s onwards would have generated bus feeder traffic to key stations, benefitted from intensive bus frequencies – notably Dalkeith (whose branch line had closed to passengers in 1942) and peripheral mining estates like Easthouses and Mayfield which had never been served by rail. All the Midlothian branches had closed by 1962, hamstrung by topography which forced a wide rail sweep to the east to reach Edinburgh via Millerhill, unlike the bus networks which followed the direct northwards 'desire line' of travellers. By 1968, just one train a day called northbound at Gorebridge and Newtongrange on Mondays-Fridays – a very far cry from the half-hourly frequency of the re-opened Borders Railway commencing in 2015.

Aspects of the *quality* of rail service offered also attracted criticism at the time. In a talk to Hawick Round Table in January 1969, Madge Elliot referred to an ex-railwayman who claimed that BR had 'sabotaged' the line, in part through persisting with inferior and poorly-maintained rolling stock. She said:

> I have heard many complaints about cold trains. Now you know why. Perhaps we ourselves are to blame. I think we have all been far too complacent and prepared to accept it all. One lady told me she stepped into a carriage at Hawick Station, intending to go South, and she thought she had got into a first class compartment. It turned out there had been a derailment on the East Coast line and this was an East Coast train which had been diverted.

John Hibbs was in no doubt about BR's failure in the tourist market:

> Melrose Abbey, the most visited of all the older sites in the area, is close to the station, while combined rail and coach tours could be run to the more distant places . . . It is indeed surprising that British Railways have not developed this traffic in the past.

It is clear that BR failed to make the most of potential passenger markets – and as a consequence the projections for annual subsidy to keep the railway open were much higher than they needed to be. Increased tourism business – based in part on a regular interval timetable which would have transformed travel for all rail users – could have had a significant impact on the £220,000 subsidy suggested for a 'radically modified service' north of Hawick.

On the local freight front – and as on the rail network nationwide – domestic coal remained a staple traffic on the Waverley Route (albeit a declining one, reflecting wider lifestyle changes) to railheads at Galashiels and Hawick (handling 13,480 tons and 11,552 tons respectively in 1967). Oil arrived by rail at St Boswells, and sugar beet (for animal feed) and road salt were handled at Hawick, but textiles were just the kind of commodity which rail was ill-equipped to retain against road haulage competition – lightweight, not suited to double-handling, and with relatively modest volumes split across fragmented destinations, other than the London market.

The Borders largely lacked demand for the kind of commodities which the emerging modern railway was well placed to handle profitably, so it would appear to be unreasonable – in general – to blame BR for failing to develop new freight markets in the Central Borders. However, as we have seen, local management in the mid-1960s seems to have ignored staff suggestions for trying to develop timber traffic, particularly south of Hawick, at the very time BR was developing this type of traffic on the West Highland Line.

In BR's defence, the Montgomery archive contains an internal BR briefing paper produced in November or December of 1968 which reveals that it had been evaluating the potential for a daily timber train from Longtown or Newcastleton to the key Bowaters paper mill at Ellesmere Port. The timber reference in the BR paper concluded with the comment that negotiations with the Forestry Commission and Bowaters Ltd 'are continuing', but cautioning that, 'it is probable that this traffic alone would be insufficient to pay for the cost of retaining the 15 miles of line between Longton [sic] and Newcastleton.'

How many passengers actually used the Waverley Route?

The number of people using the Waverley Route, and even more so their continuing decline, lay at the heart of the BR / MoT case for closure. As in the case of disputed costs, patronage data and how they were derived became a bone of contention with campaigners. Even Richard Hardy's laudatory biography, *Beeching: champion of the railway?* (1989), admitted to some doubts about the way that Beeching and his team went about their analysis and decision-making on lines to be put up for closure:

> there were innumerable critics who said, not without some justification, that our figures were suspect, that we based everything on one single week's traffic – which was true – that we closed on crude statistics – they had a point – and that both our staff and the public were bulldozed into submission.

However, irrespective of the many figures floated, there can be no argument that the Waverley Route – in common with many railways in the 1960s – was experiencing significant decline in patronage in its last years. The more important questions are (i) why this was happening and (ii) what could be done to slow or reverse the trend? Clearly, growing prosperity, and more particularly rising car ownership, was a fundamental demand factor, but on the supply side BR self-evidently failed to come up with the kind of package of measures which stemmed and reversed decline on other Scottish routes – notably regular-interval timetables, more attractive fares and imaginative promotion of the scenic qualities of the line and its convenient access to key attractions such as Melrose Abbey. Nevertheless, despite declining patronage, the Waverley Route was, by Scottish standards, still being used by a substantial number of passengers. On 19th August 1965 civil servant Frank Spaven had noted, in an internal Scottish Office memo on the planning implications of the proposed closure:

> It is relatively well used by passenger traffic. The figures from MoT . . . show 9,300 passengers a week in winter and 12,900 in summer. This is rather more than on the Perth-Inverness and Aberdeen-Inverness routes (not proposed for closure) and the Calders-Shotts line (reprieved from closure) and much heavier than on the Ayr-Stranraer line (5,500 and 9,500) and the Inverness-Wick line (2,500 and 4,800) which have been reprieved from closure.

How much subsidy did Edinburgh-Hawick really need?

A recurring feature of Waverley Route archive material is the arguments and disagreements about how much money the line was actually losing and the amount of subsidy needed to retain a service, between Hawick and Edinburgh in particular. The apparent discrepancy between official figures was encapsulated by the differences between, firstly, the £232,000 pa saving of short-term costs from withdrawal of all Edinburgh-Hawick-Carlisle passenger services as advised by BR to the TUCC in 1966, secondly, the 1968 figure of £536,000 to be saved annually in the event of complete closure of the line, and finally the same year's forecast of £700,000 pa to grant-aid a passenger service. The latter reflected the new nationwide 'Cooper Brothers' formula for calculation of long-run costs of maintaining the whole line, as opposed to the short-term saving from withdrawing the passenger service (on the assumption that freight continued, and took its share of track and signalling costs).

A number of key arguments around cost allocation emerged after the line's closure had been announced. In his 18th December 1968 letter to Baroness Elliot of Harwood, the Government's Lord Winterbottom noted that the short-term figures 'derive from the formula used in compiling Table 1 of Appendix 2 of the 1963 "Reshaping Report"' – in effect conceding that they did not reflect the *actual* expenses incurred on the Waverley Route. Related points had been identified by Sir James Farquharson – a retired railway engineer who had pioneered railway development in East Africa, and was by then the President of the Scottish Railway Development Association – in his 27th September letter to the Principal Secretary at the MoT, in which he noted that the estimated costs of grant aid were calculated by an 'agreed formula', and that as regards the contentious issue of depreciation:

> the main assets subject to depreciation – track, bridges, etc. – have very long lives and there are no grounds for closing a line just because the revenues are insufficient now to meet expenditure which may be required 20 or more years ahead. The time to consider closure would be when the major assets required renewal.

A lengthy 19th October reply from Assistant Secretary DG Fagan simply ignored this issue. 44 years later, the retired senior railway managers Richard Faulkner and Chris Austin, in their *Holding the Line* (2012), would pointedly note Beeching's failure to address the actual costs which would be saved by a specific line closure and how long it would take to achieve such savings in practice:

> Instead Beeching used average costs for track maintenance, train operations and staffing, along with an assessment of the renewals of structures and earthworks required to maintain services over the ensuing five years. The latter figure was also potentially misleading, as the maintenance of track and structures was not determined by a preset formula but expertly assessed by experienced engineers used to making accurate judgements about when a structure or length of track required renewal, given the traffic passing over it.

The force of such criticisms in the context of the Waverley Route was underlined 45 years later when contractors working on the new Borders Railway found that many of the surviving structures between Edinburgh and Tweedbank were in remarkably good condition, despite little, or more generally, no maintenance since 1968.

Together, the author and the rail campaigner Bill Jamieson have undertaken a review of the scenarios projected in 1968 for Edinburgh-Hawick to assess whether BR could in fact have produced a more cost-effective proposition for operation of a 'Basic Railway'.

Our analysis – as shown in the table on page 91 – includes a cost benchmarking exercise synthesising two key sources – the Beeching Report, and estimates for rationalised operation of the East Suffolk Line as set out in *I tried to run a railway* (1967) by Gerry Fiennes. We have used the Beeching Report's three-way categorisation of route service costs into movements, terminals and track & signalling.

In the case of movements and track & signalling (together representing 90% or more of total costs), our synthesis is based on taking the mid-point of estimates calculated using Beeching and Fiennes base data. The rationale for this is firstly that, while the Beeching Report had a lot to say about which routes lost money, it had much less analysis of reducing the cost of continuing operations (this was a key Fiennes criticism) – in other words, Beeching was too pessimistic. Secondly, in the case of the Fiennes' figures for the East Suffolk Line, we have no basis on which to judge whether his estimates were or would have been realised; the fully rationalised and modernised operation did not finally fall into place until the 1980s – in other words, it would be prudent to assume that Fiennes was too optimistic.

Our cost synthesis (and the 'Beeching' and 'Fiennes' columns) provides for inflation between 1962, 1965-66 and 1968 as appropriate, and incorporates a £55,000 'correction factor' to broadly allow for the extra costs associated with the Cooper Brothers grant-aid formula by taking the difference between the saving from complete closure of the line (£536,000) and the grant avoided (£700,000), then halving this for retention only of the Edinburgh-Hawick route mileage, and finally subtracting one third of this to allow for single-track operation with double-track structures retained. In the case of the BR 1968 forecasts it is presumed that the Cooper Brothers formula's extra costs are covered by the line of entry for 'interest and administration'.

In our synthesis, we have used Beeching's sample cost of £2,500 per station for 'a single track route with small stations', as Fiennes made no reference to this cost category. In the case of movement costs, Beeching indicated a sample range for DMUs of '4s.0d. – 6s.0d per train mile according to density of traffic', while actual costs of 2s 6d were quoted for DMU / battery rail car operation on the Aberdeen-Ballater line – we have used the 4s per train mile figure.

Track and signalling costs were often the most contentious, and by the late 1960s usually the critical, cost item in closure proposals and the Waverley Route was no exception. The Beeching Report and closure proposals focused on the direct track and signalling costs specifically attributable to a passenger service. Where a freight service still operated (and was expected to continue), the assumption was that it would bear the basic infrastructure costs necessary for that service to operate, with the passenger service only bearing the cost of additional track and signalling provision required over and above that level. This was to prove an assumption of heroic proportions as the 1960s wore on and rail freight increasingly haemorrhaged away to road haulage – the *raison d'être* of many secondary and branch lines becoming overwhelmingly the passenger market. In the case of the Waverley Route, as it became apparent that the big prize for BR was to withdraw the passenger service and switch through freight to alternative routes, the entire track and signalling cost became a key part of the equation – adding some £300,000 to the route's losses, to the dismay and disbelief of campaigners.

SCENARIO	A	B	C	D	E
data source	BR 'max'	BR 'min'	'Beeching'	'Fiennes'	BJ/DS
data reference	1	1	2	3	4
year of calculation	1968	1968	2012	2012	2012
	£ pa	£ pa	£ pa	£ pa	£ pa
Passenger movement costs	70,000	50,000	79,000	42,000	61,000
Passenger terminal costs	40,000	33,000	16,000	16,000	16,000
Passenger track/signalling costs	220,000	157,000	165,000	35,000	100,000
Interest & administration	50,000	30,000			
'Correction factor' for Cooper Bros			55,000	55,000	55,000
Total Costs	**380,000**	**270,000**	**315,000**	**148,000**	**232,000**
Total Revenue	**70,000**	**50,000**	***113,000**	***113,000**	**113,000**
Grant Requirement	**310,000**	**220,000**	**202,000**	**35,000**	**119,000**
Train service frequency	5–6 pd	5–6 pd	10 pd	10 pd	10 pd

Table: Edinburgh-Hawick financial scenarios

1 BR projection for a 'Basic Railway' in 1968, quoted in *Modern Railways*, January 1969.
2 Based on Beeching Report costs updated for inflation to 1968.
3 Based on Fiennes costs updated for inflation to 1968.
4 B Jamieson / D Spaven synthesis of Beeching and Fiennes costs updated for inflation to 1968.
* BJ/DS revenue projection has been used

The other big change in the approach to track and signalling costs between 1963 and 1968 was the arrival in the latter year – in association with the planned introduction of Government social grant aid for specific loss-making services – of the Cooper Brothers formula. As G Freeman Allen commented in the January 1969 issue of *Modern Railways*, this was 'designed to show by how much the BRB must be compensated to run the service in perpetuity.'

Broadly the same infrastructure provision assumptions are made in all the table's scenarios (single track, with one intermediate crossing loop), but the 'Jamieson/Spaven' synthesis in 2012 arrives at a total annual cost some 14%

lower than the BR 'minimum' estimate of 1968 despite the latter being based on five/six trains per day and the former on 10 trains. Given that various archive sources refer (albeit in broad, unreferenced terms) to costs being halved on two routes which were reprieved in the mid-1960s – the Far North Line and the Central Wales Line – and bearing in mind that these were already overwhelmingly single-track routes, it seems not unreasonable to project that the £660,000 annual expenses (excluding the long-run costs of the Cooper Brothers formula, or 'correction factor' as described in the table) for operating the entire double-track Waverley Route could have been reduced to under £200,000 (excluding long-run costs) for single-track operation over not much more than half the original route mileage.

Turning to revenue, BR figures quoted in the Hibbs report show rail patronage and revenue between the Border towns and Edinburgh for the years 1965, 1966 and 1967 – and if the percentage decline between 1966 and 1967 is extrapolated onwards to 1968, there would have been 113, 000 passengers and (by coincidence) £113,000 revenue. Part of this decline in the last years of the railway must have been influenced by anticipated closure, with people making alternative arrangements, and we have assumed that the decline could have been arrested in 1969 by a new service based on:

- regular-interval operation – as opposed to a highly irregular service
- an increased frequency of 10 trains in each direction – compared to seven/eight in the 1968 timetable
- faster average journey times – as all minor stations would be closed
- car parking facilities at stations, more attractive fares (reflecting elasticities of demand) and better promotion of the railway.

Bringing together costs and revenue projections to determine the estimated grant aid required to run this 'Basic Railway', the Jamieson/ Spaven synthesis suggests that a figure of £119,000 – just over half of BR's 'minimum' estimated subsidy of 1968 – might have been achievable. In his 18th December 1968 letter to Baroness Elliot, Lord Winterbottom, alluding to the projected grant aid for a simplified Edinburgh-Hawick service, admitted that, 'since this service does not exist, a substantial element of judgement must enter into the assessment of the total and the components'. The Government's Lord Shepherd went further in the next day's letter to Baroness Elliot's colleague, Lord Sieff, commenting that "it is only possible to guess at the number of people who would use a truncated service and therefore at the total value of the income to be derived from the service.' So, by their own admission, BR/MoT – with the vast array of analytical tools at their disposal – had evidently leant heavily on guess work in determining the fate of the Edinburgh-Hawick railway.

At the time of closure, *Modern Railways* magazine covered the economics of the Waverley Route in some detail. In the January 1969 issue an article by its editor, Geoffrey Freeman Allen, focused on the high track and signalling cost of maintaining through freight, from which he not unreasonably concluded that 'the withdrawal of the loss-making passenger trains is thus merely a key to open up – as was always in mind – the much bigger economy of total closure in April.' However, noting that any surviving grant-aided service would be saddled with all track and signalling costs, Allen – who was close to rail management – seemed to accept at face value 'the high rate of grant estimated by the Ministry to be necessary even if a so-called "basic railway" operation were instituted between Edinburgh and Hawick'. Yet even a back of an envelope recalculation at the time should have prompted scepticism – such as Willie Ross and the Scottish Office had voiced in private – about the robustness of the BR/MoT figures.

Our re-assessment of likely costs, revenue and subsidy suggests that while a figure of 1s 8d per passenger mile could be brandished for continuing to operate the Waverley Route exactly as it was at closure – and 11d for a 'Basic Railway' – a figure as low as 3d subsidy per passenger mile might have been achieved for a decently-promoted regular-interval service over a suitably rationalised Edinburgh-Hawick branch. Our projected grant aid figure of £119,000 is £101,000 less than the lowest figure quoted by BR – and the continuation of a rail service

An unidentified Leeds-based 'Peak' Class 45 powers the down *Waverley* away from the severe speed restriction through the platform at Riccarton Junction in 1968.
This class's association with the Waverley Route lasted from the early summer of 1961 until the very end in 1969, hauling the daytime and night trains to and from London – the only all-year passenger services which did not call at Riccarton.
The late Robin Barbour, courtesy of Bruce McCartney

would also have saved part of the cost of the (state-owned) replacement bus services, which in a confidential April 1967 Scottish Office memo was estimated as £73,356 per annum.

It can therefore be reasonably concluded that the Edinburgh-Hawick railway was sacrificed – as suspected by rail campaigners and the Scottish Office at the time – on the basis of dubious cost and revenue projections. Regrettably, by the time the BR 'Basic Railway' figures reached the public domain – where they could be challenged in conditions of open scrutiny – the closure consent had already been given.

Was the real missed opportunity further back – in the 1950s?

The Waverley Route largely lost its previous role as a premier main line after the 1923 'Grouping' left the railway as an awkward outpost of the new London & North Eastern Railway, which would inevitably prioritise its fast East Coast route to London. However, subsequent railway managements could have undertaken a strategic re-assessment in proper recognition of these changed circumstances. The Hibbs report criticised BR for not having rethought the role of the railway many years earlier:

> Tradition dies hard, and in this case it has meant that a useful railway has continued to be treated as a main line long after its early purpose had been made irrelevant, whereas it would have been better for its purpose to have been re-assessed a good deal sooner.

One example of this hangover from the pre-nationalisation period (reflecting old inter-company loyalties) was that the daytime and overnight sleeper trains through the Borders to London continued to be routed via West Yorkshire (and the East Midlands), although there was some logic in a direct link between two still-important textile districts. It may be that London Midland Region preferred the established routeing for its own internal reasons, whereas Scottish Region – if it had had the choice – might have preferred direct links from the Borders towns to Lancashire and the major rail hub at Crewe on the West Coast Main Line. But this is mere speculation. Reflecting in 2011 on general railway attitudes half a century earlier, ex-BR manager Rae Montgomery commented:

> The crux of much of BR's lacklustre performance and lack of ambition and innovation in the 1950s and 60s was that for much of Britain – and not just the Waverley Route – locomotive and operating practices continued after nationalisation much as they had before 1948, and old enmities and 'Spanish customs' died hard. This was the problem of running the railway with old men at the helm.

At various stages leading up to the demise of the Waverley Route interested parties did suggest that a recast of train services could have worked for both the Borders and the wider network interest. The SRDA draft report on the Waverley Route which was circulated within the Scottish Office in February 1967, for example, had not failed (characteristically for its author, Tom Hart) to explore 'blue skies' visions of alternative options for route development, including abandoning the whole mileage of the West Coast Main Line between Midcalder/ Motherwell, Carstairs and Gretna.

Once the die was cast for the Waverley Route, the *Scotsman* reported (in a 20th December 1968 story under the headline 'Border line grant ruled out by Minister'):

> The possibility of diverting all Edinburgh-London (Euston) traffic from the Edinburgh (Carstairs) line on to the Waverley line had been considered but discarded, because this would have meant saving only about 15 route miles of track against the 98 route miles of the Waverley line.

Marsh's response had, of course, ignored the issue of intermediate population and the associated regional development argument, but this was par for the course in the whole Waverley Route saga – rail policy and regional policy being controlled by two different Ministries, one in London and the other in Edinburgh. Only with devolution of power to Scotland in 1999 would this frustrating anomaly be resolved, but much, much too late for the Borders.

There *was* a good case in the early 1960s for closing Midcalder Junction to Carstairs, and routing Edinburgh-Liverpool/Manchester/Birmingham trains via Hawick. Admittedly the route through the Borders was more arduous for train haulage, AJ Mullay commenting in *Rails across the Border* (1990) that, 'With two summits of around 900–1,000 feet, and a serpentine succession of curves throughout, the 98 miles of the Waverley Route was arguably the most operationally difficult main line in Britain'. However, the line's key advantage over the Carstairs/Beattock route was intermediate population – the latter's biggest intermediate settlement was Lockerbie, with fewer than 4,000 people, whereas the Waverley Route directly served a population in excess of 35,000 at its four main intermediate stations, plus a further 35,000 in the surrounding catchment.

Some support for the argument for strategic diversion comes from experience of trains diverted due to engineering works. On Sunday 3rd November 1968, Bruce McCartney and fellow-campaigner Andrew Boyd travelled on the 10.50 train from Edinburgh to Liverpool which took only two hours to reach Carlisle via the Borders (including a signal stop at Kershopefoot). Fast-forward 32 years, and as Allan McLean of Virgin Trains recollected in 2010, the 2000 Borders

Railway Feasibility Study (part-funded by Virgin) modelled a future Edinburgh-Hawick-Carlisle time of just 82 minutes with tilting diesel trains, compared to 70 minutes on the Beattock route.

An early 1960s' rethinking of the role of the Waverley Route could have significantly reduced costs south of Hawick – by diverting away some or all of the through freight traffic, track singling (and elimination of a majority of the signal boxes), closure of the seven smallest intermediate stations plus the unadvertised Harker, Parkhouse Halt and Whitrope (leaving just Newcastleton and Longtown), and diversion of Up passenger trains via the Longtown-Mossband link, as was done for freight in 1963. Perhaps another benefit of singling the southern half would have been a growing perception of two distinct railways – north of Hawick and south of Hawick – rather than a lengthy double-track through route which had lost much of its *raison d'être*. As Rae Montgomery said in his March 2007 address to Hawick Archaeological Society:

> My conclusion is that, had the line been separated into its original parts when it was reviewed by Dr Beeching in 1962, the Edinburgh to Hawick section would probably still have been with us as a simplified single tracked railway serving the Borders.

Would an earlier rationalisation of the line south of Hawick have been enough – without Edinburgh-Carstairs being abandoned – to avoid the southern part of the line being listed for closure in the Beeching Report? This seems unlikely, not least because the big prize for BR was the financial saving to be secured from complete closure to passengers and freight. By summer 1968 just eight through freight trains and one parcels/mail daily in each direction needed to be diverted to the West Coast Main Line – and each extra train on the WCML north of Carlisle potentially boosted the case for its resignalling as part of the long-sought electrification scheme.

However, it does not need hindsight to say that the Waverley Route could have been extremely useful to BR as a diversionary route (particularly with a connection installed in both directions at Mossband Junction) during the five years of work on the electrification and resignalling of the West Coast Main Line. Allan McLean (a Press & Public Relations Officer with BR Scottish Region in the early 1970s) supports the widely-held view that scrapping the Waverley Route was part of a wider *quid pro quo* package for Government funding for WCML electrification – others being singling of parts of the Kilmarnock-Gretna route, closure of (a) Kilmarnock-Barrhead (which did not happen), (b) Penrith-Keswick (which did), and (c) the Settle & Carlisle S&C line – the latter proposal being thwarted at that time by Her Majesty's Railway Inspectorate refusal to allow 'catch points' on the West Coast Main Line to cater for freight trains not

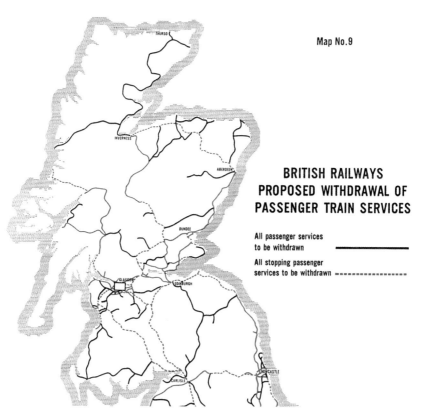

BRITISH RAILWAYS PROPOSED WITHDRAWAL OF PASSENGER TRAIN SERVICES

All passenger services to be withdrawn ——————

All stopping passenger services to be withdrawn ·····················

The March 1963 Beeching Report proposed draconian passenger rail route closures the length and breadth of Scotland. These were fully implemented in the Borders and indeed across most regions of the country, but only partially in Galloway, the Highlands and Greater Glasgow. The Waverley Route was by far the longest line to be closed

By now only a truncated freight railway, the junction at Longtown is seen looking south in spring 1969, with the former Waverley Route to Carlisle curving to the left and the single-track connection to Mossband Junction on the West Coast Main Line to the right. In August 1970 the former was closed completely between Longtown and the Harker / Brunthill RAF depot on the north side of Carlisle.

Ian Holoran

Stow swansong: an English Electric Type 4 (aka Class 40) powers the 09.20 Carlisle-Edinburgh service non-stop through Stow in December 1968. Demonstrating the poverty of vision of local and central government, permission was given in the mid-1990s for a large bungalow to be built almost exactly where the locomotive is seen here.

The late Robin Barbour, courtesy of Bruce McCartney

Lots of track, but no traffic. This desolate scene, looking north from a signal gantry north of Hawick station – and illustrating the considerable capacity and once busy times here – was captured a few weeks before the line closed completely after the withdrawal of the Millerhill-Hawick trip freight on 28th April 1969.

Ian Holoran

BRCW Type 2 (aka Class 26) No. D5307 hauls a southbound inspection saloon south
of Whitrope Tunnel on 1st April 1970. This saloon was said to have been operated to allow demolition
contractors to view the extent of track available for recovery, but it may – alternatively or additionally
– have conveyed a portable Hallade Track Recorder, rumoured at the time to have been deployed
by BR as part of a brief reconsideration of the railway's future as a timber carrier and
diversionary route for the West Coast Main Line.

Bruce McCartney

In the spring of 1971, two years after the last freight train had departed, much of the physical
infrastructure of the railway – including a road-served parcels and sundries depot – remained intact
at Galashiels station. Today the scene is (almost) unrecognisable, with the former railway footprint
swallowed up by new roads, a large Asda supermarket and light industry, leaving just the narrowest
of corridors to thread the single-track Borders Railway through the town. However, the metal gates
and two stone columns (plus a further two off-camera to the right) have survived, as the last
evidence that there was once a railway station here.

David Spaven

A station which should never have closed – leaving Hawick further from the rail network than any other town of its size in Britain. A poignant shot of Hawick station on 11th October 1971, just six months after the tracks had been lifted. The signal box was demolished nine months later, and the station in early 1975 – making way for a leisure centre.

Norman Turnbull

One of the most needless obstacles placed in the way of cost-effectively reinstating the Borders Railway – the garage of the large bungalow built on the railway solum at Stow station in 1995.

Ewan Crawford

fitted with continuous brakes. By the time that 'unfitted' freights had almost entirely disappeared from BR freight operations in the 1980s, the political climate had changed, and the S&C famously survived, despite serving an intermediate population one fifth the size of the Borders.

Tom Hart of the Scottish Association for Public Transport (the renamed SRDA) recollected in 2010 that 'Richard Marsh did say that total closure of the Waverley Route would send out a signal about the drastic action required to modernise the rail network' (and presumably help secure the funding for electrification of the West Coast Main Line). Of course, as Hart also commented, 'this needs to be seen in the context of other evidence that the major scope for rail savings and revenue gains lay not in closures, but in revised approaches to the core existing network, such as well thought-out investments in restructuring, changed work practices, ticketing and better integration of rail into the wider public transport network.'

Unfortunately too many railway managers fell into the category of the 'bandwagon of nihilists' described by Gerry Fiennes in *I tried to run a railway*: 'For a while not only no traffic but no piece of railway was safe from them.'

Considering rail management and political attitudes in the late 1960s – plus the five years until 'Section 8' Government grants were introduced for new rail freight facilities, and more large swathes of timber reached harvesting age in the Kielder, Wauchope, Newcastleton and Kershope Forests – perhaps at best a single track could have been retained from Hawick to Longtown. Together with Edinburgh-Hawick retention, this would have provided a diversionary route during WCML electrification and resignalling ready for the really big harvests of timber to be moved by rail from the 1980s onwards. Unfortunately this was just the kind of long-term thinking for which the UK has not been particularly noted since Victorian times.

Intriguingly, however, an internal BR memo of 4th September 1968 from the General Manager Scottish Region to the Director (Passenger Studies) at the BRB begins by stating opaquely: 'For the record I would like to correct the Ministry's assumptions on the withdrawal of the services and closure of the line'. It concludes with the comment:

> In spite of the Ministry's remarks *with regard to running a passenger service via Gretna Junction* I am advising the Estate Surveyor to make an application for permission to dispose of the formation between Hawick and the Regional boundary in advance of the closure date. [author's italics]

Does this imply that, just a month after Marsh's closure announcement, the MoT was having second thoughts about retaining the Waverley Route for a diversionary role during WCML electrification and for timber traffic, with trains routed via Longtown-Mossband? If so, it would have been an extraordinary *volte face* after so many years of arguing the case for closure in the face of the steadily worsening finances of the southern section of the line. The answer may lie in the 220 plus BR files on WCML electrification at the National Archives in Kew.

Where does the Waverley Route rank in British rail closure history?

No other closure in Scotland – or Britain – left so large a population so far from the rail network. When the Waverley Route fell in January 1969, the only major Scottish closure outstanding (but not a Beeching proposal) was the direct Kinross line from Edinburgh to Perth, to make way for the M90 motorway. The loss of this route was crass, but the intermediate population was not on the scale or distance from the rail network of the Central Borders.

South of the Border, a few corridors of similar length to the Waverley Route did succumb to the closure programmes of the 1950s and 60s, but these were cross-country lines – such as the Somerset & Dorset (S&D) railway – which essentially duplicated other more important routes, albeit in the case of the S&D serving some intermediate towns of significance and growing population. In essence, BR could get rid of lots of track mileage with minimal loss of traffic volume. The overwhelming majority of the stations which were lost served scattered villages and small towns, none of which were left anything like as far from the rail network as Galashiels (33 miles) and Hawick (45 miles).

The only Beeching closure involving a line longer than the Waverley Route was the 1966 demise of the majority of the Great Central Railway from London through the East Midlands to Sheffield, with the rest succumbing in 1969 (a route length of 126 miles). The Great Central was also a major loss in terms of cross-country connectivity, but the small towns which lost their train service were virtually all left within ten miles of the nearest surviving railheads. The closure of most of the East Lincolnshire Line from Spalding to Grimsby in 1970 left one town of comparable size to Galashiels or Hawick – Louth – cut off from the rail network, but by less than 20 miles.

Probably the worst of the 'post Beeching' closures – that is to say routes which were not listed for closure in the 1963 report but did nevertheless close – was the 77-mile cross-country line from Oxford to Cambridge. While never regarded as a 'main line' as such, it connected two important cities of around 100,000 population each in a region of growing affluence, but its closure (other than the reprieved section from Bletchley to Bedford) in 1968 left only small towns and villages without a rail service, with surviving main line stations never more than ten miles away.

As John Yellowlees has observed, when the BR Board put up the Settle & Carlisle Line for closure in 1983 it encountered forces of external and internal resistance that, had they existed a generation before, would surely have kept Midlothian and the Borders connected to the rail network. Casting an eye over the principal routes which were reprieved in Scotland, Borderers could be excused a jaundiced view of the rough justice which the closure proposal process had delivered. Less well-used lines than the Waverley Route had survived to Kyle, Wick/Thurso, Shotts and Stranraer, while others such as Perth-Inverness, Aberdeen-Inverness and Fort William-Mallaig had never even been proposed for closure. The treatment looked disproportionate, but the contrast with rural mid-Wales (with its three marginal constituencies) was even starker, as Charles Loft notes in *Government, the Railways and the Modernisation of Britain: Beeching's Last Trains* (2006):

> The Waverley closure seems particularly hard to defend, given the outcome of the [second] proposal to close Shrewsbury-Llanelli which ministers discussed in the summer of 1969 . . . This would leave a substantial area without a rail service but usage had declined significantly since 1964 (when Marples had refused his consent for closure) and the line had only six regular daily passengers. It served no intermediate place of comparable significance to the Border towns and required a subsidy of 21d per passenger mile compared to 16.8d which would have made Edinburgh-Carlisle one of the most expensive lines to keep, nor was there the prospect of any economies in operation.

Despite these seemingly hopeless finances, a Ministerial meeting chaired by Harold Wilson concluded that 'with the development of mid-Wales, the use of the railway for passengers and freight could develop markedly' and the line was eventually reprieved for a second time. Given that this railway had just four passenger trains daily in each direction and had not carried regular freight for five years, the contrast with the dismissal of rail's role in the Borders economy was breathtaking – except from a crudely political perspective.

In an 'ideal' world, Beeching would have proposed, at worst, complete closure south of Hawick, but only withdrawal of stopping services on the northern section of the line. However, 1960s Britain was far from an ideal world for rural rail development in regions where strategic political advantage was lacking (unlike, for example, in the Highlands).

Reflecting on what might have been, ex-BR manager Allan McLean pointed out in 2010 that when the North Berwick line was reprieved from closure in 1969, the train service was scaled back to a handful of trains at peak-time only and yet now it is an hourly and exceptionally busy service used by more than 1.5

Emerging from the mist to cross the England/Scotland border, English Electric Type 3 (aka Class 37) No. D6851 hauls the 12.40 Kingmoor-Millerhill special freight along one of the Waverley Route's few stretches of level track, at Kershope Foot, on Friday 3rd January 1969. The next morning it would head the very last northbound Anglo-Scottish freight train over the Waverley Route – but remarkably, reincarnated as 37 667, it was still hauling main-line freight in 2015.

Kenneth Gray

million passengers a year, around five times what it was carrying when closure was proposed. This was a line that very nearly suffered the same fate as the Waverley Route, yet could you find any politician, civil servant or railway manager who would nowadays say it should have been closed?

CHAPTER 5

Stand up and be counted
1968–69

WHILE John Hibbs was embarking on his eleventh hour analysis of the case for retaining some kind of rail link, the *Hawick News* of 27th September 1968 reported the belated formation of a broad-based campaign which would seek to give voice to grassroots protests through a variety of tactics, including a petition.

The 13 members of the Waverley Line Action Group included Roxburgh County Council, Galashiels and Hawick Trades' Councils, Edinburgh and the South of Scotland Chambers of Commerce, Hawick Knitwear Manufacturers' Association, the Scottish Trades Union Congress, the SRDA and three MPs including David Steel.

With hindsight, one cannot avoid contrasting the swift and successful mobilisation of popular opposition in the Highlands with this delayed and unsuccessful reaction in the Borders – more than two months after consent for closure was announced, two years after BR had published their proposal to close the line, and no less than *five and a half years* after the publication of the Beeching Report.

When Madge Elliot had spoken of a few 'prominent individuals who, for a long time, fought a lone battle' in the face of widespread apathy about the threat of closure, one person she had in mind was the Reverend Brydon Maben of Newcastleton. After the closure consent was announced, Maben organised a petition in Liddesdale and beyond, which secured 800 signatures. It was agreed that to get the maximum publicity the local group would endeavour to present the petition to the Queen while on holiday at Balmoral. As the *Scottish Daily Mail* reported on 9th October, under the banner headline 'Royal petition "snub"', the logistics did not quite go to plan (although the publicity aim clearly worked a treat):

A three-man deputation protesting about rail closures in the Borders travelled more than 250 miles yesterday to present a petition to the Queen. They arrived at Balmoral Castle, but caught only a fleeting glimpse of the Queen. And they left the castle grounds under protest after a Post Office official had refused them permission to see one of the royal secretaries.

On a wider front however, while the full extent of the official Action Group's campaign activities is not clear from archive material or the recollections of key protagonists, it would appear that the initiative ran out of steam. Madge Elliot, hearing 'a constant rumbling of anxiety coming from women shoppers' in Hawick High Street certainly concluded that not enough was being done. Elliot had hoped that the local authorities would get the ball rolling but by late November it was plain to her that she would have to take the initiative herself.

Characteristically modest, Elliot had asked herself, 'How could I, a mere housewife, set about such a project?' She turned to the Reverend Brydon Maben, who had already delivered the Liddesdale petition to Balmoral. Maben thought the Hawick initiative was late in the day but nevertheless was pleased to hear about the planned protest and offered to draft the wording.

With a team of more than 50 volunteers, Elliot spread the coverage of the petition not just across Hawick, but also to St Boswells, Galashiels and further afield. A letter dated 28th November came from two Borders students based in Edinburgh saying, 'We would like to express our sympathy and support for your efforts to keep the Borders line open and assure you of our assistance during the Christmas vacation which begins on December thirteenth.'

Elliot later reflected:

I received a visit from Bruce McCartney and Eric Glendinning. Was I glad to see them. Both these lads were frequent users of the railway and had reason to feel strongly about the closure . . . I received a phone call from Christopher Harvie, a student in Edinburgh [latterly an MSP in the Scottish Parliament]. I wasn't sure if I was hearing properly, so I asked him if he would repeat what he had just said. He did. He had written an article on railways for the *New Statesman* and had just received a fee of 21 guineas and he would like to donate this to our cause. I felt ashamed when I thought of the few coppers which had come in from local clubs, pubs and hotels . . . Chris Harvie, not content with giving a wonderful donation, he painted our placards, with assistance given by Bruce and Eric. These sort of people make you feel the job you are doing is worthwhile.

The *Hawick News* reported that, 'three young men including two Hawick students, have decided to wage their own "war" against the closure of the Edinburgh Waverley-Carlisle rail link.' McCartney, Andrew Boyd (from Edinburgh) and Tom Bogle had ordered 300 pens inscribed 'Help Save the Border Railway' and had begun distributing these and stamped addressed envelopes to Richard

Marsh on the trains. Word of the people's fightback spread fast, and the rumour mill was soon at work, Madge Elliot recollecting that on one particular day:

> my husband, Bob, flung the door open and called 'Have you seen the *Scotsman?*' I grabbed the paper from his hand and what I read caused my stomach to lurch. It stated I was going to call out 5000 hosiery workers to sit on the railway-line. I didn't know there were 5000 hosiery workers in the town.

The paper published a correction the next day, but the police were beginning to take an interest and paid a visit to Elliot's home which prompted her 'to play this down a bit with the newspapers.'

From an early stage it had been Elliot's intention to present the petition somewhere in London's corridors of power, and David Steel fortunately managed to arrange for a small delegation to be received at 10 Downing Street – but the petition had to be delivered before Parliament went into recess for Christmas on Friday 20th December. It became a race against time. However 11,678 signatures had been secured by the time the Borders delegation caught the overnight train from Hawick to London on Tuesday 17th. The party consisted of 'five adults [including piper Harry Brown in full Highland regalia] and one child from Hawick, two young ladies from St Boswells, Mrs Forsyth and her two children from Galashiels, and Dean of Guild Goss from Jedburgh.' Early the next afternoon the party rendezvoused with David Steel and the Earl of Dalkeith at the House of Commons. Here Madge Elliot completes the story of their last-ditch effort to save the line:

> Some high ranking officials from the Police Force arrived and David Steel told us that we must walk over London Bridge and down Whitehall in single file, five paces apart. We stopped opposite Downing Street where we were met with a barrage of photographers and pressmen. Good, this is what we wanted – publicity in London. Mr Steel asked my son, dressed in his kilt, if he would like to carry the one placard into Downing Street. The Police stopped the traffic in Whitehall so that we could cross the road. All the other placards had to be left at the entrance of Downing Street.

> Kim [Elliot's son] walked in front, our piper next, and then I followed with Mr Steel on one side and the Earl of Dalkeith on the other. When Harry struck up with 'Blue Bonnets over the Border' a lump came in my throat, and the tears started to well up in my eyes. I hung my head and said to myself, 'not here please'. I threw my head back and was confronted with a sea of faces at all the windows, and that did the trick. When we reached No 10 the door opened. Mr Steel asked

⇕ Protestors and press representatives foregather at the Carlisle-bound platform of Hawick station on the morning of Saturday 4th January 1969, ready to greet the arrival of the last day-time train to London. Campaigner Andrew Boyd (from Edinburgh) is clad in undertaker's garb, guarding the 'Waverley Line coffin' which would later be sent by the last (night) train to Transport Minister, Richard Marsh, in London.

Kenneth Gray

Waverley Route protestors muster in London on 18th December ⇑ 1968, prior to a three-person delegation proceeding to 10 Downing Street. David Steel MP can be seen on the left, with Madge Elliot beside him, then Bruce McCartney and Eric Glendinning. Madge's son Kim is in front of Steel.

Unknown

⇓ Police and protestors greet 1M10, the last daytime train to London, at Hawick on Saturday 4th January 1969, hauled by 'Peak' Type 4 No. D160.

Bruce McCartney

me to turn round for the benefit of the photographers, then he ushered me inside saying that he had never been there before. I certainly hadn't bargained for this.

Inside a policeman asked about the Petition and took notes. After what seemed an eternity a gentleman appeared in morning suit and shook hands with me. He accepted the Petition and remarked on the very nice wrapping [red paper for the Labour Party and black ribbon for the death of the railway]. He said he would see the Prime Minister received it. I stressed it was from the ordinary folk in the Borders.

Immediate mission completed, a very tired delegation returned by overnight train to the Borders. In their heart of hearts, they must have feared that it was too little, but above all, too late.

Protest in the corridors of power

At 3.55 pm on Thursday 14th November, Baroness Elliot of Harwood had risen from her seat in the House of Lords to open the debate calling for the

Signalman Cairns watches over the railway from Hawick South signal box – rebuilt in 1913 to improve visibility – on Saturday 4th January 1969, as the 13.00 Carlisle-Edinburgh train prepares to depart, hauled by BRCW Type 2 (aka Class 26) No. D5317. Sitting in the background is the Hawick pilot loco – 'Clayton' Type 1 (aka Class 17) No. D8606 – which had arrived 'light engine' from Edinburgh one and a half hours earlier, and would play a key part in the dramatic events at Hawick and Newcastleton the following night.

Stuart Sellar

Government to 'issue a directive preventing the impending closure of the "Waverley Line", in view of the considerable hardship this will cause to large numbers of people.' Harwood, who was made the first life peeress in 1958, was the widow of Walter Elliot MP who had been a moderate Conservative Secretary of State for Scotland in the 1930s.

Over the next 2 hours 50 minutes, no less than 14 Lords spoke out against the closure, with Lord Shepherd responding for the Labour Government (which had presided over the implementation of the vast bulk of the Beeching closures). Shepherd was Deputy Leader of the House of Lords, but with no specific transport or Scottish responsibilities; ironically, he went on to head the National Bus Company. In a memorable quote during her introductory comments, Baroness Elliot noted that the alternative Edinburgh-Carlisle route via Carstairs 'serves no population of any kind, only black-faced sheep and grouse, neither of which have much use for the railway' – contrasting this with the large population served by the Waverley Route.

In a notably visionary contribution, the Duke of Buccleuch and Queensberry (father of the Earl of Dalkeith MP, who was part of the 10 Downing Street delegation) reminded the House that no less that 600,000 tons of timber annually were projected for harvesting in the line's catchment by the year 2000.

But it was all to no avail. Lord Shepherd responded that, the Minister having made his decision, remaining responsibility rested with the BRB 'exercising their commercial judgement'. He referred to the line incurring the 'highest loss per passenger mile in this country', which of course applied to the whole route rather than a retained 'Basic Railway' between Hawick and Edinburgh. His dismal response is perhaps summed up by a closing comment – intended to underline the authority of the closure case – that 'the figures produced by the Railways Board . . . are closely examined by an economic department in the Ministry of Transport.' Hardly a convincing argument, when it was widely perceived that the Ministry was ruthlessly pursuing closure, irrespective of the case for retaining some kind of rail link to the Borders.

The *Scotsman* the next day reported that David Steel said later that the reply to the debate was 'a dreary repetition of what we already knew'. Asking why Lord Hughes, Under Secretary of State, Scottish Office, had not replied to the debate, Steel had said that to have Lord Shepherd, Minister of State, Commonwealth Affairs referring to his constituents as 'provincial country persons' made him 'hopping mad'.

Meanwhile BR was preparing an internal briefing paper responding at some length to criticisms made by the Lords. This paper (undated, but evidently compiled in November or December) is part of the Montgomery archive; in it

BR is at pains to counter the criticism that it had failed to make appropriate economies in the cost of operating the railway:

> Since 1962, surplus sidings have been uplifted, 20 signalboxes have been closed and 14 stations have been unstaffed. Motive Power Depots at Galashiels and Hawick have been eliminated and economical diesel locomotives introduced: DMU's [sic] have been employed on certain of the services. On the engineering side, the workshops at Hawick have been eliminated, and mechanical maintenance has been introduced . . . Since 1963 there has been a staff reduction of 165.

Overall this was a reasonable defence of BR's actions on costs, but it carefully glossed over one failure which had both cost and revenue implications – the fact that other than one daily Carlisle- Hawick return working, and two Edinburgh-Eskbank/Gorebridge return workings, DMUs were only used at weekends and seasonally on Mondays to Fridays. Admittedly there were operating synergies and efficiencies in using locomotives across a range of passenger, freight, parcels and newspaper trains – but these were all declining traffics and only a passenger service would be sustainable in the long term on a reprieved and rationalised railway. Nor did the BR paper address the complete failure to improve the timetable to meet changing competitive requirements.

In the House of Commons on 18th December, David Steel asked the Secretary of State for Scotland if he would make a statement on the Hibbs report. Ross responded that he had 'noted [it] with interest', but that 'any action to be taken on this report is, however, a matter for my right honourable friend the Minister of Transport or for the local authorities concerned in discussion with British Rail.'

Just two days later, any remaining hopes were dashed, the *Scotsman* reporting that the Minister of Transport 'has refused to give a three-month grant for the railway line between Edinburgh and Hawick until the local authorities have decided whether they could run the service.' Marsh had told Steel in a 19th December written reply that within the Hibbs report there was nothing . . .

> to persuade me that the figure of about £250,000 a year for a grant for a radically reduced service between Edinburgh and Hawick was exaggerated, and I do not consider that this would represent value for money.

The *Scotsman* of 20th December reported under the headline 'Last attempt to save Border rail link', that members of the Borders Consultative Group had agreed to go on a Border TV programme with Richard Marsh in the hope of securing a stay of execution at least until 1st April. Chairman Ernest Tait admitted it was only 'a faint hope' and added that 'we regret the closure, which will be a psychological and social loss, but from the economic standpoint we do not have a strong case.' Ironically, from both regional economic development and railway economics perspectives, they *did* have a good case for retaining the railway north of Hawick, but clearly *realpolitik* was kicking in, and the ground was being prepared for an alternative transport future in the Central Borders.

The day before the last train departed from Edinburgh to Carlisle via Hawick, the *Glasgow Herald* reported that David Steel, Ernest Tait and Gordon Stewart (BR Scottish Region General Manager) 'met yesterday in an eleventh hour review of the closure proposal and alternatives.' After the meeting a railway official had commented about the idea of a modified service and the local authorities contributing to its operation: 'The possibility of an experimental service of this nature during the next three months was examined and found to be impracticable.' Corresponding with the author in 2010, Steel commented that he had found Stewart to be 'wholly intransigent'.

One can only conclude that BR and the MoT refused to fund the service for a further three months, as by this stage the collective view of the various local authorities had not yet been settled. Given the blunt rebuff from Richard Marsh on any central government funding – and later confirmation that the local authorities would not pursue Hibbs's consortium recommendation – David Steel would, unexpectedly, have to turn his attention in 1969 to the even more radical option of a private sector take-over by the Border Union Railway Company.

The last rites

The last seven days of the Waverley Route were not a normal week, including as they did the traditional holiday on New Year's Day. Andrew Boyd recollected in 2010 that when he was in Waverley station on Monday 23rd December, there was a chalked notice to the effect that due to a derailment at Abington, the 10.40 to Birmingham, scheduled that day to run via the Carstairs 'avoiding line' as an independent train separate from the Glasgow train, would be diverted via Hawick. This was presumably the last occasion on which the Waverley Route was used for diversions. On Wednesday 1st January, only a skeleton service was operated. The normal Monday to Friday service resumed on Thursday 2nd (including the usual 03.50 parcels train from Carlisle to Edinburgh). That day the author had his last run on the line, leaving a dark and cold Edinburgh on the stopping train at 07.06, bound for Riccarton – accompanied by his father and many thoughts of 'what if'.

Over the previous three months, despite the competing attractions of Cream albums and, increasingly, the opposite sex, the author (then 16 years old) had written twice to the Minister of Transport and once to David Steel. His 13th October letter to Marsh may have been guilty of teenage hyperbole in places, but he did echo a recurring criticism of the management of the line:

> Victorian methods are still used in the operation of the railway – double track throughout, too many unimportant stations and a badly planned timetable . . . If a businessman wishes his firm to make a profit he attracts customers with a better, well-publicised service; naturally, he does not continue out-dated methods and keep quiet about the existance [sic] of his firm. The lesson for British Rail and you, Minister, is glaringly obvious!

As a parting shot, the author even wrote to Harold Wilson, and still 'treasures' the reply from 10 Downing Street on 23rd December 1968, to the effect that, 'The Prime Minister has asked me to thank you for your letter of 15 December, which is receiving attention.' It would be another 43 years before the author discovered the evidence that it was indeed the highest political authority in the land who finally determined the fate of the railway.

On Friday 3rd January the *Hawick News* had the unhappy task of previewing the last days of the railway and confronting the reality that 'Borders will be faced with the harsh facts of surviving in a community which lacks a main rail link.' It reported criticism of BR running a special excursion train the day before closure, not least from Madge Elliot who described this in other columns as 'adding insult to injury'. The paper reported David Steel's comment:

> I do not regard this as a disaster for the Borders because Borders people are tougher than this. I do, however, take a very serious view as a Member of Parliament to a process of Government decision which involves ignoring all the Government bodies in Scotland, including the Secretary of State.

The paper continued:

> Although goods will still be carried over the line until April, Borderers hope that during the two-year retention of the track, local authorities will succeed in formulating a scheme for the re-introduction of a rail service . . . But for many this is a gloomy prospect. Their fighting spirit has been broken. Meetings have been held, petitions have been raised, surveys have been made and questions have been asked in the House – but all have failed.

In an adjacent column, a past president of the Scottish Commercial Travellers' Association paid tribute to the railwaymen of the Waverley Route – 'as a class of men they were invariably polite, courteous and helpful and that compliment is intended for all railwaymen in all grades'. A week later Baroness Elliot of Harwood, who had fought so hard for the railway in the corridors of power, commented in the same paper, 'It is with real sadness that I say goodbye to the many friends I have made as a member of the travelling public, and I would like to say "thank you" for your service to Borderers.'

Friday 3rd January was also the last day of full passenger and freight operation over the Waverley Route – with no less than 40 train movements being recorded in Hawick South signal box train register. Sixteen were scheduled passenger services, but there were also nineteen freight trains, seven of these being specials to catch up on the New Year holiday backlog. Two mail/parcels trains and three 'engine & brake van' movements complete the story of the final peak performance of the Waverley Route as an Anglo-Scottish main line.

Saturday 4th January was the last busy day of operation on the line, including a controversial BR special train, *Farewell to the Waverley Route*, which campaigners had urged rail enthusiasts to boycott. The January 1969 issue of *Railway Magazine* carried a letter from Messrs Bogle, Glendinning, McCartney and Irving at Edinburgh University Union, which said;

> The imminent closure of this line should not be an occasion for sentimentality over the end of an era, for the closure denies the whole Borders adequate transport connections; thus the nearest railhead to Hawick is over 40 miles of tortuous road covered by bus at a crawl comparable to that of the stage-coach more than a century ago. Accordingly, we call on all enthusiasts not to participate in this flagrant example of profiteering and bad taste which adds insult to the injury already done to the Borders.

This special, hauled by Brush Type 4 diesel No. D1974, was late at Hawick because of a telephoned bomb threat. Bill Jamieson was on the train and comments that 'none of the passengers took the threat seriously, but the special was only allowed to proceed 24 minutes late', once four policemen, three bomb disposal experts and two railway workers had completed an examination beside Millerhill Yard. The hoax telephone call was never traced – not surprisingly, as the hoaxer worked in Galashiels telephone exchange! Other extreme responses to the imminent closure which were discussed clandestinely even included blowing up a span of the Royal Border Bridge at Berwick. In 2011, one of the campaigners recollected calling at a colleague's house to be confronted with a broom handle cut into pieces around which brown paper had been wrapped – creating a remarkable resemblance to sticks of gelignite. The chemicals which might be required for the real thing were discussed very briefly, but the plot went no further – a daft and dangerous idea, but indicative of how just how much anger and resentment the closure provoked amongst some Borderers. The *Hawick News* on 10th January reported that once the 4th January special had been cleared to proceed by the police:

Hundreds gathered at Hawick Station on Saturday morning to 'welcome' British Rail's 'special' excursion train – one of the last to travel over the Waverley line. The protestors, many wearing black armbands, were led by a group carrying a black mock funeral coffin . . . Police stood by as the train with over 400 passengers in nine coaches pulled into the station.

Despite the brouhaha, the train got out of Hawick unscathed, as did a further special that day – an 11-coach train from Newcastle hauled by one of BR's elite 'Deltic' locomotives, No. D9002 *King's Own Yorkshire Light Infantry*.

Saturday also saw the last through freight trains – the 08.30 Kingmoor Yard to Millerhill Yard, hauled by English Electric Type 3 No. D6851, and the 09.55 Bathgate to Kings Norton hauled by 'Peak' No. D43. Remarkably, the former locomotive (which had been built in 1963, and was renumbered 37 667 in later years) was still on main-line freight duties in 2015 for Direct Rail Services, appropriately headquartered in Carlisle.

The signal box train register, rescued for posterity by Ian Bell of Hawick – one of a band of dedicated local rail enthusiasts – records that more than 30 different locomotives (of nine different classes) worked through Hawick during the last three days of the Waverley Route. Surprisingly – over and above D6851, the only loco still in day-to-day commercial main line service – a further four have survived the breaker's torch. D1778 (aka 47 579) – now preserved on the Mid Norfolk Railway – worked passenger and parcels trains between Edinburgh and Hawick on the 3rd, while D5311 (aka 26 011) – recently in preservation at Burton-on-Trent – worked passenger trains between Edinburgh and Carlisle on the 3rd and 4th. D6851's sister loco D6846 (aka 37 146) – recently under restoration at Kirkby Stephen East – hauled freight trains between Millerhill and Kingmoor on the 3rd and 4th.

D6851 itself had a very busy 3rd January on freight duties – demonstrating a degree of operational efficiency which may come as a surprise to some advocates of today's privatised railway – hauling the 09.05 Millerhill-Kingmoor, returning on the 12.40 Kingmoor-Millerhill, then hauling the 20.10 Millerhill-Kingmoor, before completing an intensive day's work at the head of the 23.45 Kingmoor-Millerhill. On the 4th it worked the 05.00 Millerhill-Kingmoor freight, prior to performing the Waverley Route's northbound freight swansong later that morning. Finally, as we have seen, D9002 *King's Own Yorkshire Light Infantry* (aka 55 002) – now preserved at the National Railway Museum in York

– headed a Newcastle-Edinburgh charter over the Waverley Route on the morning of 4th January.

The final special over the Waverley Route ran on the last timetabled day of operation, Sunday 5th January – a Leeds-Edinburgh train for the Railway Correspondence & Travel Society, hauled by Deltic No. D9007 *Pinza*. This was not without controversy either – a posse of members of the Master Neverers Association (a reclusive group of North of England railway photographers-cum-engine cleaners) ensured, in the words of one of those present, that 'the rails were well lubricated with point oil for about 200 yards beyond Riccarton Junction, and the Deltic certainly had some adhesion problems getting away from its stop at the station!'

A few hours later, the final act of Waverley Route operation as an Anglo-Scottish railway was being prepared in Edinburgh – specifically at Haymarket locomotive depot, where Driver W Fleming and 'Fireman' G Patterson (the old steam age term was still being used) were checking over 'Peak' Type 4 diesel No. D60 *Lytham St Annes*, in readiness for running 'light engine' down to Waverley station, where they would take charge of the very last passenger train on the line, the 21.56 sleeper departure for St Pancras.

The author has multiple sources for the story of what happened in the subsequent dramatic scenes involving D60 at Hawick and Newcastleton (which have gone down in British railway history) – including eye witness accounts from Brydon Maben and Bruce McCartney; reports from the *Scottish Daily Express*, the *Hawick News* and the *Southern Reporter*; the BR Hawick Area Manager's report; and the Berwick, Roxburgh and Selkirk Constabulary's complete dossier on the events of 5th / 6th January. Unfortunately these accounts do not agree in every detail – perhaps inevitably, on a night of high emotion and conflicting perspectives. The report by the BR Area Manager was written by Osmond 'Ossie' Simpson – who subsequently became well known to the author when the latter was the BR Speedlink Coal Marketing Manager for Scotland, and the former was the BR Area Freight Manager based at Millerhill in the late 1980s. Simpson's report begins:

> On my Traffic Inspector examining clipped trailing crossover at Whitrope at 22.30 as a precaution following rumours of trouble he found padlock burst and clamp removed. On reclipping and advising me proceeded to Newcastleton arriving there at 23.15. In the interim local Police had called at his house there and informed his wife that the crossing gates had been chained and wired. They had found detonators on the line and were suspect of interference at other points.

Due to the disruption at Newcastleton on the night of 5th January 1969, signalman Gordon Hall had to leave Hawick South signal box and cross to the south end of the Carlisle platform to pass a written 'permission to proceed' to Driver Fleming of the 21.56 Edinburgh-St Pancras train. Captured for posterity by Bruce McCartney, David Steel MP – who was a sleeper passenger on the train – looks on as Hall climbs back down from the cab of 'Peak' Type 4 (aka Class 45) No. D60 *Lytham St Annes*. *Bruce McCartney*

Having mobilised engineering staff, Simpson decided that the line should be examined before allowing the last train to proceed, and a pilot locomotive ('Clayton' diesel No. D8606) departed south from Hawick at 23.19. Prior to its departure from Hawick, the leading light of the aforementioned Master Neverers Association, the late Paul Riley, had walked south placing detonators on the track at intervals to replicate the distinctive beat of the V2 steam locomotive so long associated with the Waverley Route – a stunt planned of course for the very last train. In any event, the detonators exploding under the Clayton to the beat of a V2 – recorded for posterity by Bruce McCartney – made for an eerie and fitting finale for the penultimate southbound locomotive movement on the last day of public operation.

The Berwick, Roxburgh and Selkirk Constabulary's dossier reported that the 21.56 from Edinburgh arrived at Hawick at 23.27 (10 minutes late), since 'the railway authorities had arranged for the train to be late in arriving at Hawick so that it would remain at the platform about 3 minutes' [doubtless to minimise the impact of any protests]. The dossier continued:

> Prior to the arrival of the train at least 200 people had assembled on the south-bound platform. Previously a black painted simulated coffin of cardboard material bearing the words 'Waverley Line – Born 1849, Killed 1969 – aged 120 years' addressed to the Minister of Transport had been accepted by British Railways as a goods parcel for delivery in London. A few minutes prior to the train's arrival the coffin was paraded along the platform led by a piper and followed by approximately 20 people. When the train arrived the coffin was loaded into the guard's van.

Around midnight on Sunday 5th/Monday 6th January 1969, the Reverend Brydon Maben patrols the Newcastleton level crossing gates which earlier had been forcibly closed by village protestors.
Bruce McCartney

Hawick South signal box was manned by Gordon Hall, who had swapped shifts with Jimmy Douglas so that he could be the last permanent signalman on duty at the box. Because of the disruption further down the line, and the recent departure of the pilot loco 'under caution' for Newcastleton, Hall was unable to pull the levers to clear the signals for the last train. Instead, he had to leave the box and cross to the south end of the Carlisle platform where, watched by David Steel MP (who was a sleeper passenger on the train), he climbed aboard D60 and passed a written 'permission to proceed' to Driver Fleming. Hall then stepped back down on to the platform – as captured for posterity by Bruce McCartney – and the train left Hawick at 00.02, 35 minutes late. In the meantime at Newcastleton, according to the Area Manager's report:

> [the Traffic Inspector] quickly burst the chain and wiring on the L.C. gates with a crowbar, but before the gates could be closed and secured across the roadway, about 40 villagers suddenly appeared and flung their weight against them and forcibly prevented further movement. Within a few minutes the crowd had doubled [forming a 'human barricade', according to the police dossier]; they jammed the gate lock and damaged gates, lifting off nearby hanging gates and jamming them against L.C. gates, actively led by the local minister, Mr. Bryden [sic] Maben.

Police reinforcements subsequently arrived from Hawick, including a nervous PC Graham Maben, the minister's 20-year old son, who reflected in 2014, 'I felt very uneasy, knowing, as I did, that Dad had told me there would be a demonstration. Of course, I had no idea of the scale, otherwise I would probably have had a dreadful dilemma facing me as to whether or not I should forewarn

Police officers (*l to r*, Sgt Albert Murdoch, DC Andrew Farquhar and DS Bobby Tait) lead the Reverend Brydon Maben away from the villagers' blockade of the level crossing gates at Newcastleton around 01.00 on Monday 6th January 1969. *Bruce McCartney*

my Senior Officers. I'm glad that I didn't find myself in that position!' According to Ossie Simpson, the BR Area Manager 'some scuffling took place', but the crowd remained solid at the crossing, awaiting the last train from the north. Iain Purdon, one of the passengers, subsequently described the experience in an unpublished epitaph:

> For this part of the journey, ours was the last revenue-earning train of any sort to traverse the line and circumstances combined to make sure nobody would forget it. As we stormed through the rolling hills, lit in black and white by a ghostly full moon, graced with sub-zero temperatures and the odd snowflake, the night was further lit by sudden showers of sparks from the wheels as the train frequently came to unexpected, mysterious halts. It may be that the communication cord was in on the secret but no-one was actually seen to operate it.

> Many houses on the hills were conscious of the passage of their lifeline. Against the bright background of lit doorways and windows could be seen Border folk, still up and about, watching the passing train. Some waved, others stood sullenly. For them it was the end of an era.

> . . . What happened next was undoubtedly the climax in the drama, a demonstration of protest without parallel that will not be forgotten even by the non-enthusiasts on the train. To [a] shower of sparks we came to a very decisive halt halfway down the platform at Newcastleton. The station lights were all burning yet it was difficult to see why we had stopped.

> Attempts to get out of the train in order to investigate were subverted by worried policemen and furious BR staff.

What was actually happening at the level crossing was recounted to the author by Brydon Maben in 1993:

> The pilot engine arrived and the express drew in behind it . . . and then the pilot engine driver said 'Are you going to stand there?' and I said, 'I'm going to stand here.' The station master came across and said 'put pressure on the gates,' but the pilot engine driver said, 'Oh no. If you want to drive the bloody engine you can drive it yourself!'

Asked whether the stationmaster (actually the Traffic Inspector) was a local man, Maben responded 'No, he was an idiot, and he nearly had one under the jaw from me I'll tell you.' Here David Steel takes up the story in his 1989 autobiography:

> About half an hour [after leaving Hawick] the train halted and after another quarter of an hour I was aware of my name being called. I opened the top window, looked out, and there was a railway inspector standing with a swaying lamp looking for me. 'We're just outside Newcastleton. The people are blocking the line and you're the only one that will persuade them to move.' I dressed hurriedly, clambered on to the line and was escorted alongside the carriages in the freezing darkness.
>
> There in front stood the pilot engine at the level crossing whose gates were firmly open [he meant 'shut'] – across the line – with what looked like half the population of the village, at least two or three hundred people. Newcastleton is a village largely created by the building of the railway and they felt more strongly than most about the closure because of the loss of employment as well as transport. I was met by the parish minister, the Rev. Brydon Maben. 'They'll expect you to make a speech,' he said. 'It's midnight and the temperature is about ten below freezing.' I replied, 'so it will be a short one.'

Meantime, passengers in the seating coaches were beginning to realise what was going on, Iain Purdon recollecting:

> From the end of the train we missed much of the detail but often heard loud cheers from an evidently sizeable crowd, acclaiming the failure of efforts to move the angry villagers. One ordinary passenger leaned out of the window and shouted at the multitude on the platform that she had to get to Kettering and they were being most inconsiderate towards the fare-payers on the train. There were various answers to this, none of them sympathetic and many of them unprintable.

The *Hawick News* described a festive atmosphere rather than an aggressive occasion:

Exploding fireworks added to the unaccustomed night noise. By this time more demonstrators began to converge on the scene, newly awakened from their beds. Suddenly silence fell on the crowd as they saw a familiar figure standing on the bridge, his hand raised for silence. It was David Steel, MP for the Borders constituency, who had been travelling on the train.

Ossie Simpson's report continued in inevitably terser style:

On arrival of the 21.56 at home signal at 00.44 Traffic Inspector contacted local MP Mr David Steel and persuaded him to alight from train and address the mob with a view to getting reason to prevail. Mr Steel's appeal looked likely to succeed, but was vitiated by the Rev. B. Maben's exhortation to them, and I quote, verbatim: 'I suggest we stay here until we are forcibly removed.' This incited the mob to greater pitch and unruliness. Following a bit of disorder, Mr Maben was escorted away by the Police.

The Berwick, Roxburgh and Selkirk Constabulary's dossier, perhaps wishing to draw a line under the events of the night, reached a somewhat different conclusion:

There was no hostility or violence by the demonstrators towards the police . . . No person was injured . . . The demonstration appeared to be spontaneous although it was rumoured that the incident may have been prompted by *railway employees*. [author's italics] . . . A small percentage of passengers in the Pullman showed annoyance at the delay, but it was felt that the remainder appeared to be in sympathy with the demonstrators . . . So far as is known apart from the severing of the hosepipe of the vacuum braking system in the rear coach the level crossing gates were the only railway property which suffered damage . . . No person was apprehended and no-one has been charged with any criminal offence . . . It is understood that no further action is being taken by the railway authorities and that they now consider this matter closed.'

Surviving protagonists insist that the rumours of rail staff being involved in instigating the demonstration are false – this was a community protest at Newcastleton's overnight transformation from a village well-served by public transport to one thrown on the mercy of inadequate and unreliable bus services. The local doctor Arthur Bethune recollected in a 2013 letter to his grandson Nicholas (by then a key activist with the Campaign for Borders Rail) that 'the demonstration at the level crossing was by no means spontaneous though only a few of us knew what was planned.' Bethune cited three locals who had collaborated with him, but could only recollect the names of two – the Reverend Brydon Maben and a Jim Robson.

Returning the story to the concluding scenes of this extraordinary occasion, David Steel again addressed the crowd, and finally got their promise to disperse if Brydon Maben was released and no charges preferred. In due course, the police having released Maben, the level crossing was cleared and the last train continued its journey south, reaching Longtown 117 minutes late and proceeding onwards to Carlisle and London. The pilot engine – which had run ahead to Kershopefoot – returned north, arriving at the sidings in Hawick at 02.38; the final unsung act of the Waverley Route as a through Anglo-Scottish railway had been completed.

This profound moment was complemented by a prosaic footnote at Newcastleton, as recalled by Graham Maben in 2014: 'Once the London train had departed, my mum invited all the police into the manse for tea and Marmite sandwiches. Later on, the two Senior Officers who had been entertained in the manse were carpeted for co-habiting with a criminal. How bizarre – and how embarrassing for me!'

Why was the Waverley Route lost?

On Monday 6th January 1969, Hawick – a town of 16,000 people – suddenly found itself 45 miles from the nearest railhead (Carlisle) and 51 miles from Edinburgh by a very slow and basic bus service, while the 13,000 residents of Gala were left 33 miles by road from the capital. No other towns of their size in Britain were now so distant from the rail network, and the Borders had become the only region of the country with no train services. The closure of this railway is widely recognised as the biggest and most damaging of the Beeching era, and many observers, including people in the Borders, simply blame 'Beeching' or 'BR' for the injustice. However, this was ultimately a political decision taken by politicians and their civil service advisers, supposedly representing the public interest. Those who have written about the railway have suggested a number of reasons for the closure – not least the way in which the campaign was conducted.

HP White in *Forgotten Railways* (1986) takes account of wider political factors, and effectively concludes (like John Hibbs) that the through route was a lost cause:

> Protests were voluble, but the Borders lacked the political power of the Highland and Welsh lobbies. The protestors also probably made a tactical error in concentrating on trying to keep the whole line open, for by doing so they drew attention from the less costly alternative of a 52 mile, DMU-operated, 'basic' railway between Hawick and Edinburgh.

However, given the traditional inter-town rivalry in the Borders, and the fact that David Steel's constituency embraced Newcastleton as well as the Central

Borders towns, White's suggested tactic of campaigning only to keep the Edinburgh-Hawick section would surely have risked fragmentation in the ranks of those opposing closure. As events unfolded, the option of retaining a simplified service between Edinburgh and Hawick, and closing the line south of Hawick, was still on the table (and backed by Secretary of State for Scotland Willie Ross) at the crucial final Ministerial meeting in London.

So, what can one conclude about the definitive reasons for the loss of the Waverley Route? The primary and secondary research for this book has revealed the importance of factors which have hitherto been hidden from public knowledge or not fully understood. There were indeed multiple political, social and business reasons why this strategic blunder was perpetrated, and these can be summarised under six headings in broadly descending order of importance.

The lukewarm support for the railway in the **Central Borders Plan** proved to be the critical factor at the 21st May 1968 meeting of the Ministerial Committee on Environmental Planning which approved closure. If there is a single 'silver bullet' which killed the Waverley Route it is this report produced by Edinburgh University for the Scottish Office. It conspicuously failed to acknowledge the potentially key role of the railway in providing a fast, reliable and civilised transport spine for the planned population expansion along the line corridor between Galashiels and St Boswells. Ministers, who knew how much importance Willie Ross attached to the linkage between the Central Borders Plan and Labour's wider Scottish image on economic development, were keen to see public expenditure minimised – and seized on the report's equivocal support for the railway to press the case for complete closure.

None of the author's research has found vindication for **the 1960s' performance of British Rail management**. In the words of Roy Perkins in 2011:

> Overall one has to reach the conclusion that BR management's unresponsiveness to changed circumstances was largely if not totally responsible. They failed to adjust their timetable, they failed to adjust their fares and they failed to adjust their working practices (staffing levels, number of stations etc).

While BR did significantly reduce staff costs in the late 1960s through mechanised maintenance, signal box closures and destaffing of stations, on the revenue side of the equation it did little or nothing to improve the timetable or to promote the tourist attractions of the line. It evidently had a schizophrenic attitude (depending on the managers involved at any given time) to the potential of timber traffic, and none ever moved over the Waverley Route despite its growth elsewhere in the Scottish Region. Although the Kielder dam and reservoir – Britain's largest – was being planned in the early 1960s (and constructed in the 1970s) there is no evidence that the potential for transporting aggregates and cement over the Waverley Route to the site – just seven miles down the old Border Counties line from Riccarton – was ever properly evaluated by BR. However for several years in the late 1970s BR did run trainloads of cement from Clitheroe to Hexham for onward road delivery to Kielder.

In fairness, the prevailing convention of the era that major changes to a threatened line's service or infrastructure were not made until a Ministerial reprieve decision had been announced may have inhibited management action. The Waverley Route's relative isolation from Scottish Region HQ may also have been a contributory factor – it was the only double-track main line in Scotland (other than Aberdeen to Keith) which did not have a direct train service to or from Glasgow – and there have been (as yet unproven) assertions that the split in control between Scottish Region and London Midland Region undermined the efficient management and marketing of the line.

With evident MoT lack of interest in the scope for economies on a 'basic' Edinburgh-Hawick service, BR managers (for many of whom securing big closures was still a mark of career achievement) got away with dubious cost and revenue projections, which allowed Richard Marsh to argue that the level of subsidy would be too high – and too much of a precedent for the rest of the rail network. Interestingly, ex-BR manager Allan McLean speculated in 2010 that, 'had Gerry Fiennes been in Scotland [rather than Eastern Region] then I believe Edinburgh-Hawick would have been saved, but not Hawick-Carlisle – and East Anglia would have lost out instead.'

At the end of the day, the London-based Ministry with statutory responsibility for railways throughout Britain got its wish when all 98 miles of the railway were closed to passengers. **Governmental structures** were therefore a crucial factor, not just the fact that the Scottish Office had powers over roads but not railways, but also the fragmentation of local government along the Waverley Route, reinforcing traditional rivalries between the Borders towns. Although the disparate group of Scottish local authorities did come together under the leadership of Roxburgh County Council for the purposes of official protest, a more powerful united lobbying force would have been Borders Regional Council, which did not come into being until 1975.

Just as powerful as formal structures was the *realpolitik* surrounding the demise of the railway, not least the pressure on public spending following UK devaluation and the evident financial symbolism of Waverley Route closure. The Ministry of Transport had a cost-led objective, with little or no concern for the qualitative reality of replacement bus services or wider regional development issues, and Richard Marsh was evidently determined to demonstrate that he 'meant business' in sorting out the railways – both in general, and specifically in terms of re-allocating resources to fund the West Coast Main Line upgrade.

The parliamentary constituencies straddling the Waverley Route were split between the three main parties (with no key marginals) and the Borders lacked the political resonance of the Highlands. In a situation which it is now clear was finely balanced to the very end, it was unfortunate – as David Steel has admitted – that the key political campaigners did not seek (privately) to enlist the support of Secretary of State for Scotland, Willie Ross. As Steel commented to the author in 2011: 'I wish I had known Willie Ross's thoughts at the time!' – but in fairness, as he said in his address to the 5th January 2014 Newcastleton dinner to mark the 45th anniversary of closure, 'politicians in those days tended to be party-parochial'. Ironically, it is conceivable that the Government's final decision went one way and not the other simply due to the absence from the crucial 21st May 1968 Ministerial meeting of two Ministers – Anthony Crosland and Lord Brown of Machrihanish – whom Willie Ross had previously prayed in aid as supporters of retaining the Edinburgh-Hawick section. The course of Borders' history may have been altered by the most mundane of chance occurrences.

Previous railway managements did have – in theory at least – the opportunity to put at least part of the railway on a sounder footing. The 1955 BR Modernisation Plan has been widely and rightly criticised for its failure nationwide to take on board the nature of growing road competition by investing selectively in the traffic and technologies of the future. Whether their ultimate implications could reasonably have been foreseen or not, it is arguable that key **BR strategic decisions taken in the 1950s** were to reduce the prospects of the Waverley Route's role being re-appraised and a 'railway of two halves' emerging to give the Hawick-Edinburgh section a stronger chance of survival, rather than being dragged down by the eventually desperate economics of Hawick-Carlisle.

The re-routeing of additional through freight trains on to the Waverley Route in the 1950s, and the consolidation of that move by the opening of Kingmoor and Millerhill marshalling yards in 1963 and 1962–63 respectively, ensured that it was a 98¼ mile heavily loss-making double-track route which presented itself to Beeching in 1962 – as an iconic symbol of what needed to be removed from the rail system. In the words of Allan McLean in 2011: 'I can't help thinking that a more rational view would have been taken of the Waverley Route's potential if management focus and investment hadn't been wasted on huge marshalling yards.'

Last, but possibly not least, is the conduct of **the campaign against closure** and the associated issue of wider **Borders attitudes**. Spirited as the final months of the campaign clearly were (and the author has unstinting admiration for those involved), the fact that the Action Group to fight closure was not set up until September 1968 says much about the importance that most Borderers attached to their railway. As we have seen, patronage of the Waverley Route was declining over a long period, and this continuing decline was a key element of the MoT/BR case for closure. The author's research uncovered the word 'apathy' on a number of occasions, and surviving campaigners have also mentioned unprompted the 'aye been' factor, the Borders saying which loosely translates as 'that's what's going to happen and there's nothing we can do about it'.

Unlike the energetic response to the Beeching threats in the Highlands, too many people in the Borders either believed the railway would never close or were not sufficiently concerned to do anything about it.

CHAPTER 6

A strange half-life becomes a lingering death

1969–72

B RITISH Rail did not hesitate to demonstrate that this really was the end. As HP White records in *Forgotten railways*, '[on Wednesday 8th January] BR, in the presence of media representatives, symbolically lifted a length of rail at Riddings. They had forgotten the Churchillian wisdom: In victory, magnanimity.'

While the timing of the lifting, and the media invitation, do suggest a conscious 'symbolic' motivation, this stretch of track was relatively modern (laid in 1954) and was just one part of a wider programme of removal and redeployment of rails and sleepers to other sections of the network which took place in the January to early March period, on the Up (to Carlisle) line only, between Hawick and Longtown.

The entire route had closed to passengers, but contracts with the coal trade forced BR to maintain a daily freight train from Millerhill Yard to Galashiels, St Boswells and Hawick, through to 25th April 1969. The existing signalling system was no longer required and arrangements were downgraded on 6th January to 'Telephone and Notice Board' between Lady Victoria Pit and Hawick, permitting just one train to operate at any one time on this 42 mile 1,078 yard section, which was reported in the railway press at the time as being the longest 'block section' on British Railways.

A travelling signalman joined the freight train at Galashiels each weekday to operate levers in the remaining signal boxes for the sidings at Galashiels, St Boswells and Hawick. As well as coal to Galashiels and Hawick, oil tank wagons were delivered to a rail-linked distribution depot in St Boswells.

In the early days it was almost as if the railway couldn't quite believe what had happened – an odd anomaly reported in the *Sunday Post* concerned engine drivers based at Hawick still having to report for duty to the station for six weeks after closure despite there being no engines for them to drive (the daily freight being crewed by Millerhill men).

A Type 3 (aka Class 37) provides unusual motive power for the Millerhill-Hawick trip freight only weeks before the withdrawal of this service on 28th April 1969. Seen just east of Melrose, the train also has an unusual complement of vans, over and above the standard consist of coal wagons and oil tanks.
Ian Holoran

On 24th March 1969, Edinburgh University Railway Society enjoyed a 'brake-van trip' on the surviving daily trip freight from Millerhill to Hawick. Seen here at Galashiels freight depot, BR Type 2 (aka Class 25) No. D7608 shunts coal traffic for the depot, with oil tanks for St Boswells next to the loco.
Bruce McCartney

Rail traffic survives at Galashiels freight depot in March 1969, but the entire railway estate has something of a *Marie Celeste* feel. Today, every last piece of evidence of the railway in this view has long since disappeared, including the Station Brae bridge in the right background – then spanning multiple tracks, unlike its modern replacement which has room for just a single track.
Ian Holoran

During the period of freight-only operation (when, as we shall see, the Border Union Railway Company was pressing the case for reinstatement of passenger services), campaigner Madge Elliot put in a request for a special train to be run to a rugby international at Murrayfield in Edinburgh. BR's reply stated that the signalling system was not up to passenger standard, and in 2011 Bruce McCartney recalled his wry 'amusement' that BR managed to run rail tours in 1970 and 1971 from Millerhill to Lady Victoria Pit, where exactly the same signalling system was in place. One can only assume that BR in 1969 was much more concerned about the potentially dangerous politics of running a passenger train to Hawick than the revenue which this would generate.

The lingering freight-only railway could readily turn a blind eye to practices which might have been frowned on while the Waverley Route was still a 'main line'. Ralph Coleman, who as we have seen was probably the youngest official objector to closure, recollected in 2012 how as an enthusiastic 12-year old he kept pestering the local Galashiels parcels clerk (who had not been made redundant on 6th January 1969) to speak to the freight trip driver and ask if he could have a footplate ride to Hawick and back:

I was usually given the 'green light' and had a number of memorable trips, including one occasion when the usual low-powered Clayton Type 1 diesel was replaced by a 2,750 horse power Brush Type 4 which allowed some pretty fine running between St Boswells and Hawick.

The last freight train from Millerhill Yard to Hawick ran on Friday 25th April, hauled by the same type of locomotive – the distinctive Clayton with its elevated central cab – which had played a key part in the dramatic events of 5th/6th January at Hawick and Newcastleton. The Claytons were one of the least successful of the BR Modernisation Plan diesels – and all were withdrawn by 1971 – but will always be associated with the Waverley Route because of their role in these events and their frequent use, double-headed, on through freight trains.

On 28th April 1969, the signal boxes at Hawick, St Boswells, Galashiels and Lady Victoria Pit were shut, and now the railway had carried its last revenue-earning traffic over the 43 miles from Hawick to Lady Victoria. A road-served BR parcels and sundries operation was however retained at Galashiels for a number of years. Coal traffic from Lady Victoria survived until December 1971 when the remaining branch was cut back to the Butlerfield washery a short distance to the north in Newtongrange – and this in turn succumbed to complete closure in June 1972.

Over the southern stub of the Waverley Route, the initially surviving local freight services ceased between Stainton Junction and Canal Junction in Carlisle in August 1969. In August 1970 the line closed completely between Longtown and the Harker/Brunthill RAF 14 Maintenance Unit one mile north of Stainton Junction, thereby avoiding a bridge requirement for the new M6.

The fate of the Waverley Route employees

By the time it was all over, 200 railway jobs had been eliminated. The fate of the redundant employees was fortunately recorded for posterity in an MBA dissertation – *Redundancy and Manpower Policy on British Rail* – undertaken in 1970 by Douglas Paul, who as we saw in Chapter 3 spent eight formative weeks of BR management training on the Waverley Route in 1965–66. Paul's MBA at Glasgow University was sponsored by BR, and his dissertation covered two case studies – the Waverley Route and the Kyle line, which at the time was facing a possible closure threat.

In an article in the North British Railway Study Group Journal of December 2010, Paul recalls that the long drawn-out closure process for the Waverley Route came at the price of employee uncertainty lasting for more than five years – and 'most people who worked on the line stayed in their jobs until the bitter end in the hope that the line would be reprieved.' 60% of the railway's staff were in their 40s or 50s, 'railway folk born and bred . . . and for most of them, their once valued skills were of no use outside the railways.' Shockingly, the first that

Hawick station and goods yard look pristine – and are devoid of traffic, other than a few freight wagons – in this panoramic view taken just weeks before the final Millerhill-Hawick trip freight ran on Friday 25th April 1969.

Ian Holoran

employees knew of consent to closure was when they opened their newspapers on 16th July 1968:

> There was no official communication to confirm the decision to local management until six weeks after the announcement had been made. Even then, it came indirectly from the Financial Accountant at Scottish HQ in a letter concerning budgets for the coming year! Unsurprisingly, local employees felt they had been left in the lurch.

From a total of 200 people who were made redundant, the actual number who had to find alternative jobs was 158, most of the remainder opting for retirement. 23 of the 158 chose to remain with BR – most moving away, but with just a few able still to live in the Borders and work on the railway, like the signalman who transferred to Elvanfoot in Lanarkshire, driving there by car each day from home in Canonbie. Ironically, just five years later even that job would disappear too, as power signalling centres at Carlisle and Motherwell eliminated all the manual signal boxes on the West Coast Main Line. It was hard to escape rail rationalisation.

135 ex-railway employees were therefore left to find jobs locally, and although their uncertain future was cushioned by BR's enlightened redundancy scheme and by the local textile industry's desperate shortage of labour, this came at a price, as Paul records:

> The type of work offered by the mills was an unattractive proposition for many railway employees. Typically it was unskilled and low paid work and represented a drop in status particularly for those who had progressed up the career ladder in their railway jobs.

Paul quotes the example of a 59 year old supervisor who was earning £27 a week with BR. While he was receiving unemployment benefit and continuing weekly payments he was taking home £18 a week. He remained unemployed for the full 42 weeks of his entitlement to weekly payments before taking employment as a labourer in a mill and a wage of £13 a week:

> His wife then had to start working to make ends meet. He regarded mill life as 'just an existence' with none of the social rapport among employees which he had enjoyed on the railways. He wished he had been younger so that he could have moved on to another railway job.

So why didn't more people move to railway jobs elsewhere? Paul cites the age of much of the railway workforce and local family ties, plus their awareness that the railways generally in the late 1960s remained an insecure environment for employees – with a lingering threat of more line closures, replacement of manual signal boxes by centralised power boxes, and labour-intensive goods yards giving way to more capital-intensive container train operations. Paul notes that many people, torn between the option of a satisfying railway job elsewhere or staying put in the Borders, decided to opt for the latter. He quotes a poignant illustration of the dilemma faced by many in the case of one of the ex-employees surveyed in 1970:

A few months after the line closed, the local area manager at Hawick [Ossie Simpson] who had moved to another railway job in Edinburgh by this time, was back in the town at a rugby match when he spotted a former engine driver who was now working as a petrol pump attendant. Struck by how the driver's physical appearance had changed for the worse, the manager asked the driver's wife what was wrong. She replied that her husband was missing his job so much that, if he continued like this, he would end up 'in his box'. The upshot was that a railway job was offered to him at Millerhill locomotive depot in Edinburgh. He agreed to relocate and started a second railway career as a new entrant. When he was visited in the course of the survey, he was obviously rejuvenated and delighted to be working among his beloved engines again.

Borderers (try to) get used to buses, and track lifting continues

After 5th January 1969, if you had no car, or couldn't share a car, then your journey from, to or within the Borders had to be by bus. Gone was the accepted norm of 1 hour 30 minutes or less to Edinburgh from Hawick; the new alternative transport now took 2 hours 15 minutes.

The enhanced bus service (Eastern Scottish service 95), required as a condition of closure, certainly offered a higher and more regular frequency along the A7 (hourly through the day) than the train had done north of Hawick, but none of the quality that even an ailing railway had been able to provide. The journey time was a minimum of 50% longer, with no toilets, little room for luggage, no space to get up and stretch your legs, and no provision for prams. South of Hawick, there were seven buses a day to Carlisle via Langholm, which fortuitously gained an improved public transport service as a result of the destruction of the Waverley Route.

Perhaps the biggest loser (as predicted by the TUCC) was Newcastleton, which from Monday 6th January saw just three buses a day to Hawick (with an extra service on a Thursday) and two to Carlisle (with an extra on Wednesdays and Saturdays). Only three days previously, it had enjoyed six fast trains a day to Carlisle (one continuing to London), six to Hawick and five continuing to

Edinburgh. Almost literally overnight, Newcastleton had gone from being a very well-connected village to one with a desperately poor public transport service – a serious impact for those without cars.

However, part of the reason for the failure to save the line was perhaps unwittingly confirmed by the Reverend Brydon Maben, when asked in 1993 by the author to comment on his feelings in the weeks after closure: 'Well, naturally, sad. As I say it didn't terribly affect me personally because we nearly all had cars . . .' For non car owners however, life without the railway was a bitter pill to swallow. In that vein, Madge Elliot later wrote to the *Hawick News* (on 22nd May 1970):

> I have a friend who became so chilled while travelling from Edinburgh to Hawick that she developed pneumonia. There is no need to wonder why passenger numbers are dropping. One only undertakes such a journey by bus if it is absolutely necessary. I know pensioners who have had to keep medical appointments in Edinburgh which only lasted 10 minutes. Five hours travelling for a 10-minute appointment . . . Parents who have gone to collect children from Edinburgh hospitals have been told they must not take them by bus . . . There is no other town in the country the size of Hawick which is so far from a railhead. Isn't it about time we all cared a little bit more about each other. I am sure that this is what life is all about. If we did a bit more caring the world would be a much happier place in which to live for all of us.

This heartfelt plea encapsulated the real hardship that was being experienced by so many. In his *Scottish Region: A History 1948–73* AJ Mullay reflects on a key failure of the statutory process which determined the fate of the Waverley Route: 'Closure was concluded just before the new Transport Act reached the statute book, requiring TUCCs to be more stringent in their assessment of replacement public services' – in other words the *quality* as well as quantity of replacement buses.

While the replacement bus service haphazardly bedded in, the dismantling of sections of the railway proceeded within the constraints of the Ministerial requirement for the route formation (ie the land but not the track) north of Hawick to remain *in situ* for two years.

Lifting took place at a variety of locations along the Up (to Carlisle) line of the Hawick-Longtown section between January and March, both tracks of which were now under engineering rather than operational control. The oldest rails lifted in early 1969 had been laid in 1952, and the newest dated from as recently as 1965; stretches of concrete sleepers were also recovered. Allan McLean, who worked for BR in Glasgow in the early 1970s recollected in 2010 that a section of track for the upgrading of the West Coast Main Line near Beattock was taken from the Waverley Route near Whitrope – the BR records point to this being 730 yards of flat-bottomed track which had been laid as recently as 1962. The Down (from Carlisle) line, however, remained completely intact.

David Steel, having seen Richard Marsh reject the concept of a temporary Government stay of execution while BR operated a modified service north of Hawick, returned – in a 10th January letter to Marsh – to John Hibbs' idea of the local authorities taking over financial responsibility for a rail service. Marsh's 27th January response was long (four pages), but unhelpful. He rejected the idea of central government funding for the mooted £80,000 capital expenditure to single-track the line, and the letter's final sentence left no room for doubt about the prospects of the public sector saving part of the Waverley Route:

> As I said before, I have found nothing in Mr. Hibbs's report to persuade me to think otherwise [on justification for subsidy] and I still see no grounds for optimism that a modified Edinburgh/Hawick service would attract sufficient revenue to require only a 'reasonable subsidy', whether from central or local government funds.

The birth of the Border Union Railway Company

On the evening of 8th December 1968, a London-based exile from Newcastleton had dropped into the local Wellington Arms pub in Woolwich, to celebrate his birthday with a near-neighbour. Roy Perkins had moved from Newcastleton in early childhood but retained extensive family connections in the area, including no less than five Uncle Archies scattered across Liddesdale! The conversation between Perkins and Martin Symms ('who had rather less than no interest in railways') soon turned to the imminent closure of the railway through Roy's home village. From this unlikely beginning was hatched a breathtaking plan to take over the entire Waverley Route as a going concern.

While the embryonic private sector development was taking shape, the proposed local authorities' initiative was – probably inevitably – soon faltering in the face of a seemingly major financial commitment to keep the railway running, even at a very basic level. On 21st January 1969, writing on behalf of the Waverley Line Action Group to James Kyle, County Clerk of Roxburgh County Council, the Secretary of the South of Scotland Chamber of Commerce formally advised that at the previous day's Action Group meeting in Hawick it had been concluded that there was 'no support' for forming a local authority consortium, and that 'not all Local Authorities would be prepared to make a contribution to operate the Line'. The Action Group had accordingly decided that "there was no purpose in pursuing the matter further."

The meeting Minute in fact records that Kyle was one of the eight attendees (including Provost Pate of Gala) who heard that 14 councils which had financed the Hibbs Report had been asked for their views and that, 'from replies received from Galashiels and Selkirk Town Councils it was clear that they were not in favour of the suggestion and Mr Kyle reported that Roxburgh County Council were not prepared to support a Consortium but might consider making a contribution if there was unanimous agreement by other Authorities'. It was however noted that David Steel had approached Richard Marsh 'to verify how much his Ministry would contribute to the running of the line.' The numbers were clearly daunting, but the decision to abandon this initiative may have been made more palatable in light of a report to the meeting that 'consideration was now being given by a group of businessmen from the South to the feasibility of floating a company with a view to operating the Waverley Line from Carlisle to Edinburgh as a private venture.'

Around this time, a common acquaintance in the vintage car business introduced Roy Perkins to the TV producer Bob Symes-Schutzmann, then working on *Tomorrow's World* and a known enthusiast for rail preservation. Following their initial discussion about the Waverley Route, an urgent letter was delivered by hand to David Steel at the House of Commons. Steel came out of the Chamber to meet Perkins (who had worked for Steel's 1965 by-election campaign, and was employed in market research) and Symms (who had travel and real estate interests), and a productive dialogue began. At Perkins's suggestion, harking back to the line's genesis in the mid-nineteenth century, the name chosen for the planned new company was the Border Union Railway Company (BURCo).

Perkins, Symms and Symes-Schutzmann then got to work with a vengeance on formulating their business plan, networking in every possible direction with contacts in the railway, business, financial and public relations worlds. So committed was Perkins, a qualified economist, that he resigned from his market research job with Michelin, moved back to Newcastleton, and worked full-time on the project for the best part of a year. One of Perkins' first tasks was to produce a Draft Report on the proposed North British Railway Company, which was intended to be the operating company, leasing the line's assets from the holding company, BURCo. Interestingly, this report, which is part of Perkins' private archive, contains many more financial build-up figures to support the bottom-line conclusions than BURCo's Feasibility Study which was eventually publicly launched in late August.

By the time of Roy Perkins' 27th February letter to the Reverend Brydon Maben in Newcastleton, the former was able to advise that 'we should very shortly be a corporate body' (a limited company) and that 'BR have been approached, contact having been made with both the BRB (the British Railways Board, in a 26th February letter) and the Scottish Railway Board, and the reaction, I am very relieved to say has so far been extremely favourable.' Perkins indicated that 'talks start next week', but there were also cryptic references to difficulties in terms of reactions to the Draft Report's attribution of costs to different elements of the rail service, and to a delay in the planned survey of potential rail users. The three Directors of BURCo had taken on a monumental workload – and it showed. The theme of BR experiencing delays in getting responses from BURCo and of 'time running out', for example, are recurring features of the archive.

Perkins had also approached another near-neighbour, John Grant, who promptly suggested setting up an enthusiast support group for the company – and the Waverley Association (WA) was soon established, with Grant as the first secretary. Grant was an experienced businessman (and a future director of Bovis Homes, as well as working for the preserved Bluebell and Kent & East Sussex Railways). In addition to the encouragement to set up an enthusiast support group, it was planned to establish the North British Railway Company (NBRC) to keep liabilities separate, and during the course of 1969 an impressive list of planned board directors for the NBRC was lined up from the accountancy, business, insurance and Borders' landowning worlds. In practice, the company was never set up, but eight individuals became 'associates' of BURCo – including Lord Melgund (later, as the Earl of Minto, to be Convener of Borders Regional Council, from 1990 until 1996) who was to play the closing cards on behalf of this ambitious but unsuccessful project.

The BURCo plan was publicly launched at a press conference held at the prestigious North British Hotel in Edinburgh on Saturday 15th March, chaired by David Steel. The group faced a barrage of questions from the media, and soon received generous local and national press, television and radio coverage. A great deal of public interest was immediately generated by the prospect that the last major railway to be closed in Britain could become (to quote David Henshaw in *The Great Railway Conspiracy* (1994)) 'the test-bed for a new and radical idea: a privately-owned and fully commercial trunk line.' The Directors of BURCo (Symes-Schutzmann, Perkins and Symms) followed the public launch with a series of meetings with potential investors, and – according to Perkins, recollecting events in 2010 – initial confidential backing came from the merchant bank, Noble Grossart, and the Bank of Scotland.

Freight was one of the issues flagged up in the first detailed letter from the BRB Estates Manager to BURCo on 12th June, in anticipation of a BRB /

Border Union Railway Co. Ltd.

Directors: R.M.G.Perkins, B.Sc.(Econ) Hons.
R.A.Symes-Schutzmann, Companion R.Ae.S.
M.C.I I.Cymms, B.A.Dip.Com.

Please Reply to:

The short-lived letterhead of the Border Union Railway Company

BURCo meeting in Melbury House, London, on 20th June: 'There ought to be no difficulty in accepting freight trains into Millerhill and Kingmoor, but we shall need to have more information about the methods you propose for operating freight traffic.' The initial tone of the letter was also positive about a key issue – 'there would appear to be no insuperable difficulty in accommodating your services over the Board's lines in to each terminal [Edinburgh Waverley and Carlisle Citadel stations]' – but there were quite a few significant stings in the tail, including:

> At Waverley Station, the Board have development plans which will make it impossible for your services to run in to the east end. It should, nevertheless, be possible to accommodate you in the suburban platforms, though precise timings cannot be guaranteed, and adjustments might be necessary . . . Your company's services must at all times take priority behind the Board's services, whether the latter are running late or otherwise . . . The Board will not be prepared to offer co-operation in respect of through bookings nor in respect of excessing [fares].

BURCo tries to stack up the figures – but sees the first clouds on the horizon

BURCo was keen to take advantage of established rail experience in developing its business plan. Gerry Fiennes, who had done so much to overturn the conventional wisdom on rural railways, was approached for advice, and met Roy Perkins in London in early June 1969 and corresponded with him until late October – partly with a view to producing a magazine article endorsing the scheme. In his 13th June letter to Perkins, Fiennes commented that he 'enjoyed our discussion enormously' and asked for gaps in the traffic and financial data to be filled in so that he would be 'able to judge whether I can do the article.' One of the issues discussed was BURCo's envisaged drastic reduction in staffing – from 345 under BR (although this conflicts with a figure of 274 quoted by BR in 1968) to 100 in the new company, a cost reduction which was clearly critical to the economics of the plan. Only part of this reflected the use of volunteers, much more being attributable to securing cost efficiencies such as destaffing stations and introducing more flexible working practices. BURCo had discussions with the NUR (and, according to Symes-Schutzmann at the Campaign for Borders Rail 2009 AGM, secured an 'in principle' offer of a £150,000 investment stake from the union), who accepted the offer of sole negotiating rights for staff.

However, behind the scenes, the bad news was becoming as frequent as the good. Just 10 days after Gerry Fiennes had written to Roy Perkins querying gaps in BURCo's traffic and financial data, the Hawick Manager of the Royal Bank of Scotland (RBS), AM Turnbull, brought perhaps the first intimation that raising capital for purchase of the railway and associated rolling stock was not going to be as straightforward as the Directors had hoped or claimed. Turnbull had undertaken to write to see if the bank's own merchant bank, National Commercial & Glyns, would be interested in funding the project. What kind of financial submission or business plan had accompanied this request is not clear – and it is striking that Roy Perkins, who had undertaken virtually all the financial analysis, played no part in this initiative – but the 23rd June answer was short and to the point:

> Having examined the submissions my Head Office have now replied that the Bank regretfully cannot help and that there would be no point in having a meeting with them to discuss the matter in depth. I need not go into the terms of the reply further but there is no encouragement.

This was the bluntest of dismissals and, together with Fiennes' queries, must have been the first clear indications that BURCo's grand plan (as opposed to a more modest project on just part of the Waverley Route) was – or was seen to be – of doubtful viability. Nevertheless, on 28th July no less an authority than the office of the Chairman & General Manager of BR London Midland Region (RLE Lawrence) had written to Symes-Schutzmann advising the names of four 'possible retired railway officers who could help you in the mechanical and electrical engineering field.'

The Feasibility Study is launched

BURCo's Feasibility Study, published by the public relations company David Block Associates (but largely written by Perkins and Symes-Schutzmann), was published on 27th August, significantly later than forecast. The next day, the *Scottish Daily Express*, under the headline 'We'll lower fares, say Border men', reported that the capital necessary to get the project under way would be £1.5m (of which £750,000 would be for purchase of the line), with the company putting up £600,000 and the rest found by the formation of a public company and the issuing of shares. The key role of tourism was emphasised, with BURCo having 'provided for the purchase and development of at least two hotels, and will expand – either by buying or establishing participation in a chain of hotels and restaurants throughout the Borders.' This was a big story, and on the 29th, with the headline ' "Full steam ahead" for Border rail plan' the *Hawick News* reported:

> The Waverley Route will be in operation once more within six months and will make a profit of up to £150,000 in its first year. This is the confident forecast by the Border Union Railway Company who are about to buy the line from British Railways.

A core daily service with diesel units over a single track (echoing John Hibbs's proposals) would operate every 90 minutes between Hawick and Edinburgh, and five times daily south of Hawick. A second track was to be maintained between Hawick and Newcastleton, for steam-hauled tourist trains from Galashiels to Newcastleton, appealing to car-based tourists in Edinburgh and the Lake District. This second track was also seen as offering potential for international filming contracts – since this stretch of line had superlative scenery but, as *Railway World* magazine put it in December 1990, 'without too many features to label it with any national character'. The article also referred to the planned introduction of innovative non-British operating practices, based on knowledge of Austrian and Swiss systems:

> [Symes-Schutzmann] approached Maj Rose of the Railway Inspectorate with a proposal to use radio signalling, and got approval in principle. Another planned feature was a simple 25kV overhead electrification, tramway-style, from Carlisle to Riccarton. This would link up with the

Prima facie evidence of single-line working! The notice sunk in the former Up line of the Waverley Route near Lady Victoria Colliery controlled the local operation of this first ever Scottish Railway Preservation Society tour on 23rd May 1970 – and, as the wording indicates, had also controlled the operation of the short-lived Millerhill-Hawick trip freight south of Lady Victoria between 6th January and 25th April 1969.

Allan McLean

electrified WCML (then still incomplete) to allow BR electric locomotives to work through to Riccarton at 25mph, to collect timber trains.

While radio signalling and electrification would certainly have been innovative, it is questionable whether the cost of the latter in particular could have been justified for no more than one or two freight trains daily. But new ideas were a key characteristic of whole BURCo vision – from (for example) flexible working practices, through turnstile access to stations (although it is not clear how this would have been compatible with on-train ticket machines!), a franchised on-train catering service, and airline seats, to 'the modelling of locally manufactured garments at Hawick and Galashiels stations during peak traffic periods'. How traditional railwaymen and railway enthusiasts would have reacted to the latter is anybody's guess!

BURCo had an ambitious shopping list for rolling stock to operate its all-year and tourist services, the Feasibility Study referring to 'two diesel locomotives, seven diesel railcars and six steam locomotives, in addition to 22 passenger coaches, four bogie parcel vans and sundry goods and service vehicles.' New stations were planned at Galashiels North, Galashiels Langlee, Tweedbank (the terminus of the new Borders Railway in 2015), Hawick Burnfoot and Hawick Lynnwood.

In hindsight, however, with predictions of 8%–10% returns on investment, 'rising to possibly 23 per cent later', the financial prognosis can be viewed as hopelessly over-optimistic. BURCo had a vision which effectively aimed to use the railway as a catalyst to restructure the tourist sector of the Borders economy. The Feasibility Study – while still fascinating to peruse 45 years on – reads in hindsight more like a scoping or pre-feasibility study, with not enough of the market quantification and financial analysis that a genuine business plan would have delivered to convince potential investors. It was long on optimistic commentary on the dramatic difference BURCo would make to the fortunes of the railway, but rather short on robust justification for concluding that such a transformation would be commercially viable.

Roy Perkins had argued that selected elements of the financial build-up detail in the NBRC Draft Report would strengthen the Feasibility Study, but Symes-Schutzmann was worried that some of the figures 'would alienate BR' – this was ironic, given that the core cost data had been based on BR's own figures – so the basis for many of the bottom-line financial conclusions in the study remained unclear to the reader. This was clearly a strategic error, and BURCo would soon be alienating BR in a much more profound, indeed terminal, way.

While the primary press and public interest was in passenger traffic, BURCo had also set out big plans for freight in the Feasibility Study. A key market would be tapping into the massive Forestry Commission plantations of Kielder, Kershope and Newcastleton which had been strategically planted during the inter-war and post-war years, and forests west and south of Galashiels. Harvesting had just begun in the southern forests, and the transport requirement was forecast to grow at a rate of 6–7% pa over the next 5–10 years, causing potentially major problems on inadequate local roads. On 23rd June 1969, the Forestry Commission Conservator for North-east England advised BURCo that in Kielder Forest alone production would rise from 45,000 tons in 1970 to 75,000 tons in 1974 – with the production expected to be destined for the key rail target mills in Ellesmere Port and Workington rising from an estimated total of 33,000 tons in 1970 to 42,000 tons in 1974.

In joint talks it was concluded that two big timber trains a week (rising to one train a day by the mid-1970s) could be justified from a reinstated Kielder spur of the old Border Counties Railway from Riccarton to Hexham. In co-operation with Powell-Duffryn an innovative containerisation system for timber was demonstrated at Longtown freight depot on 3rd November 1969, allegedly offering substantial cost-savings over conventional road-to-rail handling methods.

The beginning of the end for BURCo

Following the late August launch of the Feasibility Study, routine correspondence continued between BR and BURCo for several months. There was still enough evidence to suggest that BRB were genuinely willing to negotiate, but behind the scenes Gordon Stewart, BR Scottish Region General Manager, was far from happy. In his letter of 3rd October to Roy Hammond, the BRB's Chief Secretary, Stewart's view was crystal clear:

> I am getting really concerned at the work, which I am quite sure will be abortive, which is having to be done because of the Border Union Railway. We are now, apparently in the process of drawing up a Light Railway Order etc. and meantime no effort has been made by anyone to find out just how the promoters intend to finance their scheme . . . Mr Symms[sic]-Schutzmann and his partners are having a merry game playing at railways and we are paying the piper! . . . I am sorry to be persistent about this but I really think these people are just playing a game with us and it is time somebody asked them very decidedly about money.

The bombshell for BURCo then came in the transcript of a letter from HM Herbert, the BRB Deputy Secretary, as read out over the phone to Symes-Schutzmann on the morning of 6th October. The 'terms on which the Board are prepared to proceed' included the following:

- to sell the freehold of the line between Lady Victoria and Longtown, together with the permanent way and fixed equipment, for 'between £745,000 and £960,000'
- running powers into Edinburgh and Carlisle at an estimated charge of £125,000 annually, plus an estimated £85,000 of capital works at Carlisle, Longtown and Edinburgh to permit the exercise of running powers
- payment, 'before negotiations proceed', of £10,000 towards the Board's administrative costs; 'such sum to be retained by the Board if the Company are unable to complete the transaction'
- a deposit of £250,000 to be paid into the bank on 1st December
- as from 1st December, the Company to pay interest at the rate of 10% pa on a minimum of £495,000, 'being the balance of the value of the permanent way materials which the Board would otherwise have recovered and disposed of '.

The letter concluded by advising that 'the Board would like to have evidence of your ability to meet the full capital demand as soon as possible' and 'acceptance of the basic terms by not later than the 1st December.' The read text of this letter, together with a virtually identical type-written version sent to BURCo on 4th November, was a massive setback. Not only were significant additional capital costs (up to £250,000 more) and revenue costs (up to £50,000 pa more) being quoted, but also the Directors faced a critical early deadline and associated demands for delivery of funds, some of which would not be returnable if the scheme did not proceed.

The harsh reality for BURCo was that there was still no robust analysis to demonstrate the commercial viability of the project, no private sector funding had been committed, and BR management was becoming increasingly exasperated at the lack of supporting evidence to justify continuing negotiations. The blows were now raining down hard on BURCo, and BR's serious doubts about the company's ability to raise the necessary finance were vindicated (without BR knowing it) by a response on 15th October 1969 from the Edinburgh merchant bankers, Noble Grossart Ltd, to Symes-Schutzmann's submission of the Feasibility Study for their consideration. Only the first page of their letter survives in the Perkins' archive, but its message is clear:

We have concluded that it would not be an attractive investment from our point of view for three reasons. Firstly, we think that you have underestimated the capital requirements and the operating expenses under several heads. Secondly, we do not share your belief that the anticipated traffic on the line will increase to any significant extent . . . Thirdly, we do not think that the venture has any real prospects of growth in the next few years. In our opinion this is not a venture which is starting at a modest level and growing but a static or declining situation which at best can be revived by enthusiasm and made to operate at a low rate of profitability.

Once again, Roy Perkins had had no involvement in an important initiative, and a potential funder had nothing more to go on than a largely qualitative report, with no explanation of how the bottom-line cost and revenue figures had been derived. The financial market did not believe the BURCo prognosis on costs, revenue and growth – the business plan, such as it was, did not convince.

The BURCo 'associates' take over – and BR pulls out of negotiations

The Directors of BURCo and their 'associates' met *for the first time* at Crewe on Saturday 18th October 1969. It seems extraordinary that it took so long for such a meeting to take place, presumably prompted by BRB's drastic telephone ultimatum of 6th October to Symes-Schutzmann. For some months there had been a wealth of business and financial experience potentially available to assist and support the Directors, and one cannot doubt that some or all of the associates would have been keen to work with Roy Perkins to strengthen the financial detail and identify exactly what fundable business case, if any, lay at the heart of the large body of research data which had been accumulated. Reflecting on this incredible omission in 2011, Perkins' view was simple: 'We [Perkins and Symms] were kept at arms length from the associates.' Even with the benefit of 45 years of hindsight, the motivation for maintaining that distance remains a mystery.

It was belatedly agreed at the 18th October meeting – as recommended by the associates – that the Directors would commission an independent and searching financial appraisal to substantiate, or otherwise, the original Feasibility Study commissioned by Symes-Schutzmann. It had quickly been concluded by this gathering of expert business and financial advisers – doubtless informed by the Noble Grossart letter of rejection of 15th October – that such an appraisal, taking six months, was an essential prerequisite to the raising of the necessary financial backing for the project.

In parallel, following formal receipt of the 4th November letter of ultimatum, a BRB/BURCo associates meeting was convened in London on 17th November. This was attended by Willie Thorpe (BRB Deputy Chairman, who, as we saw in Chapter 2, extolled the benefits of closing the Waverley Route when he was General Manager of Scottish Region in 1966), and by three associates including Lord Melgund. None of the BURCo Directors was in attendance, and it is evident from archive correspondence that by this stage Perkins and Symes-Schutzmann had been effectively sidelined (Symms having withdrawn during the summer). A BR memo records that 'Mr Thorpe was informed quite categorically that there were no cash resources available at all to meet any of British Rail's claims outlined in [the BR] letter of 4th November.'

Meanwhile back in Scotland the *Scotsman* reported on 26th November 1969 that 'British Rail are to begin lifting 34 miles of single-line track on the Edinburgh-Carlisle line later this week', and quoted a BR spokesman as commenting, 'I must point out that these tracks are surplus to the requirement of both the British Railways Board and the Border Union Railway Company, who are planning to reopen the line.' That same week the *Hawick News* reported that 'during negotiations for the sale of the line both parties have agreed that the figure be kept confidential but the prospective buyers are said to be "well pleased" with the asking price.' This was a rosy picture, in stark contrast to what was happening behind the scenes.

Back at the BRB, a strongly worded and uncompromising draft letter was toned down in the final version sent by the Chief Secretary, Roy Hammond, on 5th December, which noted that BRB had been holding material valued at around £0.75 million since May and now had to insist on charging interest. Nevertheless Hammond did make one further gesture of co-operation:

> I am prepared, however, to offer one final solution: it is our view that qualified consultants should be able, within a short period, to undertake a quick appraisal and establish whether or not the venture is worthwhile and that you can comply with our requirements. If that can be done, I would be prepared to recommend to my Board that the interest should not be chargeable until 1st January 1970 instead of 1st December 1969.

The BURCo associates' reply stated not unreasonably that in the short period available before imposition of interest charges (just over three weeks) BURCo and associates could not produce the evidence needed to assure their financial advisers. Hammond's 23rd December reply on behalf of the BRB was short and to the point:

> It appears to us that no real progress has been made since the meeting with Lord Melgund on 17th November towards obtaining the independent and searching appraisal which was then discussed. In these circumstances the Board must now withdraw the offer to negotiate contained in the letter of 4th November addressed to Mr Symes-Schutzmann and will regard themselves as free to dispose of the materials and equipment of the Edinburgh-Carlisle line.

Hauled by a Class 08 shunter, a track recovery train retreats slowly northwards from the remains of Steele Road station in 1970 – a far cry from the express freight and passenger trains battling through here in steam days, up the 1 in 75 gradient around Arnton Fell towards Riccarton and Whitrope Summit.

Bruce McCartney

The end of the dream had now been clearly signalled, but the BURCo associates were not ready to call a halt. A preliminary meeting (about the idea of building a multi-fuel pipeline along the route of the single lifted track) had been held with Burmah Oil 'who have expressed considerable interest'. It was hoped that at a further meeting (on 8th January) Burmah would agree to pay for a new feasibility study and possibly also the BRB interest charges. BR's formal announcement of withdrawal from negotiation was made to the press – ironically, exactly a year after the railway had closed – on 6th January 1970. Six days later Hugh McMichael (an Edinburgh accountant, and one of the leading associates) wrote a letter to the other associates, marked 'private and confidential', summarising discussions at the two crucial meetings in London on 8th January and subsequent developments. At the second of the two meetings (involving the BURCo associates only) the protagonists had finally accepted the fate of the core project:

> It was agreed by all those present at our meeting that the only course presently open to us was to ascertain from British Rail if we could purchase the land and buildings in order to preserve the 78 miles of route [from Newtongrange to Longtown] for the eventual re-opening of a transport system for the Borders.

Burmah Oil had been asked to put up the £20,000 to enable a professional feasibility study to be carried out, but this was really nine months too late, and the archives contain no further references to Burmah Oil and the associated BURCo proposal – although correspondence shows that Lord Melgund did approach the BRB in January and February of 1970 about sale of the land and buildings (excluding track) for £75,000.

141

When the June 1970 election brought in a Conservative government, BURCo supporters might reasonably have expected a more favourable ideological audience for the concept of a privately-owned and fully commercial trunk railway. Replying to David Steel in an adjournment debate in the Commons on 20th July, George Younger, the new Under Secretary of State for Scotland (who had publicly argued against closure while in opposition) may have raised false hopes that a Conservative Government would take a fresh and constructive look at BURCo's private enterprise initiative: 'I can say that we have so far received no proposals from the Border Union Railway Company. We are only too ready to receive and consider any proposal which it may have in mind.' Alarmed by Younger's positive noises, the civil service then moved into overdrive – and a 24th July internal memo by a JM Howieson to his superior JH McGuinness, was scathing about the idea of Younger meeting the BURCo Directors – rightly so, by this stage:

> They have obviously no prospect of raising the purchase price; and in the light of that it is difficult to accept that they could purchase rolling stock and operate a viable service. They are, in fact, raising a good deal of false hopes in the Borders which have no chance of materialising and the sooner they can be stopped the better.

The BURCo story then faltered towards what had by then become an inevitable conclusion. On 6th November 1970, Ian Holoran, the Secretary of the Waverley Association wrote to advise the Association of Model Railway Societies in Scotland that 'unfortunately the Waverley Association is no longer in being, since the aims of the Border Union Railway Company are no longer attainable.'

Why did BURCo (and its associates) fail?

There are far fewer informed witnesses to the BURCo saga of 1969–70 than to the story of the BR closure itself. The conventional wisdom amongst railway supporters, enthusiasts and industry people has tended to be that BURCo's failure was due to a combination of unrealistic ambition and a vindictive BR attitude north of the Border. But, based on the new evidence unearthed in the research for this book, is that a fair judgement?

There can be no dispute that the scale of BURCo's ambition was breathtaking. There was no precedent for the take-over of more than 90 miles of double-track railway as a commercial concern – as opposed to the revival of short branch lines as volunteer-led 'preserved' railways. The scale of the project was monumental in relation to the immediate resources available, and the recurring letters in 1969 (from BR and others) expressing concern about delays in replying, do underline at a prosaic level the size of the task taken on by just three Directors, two of whom were only working part-time on behalf of BURCo.

BURCo's business planning strategy was clearly inadequate to the task of demonstrating a convincing business case for the financial viability (without grant subsidy) of a Borders rail re-opening scheme. The Feasibility Study delivered in August 1969 was not a sufficiently robust document to convince BR or potential investors, and by the time the BURCo Directors and associates had acknowledged this – in October – BR had run out of patience over the time and money spent on dealing with the company. Had a more quantitative study been commissioned in the spring of 1969, then a core commercial basis (supported by volunteer labour) for re-opening at least part of the Waverley Route might have been identified in sufficient time to keep BR on board while investors were still being courted. The full BURCo proposal now looks like a classic case of, 'here's something we'd love to do – now how can we justify it?' rather than, 'here is a set of problems – so what are the potential solutions?'

Interviews with protagonists point to the internal dynamic of BURCo and BURCo's external presentation being factors in alienating some potential support, but it can be hard to disentangle this from the inevitable bitterness felt afterwards by a variety of individuals who had invested much faith and hope in the project. Nevertheless, references to BURCo quickly becoming the 'Bob Symes-Schutzmann show' pinpoint an added difficulty. Perkins and Symms were both in their early twenties (but with business backgrounds), whereas Symes-Schutzmann was in his forties but had no business experience – for all the latter's energy, innovative ideas and consummate skills amongst 'the old boys' network', his domination of the Board of Directors and his style of management appear to have been a weakness at the heart of the project. In his undoubted presentational drive, he had evidently neglected – until it was too late – to listen carefully to others, including Perkins, who had more experience and expertise in business and marketing.

In discussion with the author in 2011, Symes-Schutzmann conceded that 'I may have been dictatorial, but I was flying solo' – he was evidently happy to leave the financial analysis to Perkins, so that he could concentrate on the networking to secure finance. However, the failure to fully involve the associates of BURCo – with their wide range of business and financial skills – until it was too late, must rank as one the worst shortcomings of the project, although Symes-Schutzmann pointed out that this was a difficult period for the British economy, and some of the associates' own businesses were struggling.

Archive research has unearthed a mixed picture on the BR attitude to the sale. The British Railways Board in London, and London Midland Region, appear to have been largely co-operative (and the latter even enthusiastic) throughout most of 1969, but Scottish Region was much less positive throughout the whole BURCo saga, and may well have been determined to avoid being 'shown up' by a private company. The BRB archives at Kew suggest that the Board was in fact remarkably patient with BURCo and its associates, given the very long period of time over which the prospective purchasers failed to deliver a convincing business case or evidence of financial backing. The recently unearthed archive evidence – contrary to the received wisdom over the last four decades – does not therefore suggest that the finger can be pointed at BR as a key factor in the demise of BURCo.

One of the most intriguing aspects of the BURCo story is the Government attitude to the sale. Archive research suggests that neither Labour in its 1969-70 administration nor the 1970–74 Conservative government were enthusiastic about the project. The Labour attitude might be understandable, given that in those days the party was still overtly in favour of public rather than private enterprise, but the lack of Conservative interest is a continuing puzzle. Even Bob Symes-Schutzmann, when quizzed by the author at the 2009 AGM of the Campaign for Borders Rail, was unable to come up with an explanation as to why a Government so committed to private enterprise lacked evident enthusiasm for the BURCo project. The *realpolitik* may simply have been that by the time the Conservative Government was in place, BURCo and its associates had lost all credibility with both the public and private sectors.

Tracklifters return, and BR has second thoughts?

As noted earlier, after a hiatus of six months BR track lifting activity resumed in November 1969 – and with prospects for the railway's return fast diminishing, it was not long before alternative uses for the rail solum were being mooted. The National Records of Scotland contain a substantial body of Scottish Office / Ministry of Transport correspondence from 1970 around the politically sensitive issue of disposing of parts of the Hawick-Edinburgh formation (to facilitate new road construction) well ahead of the end of the two-year moratorium on 6th January 1971.

By 25th February 1970, reference was being made within the Scottish Office to '5 sections of the above line where considerable savings of Government money [on road building] could be effected if the formation were to be given up by BR'. These were in Galashiels, Tweedbank, east of Melrose, north of Newtown St Boswells and in Hawick. During the next month this issue was propelled to almost the highest level possible. On 25th March, Albert Murray, Parliamentary Secretary at the MoT, wrote to Dickson Mabon, the Minister of State for Scotland, to the effect that:

> I think it is now quite clear that there is no question of the restoration of a service on the line in the near future by a private company . . . In this connection I should

mention that the clerk of Roxburgh County Council has written to the Department asking whether it is still necessary to build a bridge to span the railway for the new section of the A6091 at Tweedbank. Use of the formation would considerably reduce costs in this respect.

By 8th May, Dickson Mabon – having specifically excised an earlier draft's specific reference to the sensitive moratorium – was strongly emphasising the cost advantages in a letter to Albert Murray which stated that 'quite substantial savings in road expenditure could be achieved by using parts of the formation for road works.' An undated Scottish Office advisory note to Roxburgh County Council referred to the Scottish Economic Planning Board's meeting of 28th May, when they decided to recommend that the restriction on disposal of track formation be lifted.

Track lifting now moved into top gear. On 1st April 1970, BR ran a special train with an Inspection Saloon south of Hawick – according to Robert Robotham in *The Waverley Route – the Postwar Years*, 'to allow contractors to bid for demolition work', and Bruce McCartney recollects an amusing incident that day:

> Having been tipped off about this special working, I turned up at Stobs to take a photo, and approaching the station from the footbridge I had this exchange with a man walking his dog further up the line towards Shankend, on the track itself. I shouted 'There's a train coming!', to which he replied 'Huntie gouk' [English translation: 'April Fool']. Seconds later, there was the sound from both the Type 2 diesel and the rusty track being scrunched. I took my photo facing the Hawick direction, then turned round to look up towards Shankend, and watched the gent scrambling up the track verge. As he later approached me after the train had passed, he mumbled, 'Ye bugger, ye were right!'

There is some dispute over whether around this time BR had second thoughts about having closed the line. The July 1970 issue of *Modern Railways* carried a short news item which reported:

> Following approval for the Weaver Junction-Glasgow electrification, there are indications that BR may have reopening of the Waverley Route from Carlisle to Edinburgh in mind. The immediate use would be as a diversionary route during electrification, but it is understood that BR representatives have also been actively canvassing the potential for new revenue-earning traffic should the line be restored.

The report also stated that 'it is alleged' that BR was exploiting the ground work and surveys undertaken by BURCo, in particular in relation to some 300,000 tons of timber a year. It is unclear who the source of these reports was,

National Coal Board No. 17, an 0-4-0 saddle tank, is seen hard at work at Butlerfield Washery
in Newtongrange on 1st March 1972, just three months before all rail operations ceased here.
In this view looking south, the then still operational Lady Victoria Colliery – where BR freight trains
had last called in December 1971 – is off-camera to the left. The site of the new Newtongrange
passenger station opening in 2015 is in the left foreground.
Norman Turnbull

but *Modern Railways* cited as evidence for the 'belief that re-opening is now contemplated' track lifting being confined to singling and a recent run over the rationalised route by a 'Hallade Track Recording car'. As the Hallade track recorder was in fact a piece of portable equipment, it could have been conveyed on the 1st April Inspection Saloon observed (and photographed) by Bruce McCartney, but research could neither prove nor disprove this theory. No other train workings of this type were ever observed by the continuing band of Hawick railway enthusiasts.

A year later, on 2nd June 1971, the *Hawick News* reported that proposals by Lord Melgund to have the route of the railway protected for future service to the Borders had been rejected by the County Council. Lord Melgund and his associates had found financiers who would be willing to consider the purchase of the Waverley Route – but before any authority could be obtained to commence a survey of the route, 'those involved would require a firm assurance that the Waverley Route would remain intact at least for the period of two years or so which would be required to carry out the survey.' Melgund and his associates

Both the Up and Down lines are still extant near Fountainhall in this 12th September 1971 shot of a track recovery train returning north to Millerhill Yard, headed by a Class 08 shunting loco.
Norman Turnbull

had been rebuffed by the Scottish Office, and unfortunately, Roxburgh County Council had the same poverty of vision, and 'the sub-committee agreed that the County Council should not make any representations to the Scottish Office or to British Rail about the disposal of the Waverley line.'

Despite the inexorable retreat northwards and southwards of the remaining track, occasional correspondents to the *Scotsman* still made the case for the revival of the railway. Provost Pate of Galashiels, having long adjusted to an alternative transport future for the Borders, was brusquely dismissive in a letter of 27th July 1971:

> To endeavour to resurrect [Border railways] in the face of the very competition which killed them would be folly of the first degree . . . The 90-mile strip of railway track from Edinburgh to Carlisle constitutes a barrier to progress, tolerable so long as it served a useful purpose but now a hindrance to development on every hand. The railway is dead and far beyond revival. The sooner this fact is accepted and acted upon by all concerned the sooner will its track be available for the promotion of industry, tourism and agriculture. The sooner, too, will we have a straightening of roads, a realignment of bridges and a freer flow of traffic. To cry over the past is no way in which to face the future.

Pate was to be proved right about the fate of the railway (at least until the 21st century), and the programme of track removal steadily eliminated the iron road from the Central Borders.

Meanwhile, moves to make alternative use of the solum gathered pace. On 1st March 1972 the *Scotsman* reported that, 'negotiations have started with the estates department of British Rail and local authorities in the Borders for the sale

Formerly staple motive power on Waverley Route freight trains, by the time of this shot on 27th February 1970, the 'Clayton' Type 1s were by now only visiting the Borders on track recovery trains. Here at Portobello East Junction, where the Waverley Route joined the East Coast Main Line, No. D8614 is hauling a train load of the distinctive Leith General Warehousing vans which conveyed grain between Leith Docks and the North British Distillery in Gorgie for some 70 years from 1903.
Bill Jamieson

of the former Edinburgh-to-Carlisle railway line.' Both Galashiels and Hawick town councils had said they wanted to acquire all railway land in their respective burghs – for factories, roads and, in the case of Hawick, a sports complex – and 'expect to be in possession of the land they want within 12 months.'

In September of the same year, the Countryside Commission for Scotland published *Disused Railway Lines in Scotland: a Strategic Appraisal*, which noted in the case of the Waverley Route that, 'despite great efforts by the Scottish Development Department to find alternative uses for the line, it has aroused only piecemeal interest.' It was suggested that, 'on the assumption that a decision were ultimately made to extend the Pennine Way northwards towards the Central Belt of Scotland . . . [the Waverley Route] should be examined for sections which could usefully contribute to a long distance path.'

By late 1972, after 121 years of full passenger and freight operation, four months of vestigial freight, and nearly four years of start-and-stop track-lifting, the last remnants of railway had vanished from the abandoned Waverley Route south of Millerhill Junction. As civil servant Frank Spaven had warned at the Scottish Office back in August 1965, closure had rendered the Borders region:

by far the largest population grouping in Britain with no accessible railway services . . . the population in this area who will be more than 25 miles by road from the nearest railway station will amount to 70,000 persons.

CHAPTER 7

Almost forgotten for two decades
1972–92

ONCE the last track panel of the 87 route miles between Millerhill Junction and the Harker RAF depot at Carlisle had been lifted in 1972, the lost Waverley Route settled into a long period where the solum gradually returned to nature. A few stretches were used for burying utilities and there were intermittent breaches for road building, and – even more crassly – house building.

This was of course a classic example of where government should have had the vision to step in with a strategic perspective. But regrettably, following the 1971 end of the post-closure moratorium on disposal of the formation, 20 years would elapse before there emerged any local or central government policy to maintain the integrity of the route corridor for possible future re-use as a railway, or even just as a long-distance cycle route.

In the absence of any strategic vision, some of the major structures did not last long – to avoid ongoing maintenance and to create space for alternative land uses in the town centre, demolition of the mighty viaduct across the Teviot in Hawick began on 1st September 1975. But while the rail prognosis in Hawick was by then entirely negative, some surprising official discussions – little known

A desolate scene at Riccarton Junction on 12th October 1971, nearly three years after closure, yet almost everything (including the public telephone box on the platform) has survived – except the rail tracks.

Norman Turnbull

until now – were seriously focussing on the prospects for the return of the railway just 18 miles to the north. The Montgomery archive contains a copy letter of 16th May 1975 from Keith Smith, the assistant to BR's Traffic Survey Officer to RI Hill, Director of Roads Engineering at Borders Regional Council on the subject of: 'Proposed restoration of former Waverley Line between Edinburgh, Galashiels and Newtown St. Boswells'.

The infrastructure and service package proposed by BR was broadly similar to the 'Basic Railway' package considered and rejected for Edinburgh-Hawick by Marsh in 1968 – single-track with one crossing loop, carrying 'a service consisting of a basic 7 trains each way each week day, operated by two 3-car DMU sets.' Maximum line speed would be 60 mph, and a journey time of 50 minutes to Galashiels was projected – a few minutes slower than the fastest (non-stop) trains in 1968, but substantially quicker than the stopping trains, and of course the bus.

BR estimated a capital cost of £2.1m to reconstruct what would have been 27 route miles from Millerhill to Galashiels (subject to the results of a 'very rigorous examination' of the condition of bridges), plus a longer-term requirement to compensate the National Coal Board by £60,000 for 'retention of coal pillars in order to safeguard certain bridges and culverts' and £80,000 for installation of Automatic Half Barrier level crossings at Fountainhall and Heriot. Interestingly, the letter noted that, 'Any requirement to operate heavy freight traffic over the line could involve further strengthening of bridges and culverts' – was this perhaps a reference to prospects for timber traffic in the maturing forests west of Galashiels?

The revenue forecast – 'based on number of passengers travelling on equivalent trains in 1966 (latest information available) and present day fares' – seems pessimistic at just £66,000 pa, presumably making no allowance for the

The vast area of redundant railway land in central Galashiels – and its potential for industrial and retail development – can readily be appreciated from this 5th April 1975 view taken looking south from the station site under the Station Brae bridge. Ironically, at this very time BR and the new Borders Regional Council were seriously discussing the feasibility of reinstating a passenger rail service to Galashiels or St Boswells. *Bill Roberton*

impact of a better marketed, more regular and on average faster service, nor for the scope for park-and-ride and connecting bus feeders from the likes of Melrose and Hawick. The 'annual deficit on total costs' was projected as £142,000, although this cannot have represented the full 'Cooper Brothers' costs of a grant-aided service provided in perpetuity – and a subsequent (July 1975) news story by the Scotsman's Borders correspondent Bill Chisholm reported a direct operating loss of £95,000 (this was the BR figure excluding maintenance costs), but that 'when other factors are included, the regional council would be faced with a total loss of £204,000 per year'. This would not have been a cheap bill for just seven round-trip trains a day.

A noteworthy feature of this letter is the projected impact on revenues of a seven-mile extension to St Boswells – rising from £66,000 to £144,000, and reducing the annual deficit to £98,000 through bringing two important revenue generators directly back on to the rail network – the small but important tourist town of Melrose, and St Boswells, which showed the third highest station revenue on the Waverley Route in Map 3 of the Beeching Report ('£5,000 to £25,000 per annum'). Notwithstanding the additional capital cost (and the further cost of breaching the A6091 at Tweedbank), the St Boswells option must have looked potentially attractive, reconnecting as it would the majority of the Central Borders towns which had lost their train service – including the crucial corridor for development identified by the Central Borders Plan.

BR was at pains to emphasise that 'we shall be pleased to co-operate fully with your Council', and intriguingly ended the letter with the comment that: 'we look forward to the further joint meeting with the Scottish Bus Group, the Post Office and yourselves which you propose to hold in the near future.'

How far the dialogue developed is unknown, but the July 1975 report in the *Scotsman* indicated that Borders Regional Council considered five different options outlined by officers, from asking BR to reinstate the service through to permitting BR to dispose of all property and land; in the event it decided to approach BR to determine the asking price for the track bed in order to 'retain the route without prejudice to its future use'. What then happened is unclear, although the Council certainly did not purchase the solum of the whole route – much to the detriment of the future cost of re-opening the railway.

In an unpublished paper produced prior to the submission of The Waverley Railway (Scotland) Bill to the Scottish Parliament in 2003, Douglas Muir of Midlothian Council notes that in a letter dated 11th March 1976 British Rail offered to sell the line between Millerhill and the southern Midlothian boundary to Lothian Regional Council for an estimated purchase price of £7,000, but Muir then records:

Due to the high conversion cost to convert it to a road or to reopen as a railway (estimated at £3m plus any annual subsidy), the limited potential use (an estimate of £500 to £1000 per mile was provided for the cost to convert it to a cycle track) and the potentially high annual maintenance costs (estimated at £400 per mile annually), at a Lothian Regional Council Planning and Development Committee Meeting of 22nd October 1976, the Committee recommended that the line was not purchased. The solum was then offered to adjacent landowners and much of the solum was thus disposed of.

Seen with hindsight, this looks like a bargain to protect the line of route of the railway, irrespective of the costs of any early conversion of the solum to another transport function, but the Council was presumably not thinking in terms of a future rail re-opening, despite BR's relatively recent offer to resume train services. Once again, the 'vision thing' was absent.

Back on the roads in the decades following rail closure, to the benefit of bus users – but more so, car drivers – the Central Borders section of the A7 was improved virtually throughout from the south end of Galashiels to the edge of Hawick. North of Galashiels to Falahill – fortunately for the landscape of the Gala Water valley, and for the prospects of a future railway – only a few stretches of the A7 were realigned in this period, notably the Fountainhall straight and a breaching of the railway solum north of Heriot, where the A7 bridge over the line had been on a dog-leg.

The National Records of Scotland show that as late as 1977, despite a significant number of breaches of the solum, there was still some debate within the Scottish Office about whether protection of the route was required. The author recollects arriving in Melrose on foot with his father in the summer of 1983 – after walking the Southern Upland Way from Cockburnspath – and refusing to join him on a diversion to view the state of the surviving buildings of Melrose station. Frank Spaven returned to the hotel in the centre of the town,

The lack of a strategic central or local government vision for the former rail corridor led to some crass planning decisions, not least the mid-1980s consent for construction of this housing estate on the rail solum at Gorebridge, seen here looking south.
Ewan Crawford

chastened and depressed by the semi-derelict buildings and the abandoned railway solum.

Around this time, the floodgates opened – including, near the Gorebridge station site, the construction in 1984 of a small housing estate whose gardens were crassly allowed to breach the railway corridor (see photo on page 151). Gallingly, a number of key breaches in the Central Borders took place within 10 years of the events of 1998 which turned rail re-opening into a mainstream response to the Borders's economic difficulties. The Melrose bypass was completed in 1988, taking up most (but not all) of the width of the rail solum through the former station. The line had been breached previously just south of Ravenswood Junction (north of Newtown St Boswells) when the bridge carrying the A68 over the line was removed, and the Newtown St Boswells bypass made another breach in the solum in 1990. The link road from the east end of the Melrose bypass to the A68 at Ravenswood, completed in 1995, also utilised part of the old rail route. It was not in fact until 2002 that the Scottish Borders Structure Plan was approved by Scottish Ministers, incorporating – at long last – the full and formal protection of the railway solum which more visionary government would have put in place decades previously.

In 1990 the Scottish Office announced its preference to upgrade the A7 as the main road access to the Borders, and to subsequently de-trunk the A68, but the decision was reversed in the mid-1990s (the Government claiming that this was for environmental reasons). So, fortunately, the railway solum suffered no significant road breaches along its route up the valley of the Gala Water, almost as far as the boundary with Midlothian.

North of Falahill much of the A7 was realigned or improved on line, with significant solum breaches by Scottish Office works at Shank Bridge between Newtongrange and Gorebridge, at the Dalkeith western bypass between Lothianbridge viaduct and Sheriffhall, and Midlothian Council's later (2000) creation of an A7 bypass roundabout at Hardengreen. It may seem surprising therefore that the Lothian Structure Plan 1994 Written Statement had incorporated a visionary provision (in Transport Policy 18) which stated that, 'Local Plans shall safeguard the routes of the following former rail passenger lines for possible future transport use: . . . routes in Midlothian including those to Dalkeith, Lasswade, Penicuik, and Central Borders via Gorebridge.' In practice, the best of local authority intentions were at various times and locations subverted by Scottish Office pressure to keep down costs – not least of new roads – by permitting breaches of the alignment.

How much was the Borders missing the railway? For those without cars, relying on public transport slower than it had been in 1910, the answer was not in doubt. Academic endorsement came in 1980, with a unique report commissioned by BR to reach conclusions on the impact of ten rural rail closures. *The Social Consequences of Rail Closures*, produced by Mayer Hillman and Anne Whalley of the Policy Studies Institute found that the substitution of bus services had resulted in a marked diminution in the quality of public transport and in the activities and opportunities of the communities from which the services had been withdrawn. In the case of the Central Borders, as reported by AJ Mullay in *Rails across the Border*:

> The replacement bus services often followed a different route network, producing huge anomalies in the service pattern. The inhabitants of Newtown St Boswells now had four buses per week to Hawick in place of 44 trains . . . Travelling times were also vastly inferior – Newtown to Hawick in 55–68 minutes by bus instead of 13–19 by rail.

The report recommended that there should be no more closures, and from 1980 BR made no subsequent requests to government – with the notable exception of the Settle & Carlisle line in 1983 – to approve further significant closures. It was of course 10 years too late for the Borders. If personal hardship was not in doubt, how was the wider Borders economy faring without a railway? In a February 1991 letter, Frank Spaven (by then long retired from the Highlands & Islands Development Board) reflected that the Central Borders had never had Scheduled Development Area status, 'and perhaps for that reason <u>and</u> through losing its rail link and not getting a super-highway like the A9, its development and growth has been much later and slower than the Highlands'.

Elsewhere in Scotland there were distinct signs of a change in railway fortunes and political attitudes to the role of the railway in meeting wider social, economic and environmental objectives – between May 1984 and September 1994, exactly 50 permanent new stations were added to the ScotRail network. The most dramatic re-opening of that period came in 1986 between Edinburgh and Bathgate (10 route miles, which had been freight-only since 1956), This was the era of Chris Green, the charismatic General Manager of the newly-branded ScotRail, who blazed a trail of railway development across Scotland during his time north of the Border.

Demonstrating emphatically what rail re-opening could achieve, the Bathgate line's 1994 traffic growth target was achieved by 1987. The resurgence of this railway can be seen as part of (or at least a parallel to) a growing environmental awareness nationwide, and, more prosaically, local and central governmental understanding of the important role of rail in overcoming road traffic congestion problems – with Regional Councils in particular responding to a change of mood within BR.

Back in the Borders, it was roads and nothing else for private and public transport. By the late 1980s – post bus privatisation and deregulation – the service 95, now operated by Galashiels-based Lowland, was still recognisable but was down to a core hourly Hawick-Edinburgh service from 06.30 until 16.30, with a couple of evening buses. This was significantly worse than the 1969 bus timetable, except in respect of journey times, which were ten minutes faster due to road improvements.

While few people may have been thinking seriously about the return of the railway to the Borders over the previous decade, the immediate success of the Bathgate re-opening prompted Oliver Barratt, Secretary of the Cockburn Association (Edinburgh's civic amenity society) to submit a paper on 25th August 1986 to ScotRail, Lothian Regional Council (LRC), Midlothian District Council and City of Edinburgh, urging LRC to undertake a feasibility study of rail re-opening from Millerhill to Eskbank & Dalkeith and to abandon its proposal to sever the railway solum at Sheriffhall (south of Millerhill) in order to accommodate the planned A720 Edinburgh City Bypass. Unbeknown to Barratt, on 31st July the Director of Highways at LRC had written to ScotRail requesting costings for re-opening to Eskbank and Newtongrange. ScotRail's 19th August reply indicated that it would be a major exercise to give LRC more than estimates of costs 'to meet the timescales involved' but intriguingly ventured that, 'the position of the Council in this matter is recognised and it is suggested that the following approximations *may suit the purpose of the Public Inquiry*.' [author's italics]

Was this an implicit reference to ScotRail accommodating to an LRC wish for a rail re-opening proposal not to stand in the way of minimising bypass costs? The rail proposal came to nothing, and following the Public Inquiry the City Bypass did obliterate (in 1988) the solum of the Waverley Route at Sheriffhall – the worst example of government's short-sighted approach to route protection, adding several million pounds to the ultimate bill for re-opening.

Luckily (and it was through luck, rather than by design) a number of large important railway structures survived, particularly between Galashiels and Edinburgh – notably the Lothianbridge (Newbattle) and North Esk viaducts. Nevertheless, by the early 1990s, the future bill for rail reinstatement would be much, much higher than if the route had been properly protected.

John Yellowlees recalls that in the early 1990s (after his return from London to work in BR ScotRail public relations) BR extended to Borders Regional Council the courtesy of the annual meetings offered to all other Regional Councils, despite it having no railway stations in its territory. At these gatherings (until local government re-organisation in 1996), held in the salubrious surroundings of locations like the Black Barony Hotel at Eddleston:

There was a void at their heart, since all that they had to discuss was a few matters of mutual interest such as the operation of the Borders Rail Link bus services to Berwick and Carlisle, the condition of disused railway viaducts; and sometimes the Borders Regional Council roads and transportation spokesman, the late Lt Col Alistair Hewat, would express regret that the Waverley Line no longer served his region. Fortunately soon it was time for lunch, over which there would be discussion about the continued availability of such delightful journeys as those on the Kyle and West Highland Lines, and then the BR representatives could retreat by car to their comfort zone of the rail-served Central Belt.'

But while the return of trains to the Borders might have been far from the minds of Regional Council members and officials, others were not so oblivious to how the wider rail revival could benefit the only region of Britain without train services. The dawning of a Borders rail re-opening movement came in early 1991, when Tony Clayton of the Centre for Human Ecology at Edinburgh University approached the author, then a fellow activist and office-bearer of the Scottish Green Party, about the Waverley Route. The author was still working for BR, and Clayton, who knew of his enthusiasm for railways generally, had become increasingly aware of the absence of any passenger railway in both Midlothian and the Borders. He planned to produce a short initial report for the Lothian & Edinburgh Environmental Partnership (LEEP) on the scope for re-opening at least part of the Waverley Route, and could the author help? There was only one answer to that question for the author – who had 'spent much of [his] adult life angry about the loss of the railway' – and his first step was to suggest getting some historical background from Frank Spaven, who had worked so hard behind the scenes in the Scottish Office to make the regional development case for the Waverley Route. Spaven senior's letter of 1st February to Clayton enclosed a raft of relevant documents, and commented that:

> The region appears to have not only the 'inter-urban' potential for Hawick-Gala-Edinburgh traffic, but also the resources potential for 'tourists and timber', which my researches in Norway, Sweden and New Zealand [for a post-retirement MSc thesis at Aberdeen University] have shown to be a winning traffic combination for Highland-type lines.

In mid June the two Spavens commented extensively on Clayton's first draft, which focused on population and employment trends and economic develop-ment potential in the Borders, as well as the competitive market for rail and potential costings of a re-opened route from Edinburgh to Hawick serving the main population centres. Clayton's 'Phase 1' internal report to the LEEP Board was completed in early July 1991, with a view to LEEP deciding whether or not to pursue the idea. The report's main conclusions were that:

- the rail project had 'clear development potential' for commuting, tourism, express parcels, and 'heavy freight, especially timber, if the line is replaced to full standard'
- the viability of a Borders-Edinburgh rail link was likely to depend partly on subsidy and partly on the generation of additional tourism and leisure traffic
- of four development options (to Newtongrange, Gala, Hawick and Carlisle, 'options 1 and 3 clearly represent the 'best buys'
- estimated capital costs (including rolling stock, but excluding land purchase, rebuilding bridges, and provision of radio signalling and automated loops) were £21m to Galashiels and £29m to Hawick.

Following a subsequent hiatus of more than a year, Clayton wrote on 16th December 1992 (in reply to a 5th November letter from Frank Spaven) to the effect that LEEP, for whom he had written the 1991 report, 'decided that they could not take the project much further given the uncertainty and confusion surrounding the issue of rail privatisation . . . The decision taken was to hold the matter over until some of the uncertainties were clarified.' Clayton and Frank Spaven then met in Edinburgh on 23rd February 1993, but the LEEP initiative did not make any further progress. However, there had been a new stirring in the railway undergrowth, which was to have a profound impact on the prospects for re-opening the Waverley Route.

CHAPTER 8

Simon Longland and Borders Transport Futures' vision 1992–98

B Y the Spring of 1992, architect Simon Longland had been living in Melrose for ten years, and was becoming increasingly conscious of the illogicality of there being no railway in the Central Borders. Longland had been interested in railways and environmental issues for many years and – partly through his job with Scottish Borders Enterprise – was now acutely aware of the region's complete economic and social dependence on road transport, at a time when the environmental implications of the car and the lorry were becoming ever clearer. He also knew that there had been some significant breaches of the Waverley Route solum and that more were threatened by roads and housing development.

Longland decided he had to draw this to the attention of a wider audience, and that the best way to do so would be firstly to undertake a photographic survey of the trackbed and structures of the complete route (using his trusty BMW K100 motor bike), and then to incorporate the survey results in a report setting out the key arguments for protecting the route and eventually reinstating part or all of the railway.

Outside his Melrose home in 1985, Simon Longland poses beside the new motor bike later used for his catalytic 1992 survey of the solum of the entire Waverley Route. The first meeting of the Borders Rail Reinstatement Campaign took place here on 21st February 1994.
Annemarie Kuklinski

His photographic survey, undertaken between April and June 1992, is a large and impressive document. He found that the main owners of the solum were now local authorities, the Forestry Commission, and farmers – and identified 17 breaches of the alignment (mostly by roads) and a few instances of partial or complete obstruction by housing or industrial buildings. Of 123 bridges, 85 were still extant, and the line's three tunnels remained *in situ*. Looking to the future, Longland judged that, 'the principal threat is the dualling of the A7 north of Galashiels', and in a far-sighted commentary stated that:

. . . as the route is unprotected portions will always be at risk from rubbish tipping, housing or industrial developments, bridge demolitions or road alteration schemes . . . Some of these possibilities, if carried out in critical locations and without forethought, may have disproportionate cost implications for any reinstatement, which proper consideration would have avoided without significantly prejudicing the development proposed . . .

Every new disruption to the route, no matter how small, diminishes the useability of this existing resource and further compromises the possibility of reinstatement . . .

Rationally, it is clear that before this asset is irrevocably thrown away, a full comparative economic cost/benefit analysis of the rail investment option for the region which it represents should be carried out as a matter of urgency, to at least determine whether or not it has any worth. While this is under way, the remainder of the rail route should be given temporary protection from further degradation . . .

To approach the issue in any other way is to cast aside an irreplaceable asset without ever knowing whether or not it has any value.'

The key findings of Longland's survey were incorporated in an (unpublished) July 1992 report, *A preliminary case for the reinstatement of a Borders Rail Link*, which was privately circulated among friends and colleagues. This report concluded that, 'even though the immediate tactical case for re-opening may perhaps appear unpromising, there is a powerful long term strategic case to justify the re-establishment of a rail route across the region'.

Interest widens as the 25th anniversary approaches

Longland was uncertain what to do next, and sat on his report for some time, but in early February 1993 phoned the author – whom he had known briefly in the early 1970s, at Edinburgh University and as a fellow volunteer on the Strathspey steam railway – to sound out his potential interest. Just as in the case of Tony Clayton's report in 1991, there could be only one answer from the author, who replied by suggesting four 'sympathetic and suitable individuals who might work together as part of a small, unofficial but determined lobby group' – Tony Clayton, John Yellowlees (the Edinburgh-born, former London-based civil servant in environment and transport, who had become the Corporate Affairs Manager for the British Railways Board (Scotland) in mid-1992), Lawrence Marshall (BR train driver and the leading light of the Capital Rail Action Group), and Frank Spaven.

By late March John Yellowlees had offered the Edinburgh office of the BRB as a venue for a meeting of interested parties. The meeting was held on 15th April 1993, attended by Clayton, Longland, the author, and Yellowlees, plus Alan Bailey (quantity surveyor from Hawick), Peter Fuller (Public Transport Officer, Borders Regional Council), Roddy Mackay (Planning Department, Borders Regional Council), Sandy Mullay (railway author), and Bruce Skivington (Vice-Chairman of the Conservative Transport Group). Longland's subsequent letter to Spaven concluded that, 'all present [at the meeting] seemed to agree (to a greater or lesser extent) that . . . a project aimed at re-introducing a rail link into the Borders is one that is worth pursuing'.

A few months later, to mark the 25th anniversary of Marsh's closure consent, the *Southern Reporter* lead its 22nd July front page with the headline, 'How we were dumped off the beaten track'. Reporter Mark Entwistle found that 'time has done little to heal the wound caused by the loss of rail travel', with the Chairman of Borders Regional Council's Planning & Development Committee, Drew Tulley, commenting:

> There's no doubt that the loss of the Waverley Route has affected development in the Borders. Every day that goes past proves what a tragedy the loss of the Waverley Route was . . . You just need to look at the massive problems there are in the transport of timber by the forestry industry, which has seen money having to be spent on roads and strengthening bridges.

David Steel, still the area's MP, agreed about the impact of closure and commented, 'if the same arguments were run over today, the line would be kept open.' However, when asked whether the centre of the region would ever see trains again, 'both men were very doubtful.' Undeterred by this pessimism from key players, Simon Longland managed to track down the address of the Reverend Brydon Maben, now living in retirement near Duns, and passed the contact on to the author, who was hoping to interest a national newspaper in an article on the line's closure. Spaven travelled to Berwick in mid-August to meet Maben and his wife Betty, and all the conversation was recorded on tape. Subsequent efforts

The first stretch of the Borders Railway – the 'turn back' siding just south of Newcraighall station – seen on 3rd June 2011, shortly after track works had been completed. In the foreground is the open verandah of the Royal Scotsman luxury land cruise, a likely future visitor to the railway. More than a decade of determined campaigning by the Campaign for Borders Rail finally convinced the Scottish Government in late 2012 that the Tweedbank terminus should be re-designed to accommodate 12-coach charter trains – bringing valuable additional visitor spend to the region.

John Furnevel

The green light for the Borders Railway. At a ceremony on 6th November 2012 in the National Mining Museum (adjacent to the future Newtongrange station), Transport Minister Keith Brown (right) and Network Rail's Route Managing Director, David Simpson, sign the contracts for the construction – and completion by 2015 – of the new railway from Newcraighall to Tweedbank.

© *Network Rail*

As *Modern Railways* magazine reported under the headline 'DAFT OR WHAT?'
in its November 2014 edition:

'This picture from David Spaven illustrates what is probably the most short-sighted piece
of infrastructure design on the entire Borders Railway – Overbridge 41 at Cowbraehill between
Tynehead and Falahill, seen looking south on 15 July 2014. Under Transport Scotland's original
specification, published in 2009, this section of the route would have been double track.
Following the subsequent cutback from 16 miles to just 9½ miles of double track on the railway,
the track here and the overbridge span will now just be single – and, in the absence of
'passive provision', any future attempt to double will require complete demolition of the bridge
(carrying a farm access road) plus major disruption to train services.'

David Spaven

Whitrope was until 2015 the location of the only operational railway between Millerhill Yard in
Edinburgh and Harker in Carlisle: this short stretch of track belonging to the Waverley Route Heritage
Association beside Bridge 199, looking north towards the tunnel entrance, with an ex-War Department
Ruston 0-4-0 diesel borrowed from Rutland Railway Museum.

Bruce McCartney

What should have been the terminus of the new Borders Railway – the splendid A-listed station building at Melrose, seen here in 2003, with ample space for a single-track railway beside the surviving platform.

John Furnevel

First in a sequence of three photos showing the changing face of one section of the old railway solum between 2012 and 2014. Evidence of advance works on tree and vegetation clearance for the Borders Railway in May 2012, looking south near Kings Gate – between Shawfair and Eskbank – along the footpath on the trackbed of the Waverley Route.

Bill Roberton

The advance guard of the Borders Railway rail-laying train drops rails into place
near Kings Gate Points on Monday 13th October 2014.
David Spaven

A track tamping machine heads south near Kings Gate on 6th November 2014. The alignment of the
original Edinburgh & Dalkeith Railway trailed in from the right.
David Spaven

to interview Steel were rebuffed by a 'VERY full' diary, but he then sought to contact Richard (by then Lord) Marsh, partly as a result of Longland spotting a newspaper quotation from a 9th December 1992 Transport Committee hearing, in which Marsh had said:

> The Civil Service has always wanted to close lines to save money, as Beeching did in the closure programme of the 1960s. But some of the lines closed were essential feeder lines to other lines . . . Why are we doing this?

As Longland reflected in a note to the author, 'Why did *I* do this?' might have been a more appropriate question.' Spaven got no reply from Marsh, but had more luck with BBC Scotland, whose Environment Correspondent, Louise Batchelor, he had got to know in his political campaigning days. On the *Reporting Scotland* TV news programme on 6th January 1994, Batchelor fronted a long piece on the demise of the Waverley Route and hopes for its re-opening, featuring an interview with Longland and Maben on the surviving platform at Melrose, against a backdrop of timber lorries thundering along the bypass through pouring rain. Together with two short articles by Longland published in the *Southern Reporter*, the first tentative steps in a campaign for Borders rail reinstatement had begun.

The author had a long telephone conversation that evening with Yellowlees, who suggested that the forthcoming Regional and European elections could provide an ideal platform to coax opposing politicians to address the railway issue – and within a few weeks Longland was writing to interested parties with an invitation to attend an inaugural meeting, 'to form a group to campaign specifically for a rail link, but also more generally for the establishment of a more environmentally "sustainable" future transport strategy for the Borders.' Meantime, Longland was working with a colleague from Scottish Borders Enterprise, Gordon Cox, on an initial financial analysis of the case for re-opening from Edinburgh to Galashiels, to be presented at the meeting.

The Borders Rail Reinstatement Campaign

The inaugural meeting of the informally titled 'Borders Rail Reinstatement Campaign' took place at Longland's Melrose home on 21st February 1994. In attendance – as well as Cox, Longland and the author – were Donald Grant (from Penicuik), Arthur James (Lilliesleaf), Martin Rae (Dalkeith) and Alistair Reid (a Scottish Association for Public Transport activist from Edinburgh).

The meeting notes, produced a few days later by the author, recorded that Cox and Longland's financial analysis of re-opening between Galashiels and Edinburgh, 'based strictly on conventional economics, and excluding social and environmental factors' had concluded 'that rail re-opening would offer better value than dualling the A7.' The meeting agreed that with the threatened obliteration of the route by a new A7, 'this might be the last realistic chance to save the route line', and it was decided to set up a formal campaign – with the main target being the run-up to the Regional Council elections in May. In a cautionary note – which was to have implications for the way that efforts to re-open the railway developed – the meeting notes record that: 'The biggest priority in terms of group resources would have to be to secure the involvement of several Borders-based activists who would be willing and able to front up the campaign at public meetings and press conferences'. This was in part a reflection of Longland's personal reluctance – as a Scottish Enterprise employee – to provide a public face for any campaign.

Seven further meetings were held under this campaign name between March and August 1994. Meantime in May the well-known Borders-based novelist and critic Allan Massie penned a *Scotsman* column bemoaning the loss of the Waverley Route, and this provoked a flurry of letters in the paper's correspondence column on the scope for rail re-opening. In late July, Alan Bailey, who was now the Chair of the campaign, flagged up in a letter to the author that an important new dimension had emerged:

> Very exciting responses from potential commercial users (forestry/pulp mills) have been obtained regarding the southern Borders Rail Link ie Kielder/Carlisle. It would appear that the commercial case is much easier to make on this line and it is intended to set things in motion for this southern link as soon as matters for the northern link are underway.

This new development was instrumental in ensuring that by the time of the eighth and last meeting of the campaign under its original name. the group's plans had changed significantly. The local elections had consciously not been used as a campaign platform, and instead – partly encouraged by the lobby group Transport 2000 – it had been agreed to set up a limited company, focused on the two key objectives agreed at an early stage: firstly, to protect the remaining track bed and structures, and secondly to commission a cost-benefit study, with a view to the new company participating directly in the re-opening and running of the railway. Reflecting in 2011 on this change of direction, Simon Longland said:

> We felt that a commercial approach would be going with the grain of the emerging rail privatisation; at that time there was a hope that the railway would become more open to new market-based ideas, and less bureaucratic.

The make-up of individuals involved had also changed. The author, who had moved home from Glasgow to even more distant Renfrewshire, could no longer commit the time for regular public transport trips to the Borders, and two new players had joined up with Bailey, Cox, James and Longland – Roy Brown (a chartered accountant) and John Butler (a Liddesdale farmer). The stage was set for a new organisation which would come tantalisingly close to re-opening the southern end of the Waverley Route for freight, and which succeeded in putting the northern end of the railway firmly on the mainstream political agenda.

Borders Transport Futures

The first meeting of Borders Transport Futures (BTF) was chaired by Alan Bailey in his Hawick office on 3rd September 1994, with Brown, Butler, Cox, James and Longland in attendance. Its principal objective as defined by the Memorandum of Association was: 'To explore the re-opening of the railway line between Edinburgh and Carlisle by Hawick with a view to operation of a public railway service.' The Minutes record that the discussion focused on securing funding for the planned feasibility study, with both private and public sector input envisaged.

As Longland reflected in 2011: 'We had to establish some credibility first', and the pre-production version of BTF's own *Pre-feasibility Study for a North Borders Rail Link* was soon put in limited 'commercial in confidence' circulation prior to an anticipated October launch. In practice, a BTF meeting with a Glasgow stockbroker led to the group agreeing to take on board the following advice:

> Publicity should be avoided until the [full] Feasibility Study is complete. The best chance of impressing investors would come from a strong case which was new to the market, ie make one approach only to the market. The idea should not be touted around the financial services industry.

The pre-feasibility study incorporated a spreadsheet model (extending Cox and Longland's original work early that year) to test the potential viability of the project in a variety of scenarios. The key finding was that a Galashiels-Edinburgh rail link could be viable, based on a capital cost of around £28m, 'or about

The mission –
to build and operate modern,
efficient rail links feeding
Edinburgh and Carlisle
from the Borders of Scotland.

Borders Transport Futures' 1995 publicity brochure suggested that its plan to re-open the Waverley Route was 'firmly on target to commission the initial service on 1st January 2000'.

163

£9.1m more than would have been the case had protection of the alignment not been abandoned in the mid 1970s'.

BTF envisaged deposition of a Private Bill in Parliament in 1998, securing Royal Assent in 2001, with construction over 2002 and 2003 leading to a 2004 start of railway operations – with six Edinburgh to Galashiels return services per day and 10 Edinburgh/Gorebridge return services, giving an hourly service from Gorebridge and a two hourly service from Galashiels. This could go to a 20 minute peak service north of Gorebridge without major infrastructure costs.

The principal conclusions of the study were that the project proposal should be taken forward to the next stage of detailed feasibility and that there should be urgent lobbying of local authorities to prevent further erosion of the trackbed. Despite BTF's wish to keep a low profile, news soon leaked out, with the Scotsman of 7th October 1994 reporting developments.

However, just four days later, came some very good news for the prospects of rail re-opening – the Scottish Office announced that the A7 dualling was to be dropped (allegedly due to 'an unacceptable environmental impact on the landscape and on farms within the Gala Water Valley') in favour of more investment on the A68 between Dalkeith and Leaderfoot (east of Melrose). Allan McLean, then the Transport Correspondent of the *Scotsman* reported that the announcement, 'attracted angry criticism in the Borders, where campaigners complained that it meant further delay in road improvements promised 25 years ago when the Waverley Rail route closed.' It seemed that nobody, other than BTF and a handful of rail campaigners, had spotted (or cared) that this removal of a major additional threat to the integrity of the rail trackbed was a crucial boost to the prospects of reinstating the line to the Central Borders.

Buoyed by this news, BTF pressed on with its search for project development funding and potential public and private rail investors, while also working up a pre-feasibility study of the potential for timber transport over a reinstated rail route from Kielder to Riccarton – as envisaged by the Border Union Railway Company 25 years earlier – and onwards to the West Coast Main Line north of Carlisle. BTF's long-term goal was now the complete re-opening of the Waverley Route, with its first interim objective being Edinburgh-Galashiels reinstatement for passengers, its second the proposed freight re-opening south of Riccarton, and the final aim being to complete the missing central section connecting Riccarton, Hawick, St Boswells, Melrose and Galashiels.

On 5th January 1995, the day before the 26th anniversary of closure, *Local Transport Today* reported that BTF 'will be presenting its plans this month to Railtrack and ScotRail', with Alan Bailey quoted as estimating that the [Edinburgh-Galashiels] line would be viable if just 5% of the existing 15,000 daily car journeys between the Borders and Edinburgh could be switched to rail. Just a few days later the *Scotsman* revealed that BTF 'believes trains will be running on a single track between Galashiels and Edinburgh Waverley within six years', and was 'receiving the full backing of the region's two MPs' – Sir David Steel and his Liberal Democrat colleague, Archy Kirkwood – who were 'urging the planning authorities in Lothian and Borders regions to protect the trackbed from further development or disruption.'

BTF's *Pre-feasibility study for a South Borders Rail Link* was issued in February 1995, focusing on timber opportunities within the projected 230% growth of domestic timber production over the next 30 years, but also setting the scheme in the wider context of national transport policy and growing environmental concerns. The study noted that with a reinstatement cost of around £18m, 'a Southern Borders freight railway could be commercially viable', given the availability of Government grant schemes to encourage modal switch from road to rail – Freight Facilities Grant (for capital) and Track Access Grant (a revenue subsidy). Key markets would be the forest products mills at Rockcliffe (Carlisle), Workington and Shotton, to be served by a total of five (1,000 tonne payload) trains a week throughout the year. The study found that the viability of rail freight operation was critically dependent on the cost of in-forest road haulage to the railheads on the new line, and it recommended containerisation, which could 'reduce these costs to a level that will allow the overall intermodal haul to compete at freight rates broadly comparable to those that are presently levied by road hauliers.' Like the North Borders Rail Link study, the report recommended that the project be taken forward to the next stage of a detailed feasibility study.

By April 1995, BTF was pitching for a Borders railway to be part-funded by the new Millennium Commission – but it was to lose out to the £60m Millennium Link upgrade of the Union and Forth & Clyde Canals between Edinburgh and Glasgow. The same month that stalwart of the campaign against Waverley Route closure, the Reverend Brydon Maben, sadly died before it became clear that re-opening of the railway was a realistic prospect.

BTF were meantime spreading the message widely amongst opinion formers and decision makers across Scotland, and in early November the scope for a Borders railway was flagged up at a European seminar held by the Convention of Scottish Local Authorities (COSLA) in Edinburgh. Councillor John Ross Scott – who was to become a prominent advocate of the railway in later years – drew attention to the Central Borders being 'totally reliant on roads'. But an early warning of the scepticism of a future Labour transport spokesperson in the Scottish Parliament was reported in the *Berwickshire News*:

Councillor Charlie Gordon of Strathclyde, while supporting Councillor Scott's plea [for rural rail connections] said, while good local rail links were essential, it could be that in areas like the Borders more benefit would come from pumping more money into improving road links to the main stations.

The same month, BTF published the *Border Rail Links Study* by Oscar Faber, Roger Tym & Partners, Mott MacDonald and Ryden. This professional consultants' report – funded by Scottish Borders Enterprise, Midlothian Council, Lothian & Edinburgh Enterprise and City of Edinburgh Council – found that BTF's two in-house pre-feasibility studies were broadly correct in their assessment of the potential passenger and freight markets and of the costs of rebuilding and equipping the South Borders railway (the consultants' estimate for the latter was £20m, compared to BTF's £18m). Remarkably, the study concluded that BTF had significantly *over*-estimated the cost of the North Borders (Edinburgh-Galashiels) railway at £28m (updated to £32m to take account of an extension to Tweedbank), advocating instead a figure of just £18m. Subsequent events, however, would suggest that the 'amateurs' had come up with a more robust figure than the professionals!

On 1st December, the *Hawick News* reported that the £27,000 study had concluded that it would give a huge economic boost to the region (in terms of housing, tourism and business environment gains), and that:

> Potential sources of finance for both the north and south rail links have been identified and are now being investigated by BTF . . . it is understood the total package of proposals [including the central section between Riccarton and Tweed-bank] would cost a minimum of £100 million and that BTF want to see some sort of service operating by the year 2000.

Following discussions with the Scottish Office, the report concluded that the South Borders railway would meet the requirements of the Government's Freight Facilities and Track Access Grant schemes, and possibly also European Regional Development Fund aid in the unlikely event of budgetary constraints on FFG funding. The report recommended *inter alia* that a range of rail service and transport policy scenarios should be tested and the impact these have on the cost-benefit analysis established, and that the rail route alignment should be safeguarded in the forthcoming revision of the Borders Structure Plan. However, the Structure Plan revision incorporating rail route protection (as suggested by Borders Regional Council in 1994) was not approved by the Scottish Office until after three planning episodes which illustrated the extent to which re-opening the railway had still to secure widespread credibility.

In the mid-1990s, Borders Regional Council and then Scottish Borders Council (after single-tier local government was introduced) were in favour of a new supermarket site in central Galashiels, retail development being seen as a key route to economic regeneration. The Council then received an interest from a developer in a location straddling the old station site and very largely in the Council's ownership. While maintaining a cycling/walking route through the area had official backing, rail campaigners were alarmed by the threat to line reinstatement. Bill Jamieson of Stow (later to be a leading light in the Campaign for Borders Rail, Stow Station Supporters Group and the Waverley Route Trust) recollected in 2012:

> The development proposal which eventually materialised as the ASDA super-market first surfaced around 1995. At that time, no thought would have been given to accommodating the railway – it wasn't yet on the Council's agenda and planning guidance regarding the protection of former rail routes would only appear later that decade.
>
> Far from being railway driven, the proposed supermarket threatened to block its path – something which was only eventually resolved by taking a very expensive diversion to the north-east of the store. As I was aware of what BTF were doing, I contacted the Railway Development Society [now Railfuture] asking them to object to the planning application – as a council employee I could hardly do so myself!

This potentially critical breach in the potential route of the railway was avoided – albeit at significant cost – but just seven miles to the north, a crass planning decision by Scottish Borders Council allowed a substantial bungalow to be built in 1995 straddling the entire solum at the former Stow station site. 41 Station Road, and its owner's opposition to rail re-opening, became something of a *cause celebre* in subsequent years, typifying as it did the lack of long-term vision about a potential future role for the railway.

A later, evidently bizarre, planning decision by the Council was reported by the *Southern Reporter* on 13th June 1996 with reference to an application to build houses on part of the line at Ryehaugh just north of Galashiels which had come before the Council:

> Paul Gregory, Director of Planning, told the meeting of Scottish Borders Council planning committee this week, that the Government wanted local authorities to protect the routes of former railway lines . . . But Convenor Drew Tulley warned against any moves which might lead to the council purchasing land to safeguard the line of the former railway, when there was no guarantee that it would be used

by a rail link. In the end the committee approved the application and agreed that the condition protecting restriction [sic] the line of the old rail track at Ryehaugh be removed.

Fortunately the houses were never built, but this episode illustrates the hurdles which BTF faced – and in an attempt to reach consensus and co-ordinate policy towards a rail project, BTF subsequently facilitated the creation of a railway working group comprising representatives from the Council, Scottish Borders Enterprise (SBE) and other interested parties.

Despite some difficulties in the political arena, subsequent events on the fund-raising front demonstrated that BTF's concept really had gone mainstream within the rail industry. They approached the Commercial Director of Railtrack, Michael Howell (who had a home in Midlothian), and in the early spring of 1997 were offered £100,000 to assist with project development. Following a meeting in London, Ed Burkhardt, the dynamic new Managing Director of the recently privatised freight operation, English, Welsh & Scottish Railway (EWS), had also come up with £100,000 on a similar basis (contingent on BTF and Railtrack striking a deal). Glasgow-based First Engineering offered both railway engineering expertise and £50,000 towards the project development process.

Buoyed with their success in securing external finance and expertise, BTF pressed on with putting the planned Parliamentary Bill together – this had to be a Private Bill as the route straddled both Scotland and England, and therefore could not be progressed under the Transport & Works Act. First Engineering drew up detailed technical drawings of the route for the Parliamentary process. In Scottish Borders Enterprise's newsletter of Spring 1997, Alan Bailey of BTF projected a 1999 start to construction of the South Borders railway, 'with the first train in operation possibly a year later.' The Edinburgh-Galashiels link, which would require a separate Parliamentary Act, 'would follow on a year or so later.' Support for the latter, from the heart of the rail industry, came in an address to the Capital Rail Action Group's February 1997 conference by John Ellis, the departing General Manager of ScotRail. Echoing a concept first advocated a decade earlier by the Cockburn Association's Oliver Barratt at the A720 City Bypass public inquiry, Ellis called for a cross-Edinburgh service (later to be christened 'CrossRail') to the south east of the city – which led to the three single-tier Councils of City of Edinburgh, Midlothian and Scottish Borders vowing to promote the Waverley Route re-opening in stages, 'rather in the manner of a relay race' as John Yellowlees recollects.

It was during 1997 however that the first dark clouds appeared on the BTF horizon. Due to an excess of timber availability in the Baltic countries, the delivered price of domestic timber began to be forced down by market pressures and imports took an increasing share of the market for supply to paper and board mills. This was a worrying development, and around the same time Michael Howell left Railtrack and responsibility for dealing with BTF fell to new recruit Robin Gisby. BTF were called to meet Gisby at Edinburgh Airport on 17th April, and in the words of Simon Longland they encountered someone 'who didn't seem to know much about the project'.

Meantime, with the decline of timber prices, rail freight began retrenching in a market which generally did not offer sufficient volumes for full trainload operation. While the daily full trainload volumes envisaged for a re-opened South Borders rail link might have survived the subsequent EWS cull of wagonload services, the decision by the Shotton paper mill (the planned destination of 60% of the timber volume on the railway) in the early 2000s to switch to 100% recycled fibre instead of virgin timber would surely have grievously undermined the operating economics of BTF's timber railway.

Ironically – in a demonstration of personal commitment and faith in the project, and echoing the action of Roy Perkins of BURCo back in 1969 – Simon Longland left his job at Scottish Borders Enterprise (on 6th June 1997) to work on the BTF project full time, at a time when both general and specific difficulties with the rail project were beginning to be encountered.

On 18th June, the *Scotsman* reported problems with the South Borders rail link: 'The proposed £20 million rail link has sparked a dispute similar to the fierce row which preceded the construction of the original Waverley Route 140 years ago.' BTF – who had also had positive discussions with the Ministry of Defence and the rail industry about conveying light armoured tracked vehicles to Kielder, whence they would travel by forestry road to the nearby Otterburn training ranges – were being challenged by 25 landowners and householders who might be faced with compulsory purchase 'to say how the multi-million pound projects will be funded and to provide evidence of economic viability.' Alan Bailey had responded to the challenge by commenting:

> We have been trying to talk to the [opposition] group for 14 months, but they refuse to hold discussions. We are doing everything correctly and now we are into the period of consultation before the bill is deposited in Parliament. They cannot expect us to divulge commercially sensitive information to a group unconnected with this project.

Bailey concluded that, 'We are very confident the South Borders Rail Link will become a reality'. Based on the imminent planned deposition of the Bill, the Scottish Office Transport Minister, Calum MacDonald, announced at Westminster in November that an FFG application from BTF was anticipated once Royal

Assent had been obtained. However, Railtrack, who were critical to BTF's scheme in terms of main line connection, then, 'at the 11th hour and 59th minute' (in Longland's words) failed to provide the required endorsement that the Bill should be deposited in Parliament.

After Railtrack effectively withdrew from the project, BTF approached forestry interests to try to put the project back on track, but Longland now admits: 'As soon as we had to pull the deposition of the Parliamentary Bill [because of Railtrack's withdrawal of support], I knew in my own heart that it was a dead duck.' In hindsight, Longland also has doubts that their Bill would have got through the Parliamentary process:

> Developments in the timber market were certainly not helpful, and we were dependent on a very large – up to 75% – Freight Facilities Grant from the Government. Into the bargain, the landowning interests closed ranks in the face of what they seemed to see as 'an invasion' of their property, rather than an opportunity to add value, while also aiding the wider Borders economy and environment.

Having previously prioritised the freight-based South Borders Rail Link, as it had seemed to be less 'political' and had a semi-commercial justification, BTF now began to refocus its attentions on the northern end of the line, where passenger traffic was the key. To the delight of rail campaigners, external factors in the Borders economy very soon pushed the North Borders Rail Link from being a minority interest into a mainstream objective – but ironically, Borders Transport Futures was destined to play no long-term part in this transformation of the rail concept into political reality.

One of the most needless obstacles placed in the way of cost-effectively reinstating the Borders Railway – the large bungalow built on the railway solum at Stow station in 1995, seen here in April 2007 sporting a large notice 'beware of trains and cowboys'. The minor road bridge over the railway solum is on the far left.
John Furnevel

Initially however, pressure emerged to extend passenger trains south from the East Coast Main Line on to the first stretch of the remaining northern stub of the Waverley Route. Proposals originating with John Ellis at ScotRail and promoted by John Yellowlees at Railtrack were discussed at Midlothian Council Chambers on 16th February 1998, and a Rail Development Task Group was then set up, chaired by Midlothian Council. What would eventually be known as Edinburgh CrossRail (re-opening the line to passengers services as far as Newcraighall, just north of Millerhill Yard) was seen as the first stage of phased development, with the second stage extending into Midlothian and the third taking the line into the Scottish Borders.

CHAPTER 9

Rail re-opening becomes political reality 1998–2006

Grassroots action and economic downturn propel rail to the top of the agenda

In April 1998, German expatriate Petra Biberbach had moved home from Northumberland, with her husband and infant daughter, to work as a part-time environmental adviser with Scottish Borders Council (SBC). Biberbach was amazed to find that a region as populated as the Borders had no railway. With her track record as an environmental campaigner she was soon contacted by Gordon Cox of Borders Transport Futures, which around the same time had come to the view that their business initiatives could be aided by a parallel, but independent, lobby group. Biberbach then called a public meeting in Galashiels as a first step towards establishing a campaign group supportive of BTF's aim of getting the Borders back on the rail network.

Meantime the Borders economy was experiencing its own share of UK de-industrialisation and the impact of an increasingly globalised economy, with textile mill closures across the region. During the 1990s much hope had been invested – not just in the Borders, but throughout central Scotland – in the salvation evidently offered by 'Silicon Glen', the electronics-based drive for new jobs to replace the dying manufacturing economy north of the Border. In due course, this vision was to crumble as the essentially foot-loose nature of 'branch-plant' industries manifested itself in a succession of 'here today, gone tomorrow' inward investments. The Borders was no exception – and in December 1998 the American-owned Viasystems closed its Galashiels plant, followed by the closure of its Selkirk factory in June 1999, with the loss of 920 jobs.

Fortunately for the Labour-controlled Scottish Office, there was a ready-made economic regeneration project ready to be taken off the shelf, dusted down, and turned into a convincing route forward for the Borders economy – BTF's Edinburgh-Galashiels rail re-opening scheme, which would also put Midlothian

172

Right:
Still campaigning for a railway 31 years after the 1969 closure – Madge Elliot outside the Volunteer Hall in Galashiels prior to the 27th March 2000 meeting of the Scottish Parliament's Public Petitions Committee.

Far right:
Petra Biberbach, first Chair of the Campaign for Borders Rail

Photos: Alastair Watson, courtesy of the Southern Reporter.

back on the rail map. On an official visit to the Borders on 10th December 1998, the Business & Industry Minister, Lord Macdonald unveiled plans for a £400,000 feasibility study backed by Virgin Trains and Railtrack, and accompanied by a statement of support from a previous sceptic about rail re-opening, Councillor Drew Tulley, Convenor of Scottish Borders Council. The *Southern Reporter* reported his comment: 'Just think what [the railway] might mean to the young, fit and able who currently leave for jobs elsewhere in the UK and across the world.'

The involvement of Virgin Trains may have raised a few eyebrows, but its then Public Affairs Manager for Scotland, Allan McLean, provides a simple explanation:

> Let's admit that my personal enthusiasm had something to do with it, but from a company perspective there was the prospect of running long-distance tilting trains through the Borders if the case for re-opening the entire route stacked up.

The Scottish Office package included funding a short pre-feasibility study to provide a critical assessment of previous investigations of re-opening. This contract was won in January 1999 by a team from Carl Bro, The Spaven McCrossan Partnership and ERM, and the author found himself in the enviable position of being paid to re-read and appraise 28 reports, dating back to 1966, relevant to the mooted re-opening of the railway. The pre-feasibility study concluded that 'the conclusions of the mid-1990s reports appear broadly reliable for their time (and certainly sufficient to justify taking the project forward to the substantive study stage).'

The scene was set for a substantial body of feasibility work to be undertaken over subsequent years by a team led by consultants Scott Wilson (by then including the privatised British Rail engineering design offices), examining supply and demand issues in detail and producing a costed design for the planned re-opening of the northern third of the Waverley Route – but not before a remarkable grassroots campaign took to the Borders' streets.

With rail re-opening now at the top of the economic regeneration agenda, the timing was ideal for the creation of the Campaign for Borders Rail (CBR), which fittingly had its formal launch in the restored A-listed station building at Melrose in January 1999. A large CBR committee was elected – with representation from all parts of the Borders – and with three SBC employees (in personal capacities) in key positions, networking was simplified. Biberbach – who was very much the driving force – was appointed Chair, Kathleen Fraser (Biberbach's assistant at SBC) as Secretary, and Bill Jamieson (a civil engineer and long-time advocate of rail re-opening, who had been giving advice on bridges to BTF for some years) as Treasurer. Another key activist was George Fraser (father of Kathleen) who was the campaign's Midlothian representative and came from a business background, with no railway enthusiast baggage. Regarded as the 'elder statesman' of CBR during the early years, he was a confident public speaker and one of the key CBR witnesses at the meeting of the Scottish Parliament's Public Petitions Committee in Gala in 2000. Looking back in 2015, Biberbach recalled: 'We had a lengthy debate over the title of the campaign, and very consciously chose a forward-looking name. Everyone knew the Waverley Line but we wanted to adopt something which would embrace the whole region and reflect its geography.' And ultimately that vision would be reflected in the official, and popular, 'Borders Railway' title for the re-opened line.

The new group's first newsletter was published in January 1999, and its calendar of coming events gives a flavour of the feverish campaigning activity which was to characterise much of the first eight years of CBR's existence – February children's artwork competition; March slide show in Newcastleton; May sponsored walk; July barbecue at Hassendean station; August stall at Duns Show, stall at Hawick Model Railway Exhibition, and stall at Newcastleton Show. As Biberbach said in her welcome, 'what appeared like a pipedream is now growing rapidly into a movement.' Recollecting those heady days in 2012, Biberbach commented:

> We thought it was important to speak to everybody – the young, the old, not just business interests. Big things were happening in Edinburgh, with the arrival of the Scottish Parliament, but in the Borders people seemed to be used to things 'being done to them'. I remember one woman saying to me – and this was quite common – 'it's great, hen, but it'll never happen in my lifetime.' We were determined to engage with people on the streets and encourage them to believe that they could really make things happen.

Most of CBR's early activists probably realised that they had to be in this for the long-haul, but doubtless few could have envisaged that it would be 2015 before the trains would once again be running along the valley of the Gala Water. As it turned out, the events of the next decade were to test the stamina of even the most dedicated campaigners. However, by late 1999 CBR had some 300 members and several thousand signatures on its public petition to re-open the railway – and had successfully run the first of three conferences which it would organise over the next ten years. CBR eventually managed to collect 17,200 signatures on its petition. This was no mean feat, as Cathel Kerr (a CBR office bearer) recorded in his 2004 Certificate in Railway Studies Project at the University of York: 'Most Borderers would have said they were in favour of the railway but also that it was never likely to happen' – echoing perhaps the scepticism and apathy which limited the campaign against closure back in the late 1960s?

History was made in March 2000 when the Scottish Parliament's Public Petitions Committee held its first meeting away from Holyrood – at a packed Volunteer Hall in Galashiels, where the Committee met to consider CBR's petition. The *Southern Reporter* noted that there were almost 300 people in the public gallery, 'many of whom had been bussed in from Hawick and Newcastleton', and that 'veteran rail campaigner, Madge Elliot, received loud applause even before she spoke'. A subsequent debate in the Scottish Parliament in June unanimously endorsed the petition's aims, with John McAllion MSP (Chair of the Committee) rehearsing an inter-regional comparison which the author had first introduced to the public debate at CBR's conference the previous year:

> I was struck by one comparison the witnesses made: that between the Borders and the Highland region. The Highland region has a population of around 220,000 and is sometimes thought of as a neglected area. It has 57 railway stations. The Borders, which has more than half the population, does not have one railway station in its area. That is not fair, it is not right and it is unjust.

In his project thesis Cathel Kerr attributed the success of CBR in providing a vehicle for the case for railway re-opening to a number of factors, including reaching out to the business community, railway industry and local and national government:

> The advent of the Scottish Parliament in 1999 came at the right time for CBR. The new legislative body was looking for causes to champion and the Borders railway project seemed to fit the bill. Another factor in CBR's success is that it managed to position itself away from the male-dominated world of the railway enthusiast. Petra Biberbach was the first chairperson of CBR and having a woman

at the helm made it clear that the Borders railway was a transport issue of importance to people (male and female) in the region.

The Scott Wilson study

Scott Wilson's £400,000 report – which had been commissioned by the Scottish Executive, Scottish Borders Council, Midlothian Council and Scottish Borders Enterprise – was finally published in February 2000. Its key finding was that a frequent passenger service from either the Central Borders or Gorebridge to Edinburgh could cover its direct operating costs. The highlighted (but not recommended as such) options were:

- a half-hourly frequency service from Tweedbank (mid-way between Galashiels and Melrose), with intermediate stations at Galashiels, Gorebridge, Newtongrange, Eskbank, Newcraighall and Brunstane (the latter two being part of the Edinburgh CrossRail scheme, which was then at the planning stage) – at an estimated capital cost of £73 million, substantially greater than the Oscar Faber 1996 estimate of £18m for a Galashiels-Edinburgh railway – with an end-to-end journey time of 52 minutes, or,
- a half-hourly frequency service from Gorebridge, with intermediate stations at Newtongrange, Eskbank, Newcraighall and Brunstane – at an estimated capital cost of £27 million.

The study did not find an economic case for other options south of Tweedbank – in the case of the route as far as Hawick, this reflected in part the high cost of overcoming the very significant breaches of the solum (largely for road construction) permitted by the Scottish Office and Borders Regional Council in particular over the previous 25 years. Scott Wilson had in fact identified no less than 24 'base options' for evaluation in the study – varying by terminus / service frequency / number of intermediate stations / and whether or not the train service would be an extension of the forthcoming Edinburgh CrossRail service. In summary the termini were: Gorebridge (4 options), Galashiels (5), Peebles, Tweedbank (3), Selkirk (2), Newtown St Boswells (3), Jedburgh, Kelso, Berwick, Hawick and Carlisle (2).

Politically the promoter had to be seen to have examined all possible options, but amongst the most dubious inclusions in the options for evaluation were Jedburgh (a town of just 4,000 population, with a very limited surrounding catchment, which had lost its train service in 1948) and Peebles (a significant centre, but Scott Wilson were considering the circuitous route to Edinburgh via Galashiels, which would be uncompetitive even with bus services).

Considering the inclusion of such clearly non-viable propositions, there were two very surprising omissions from the list of base options – firstly a two-tier service pattern (a more frequent stopping service to Gorebridge, overlaid by a less frequent express service to the Borders), and secondly the option of an extension less than two miles from Tweedbank to the surviving old station site at the heart of Melrose. Scott Wilson did examine four 'express' type options independent of CrossRail – including a service from Tweedbank to Edinburgh which was projected to have no intermediate stations, even at Galashiels! Unsurprisingly, as the Midlothian market was completely omitted, these 'straw men' failed to demonstrate viability.

Scott Wilson's base options were heavily dominated by services envisaged as extensions of CrossRail – 19 out of 24 – and this may well have reflected a strong 'steer' from the Scottish Executive. The specification of the largely single-track infrastructure – designed only for the standard half-hourly train service – would also severely limit the scope to carry any additional traffics such as passenger charters or freight. The Scott Wilson report did assess the market for freight (timber in particular), but the tourist charter train market was not examined.

The omission of any Melrose options was very strange – sufficient space survived at the remaining station platform to accommodate a single rail track north of the bypass road, and the big line breach problems were *beyond* Melrose, en route to Newtown St Boswells and Hawick. Securing a terminus in the heart of the town (one of the hotspots of Borders tourism), minutes walk from the famous Abbey, would self-evidently have boosted the tourism potential of the railway, as well as helping to alleviate Melrose's chronic summer parking problems.

Reflecting on the options in early 2015, Councillor David Parker (Leader of Scottish Borders Council since 2003) recollected that 'while ideally we would have liked to reach St Boswells or Charlesfield [a potential development site just south of St Boswells], we had a massive worry about getting through Melrose, both in terms of local objections and the cost of putting the railway back. In contrast, the engineering and politics of Tweedbank looked okay.' This makes sense, but leaves unanswered the question as to why Scott Wilson did not examine the feasibility of extending the railway just to Melrose as a 25th 'base option'.

However, the Scottish Executive was at pains to avoid raising expectations too high even in relation to the partially disappointing outcome of the £400,000 study. Unveiling the report, Transport and Environment Minister Sarah Boyack commented:

> As intended, the study does not make any recommendations on whether or not the project should be progressed and, if so, how. That is for the stakeholders to

decide and take forward with other interested parties, including the Scottish Executive, as appropriate.

Recollecting this period in discussion with the author in early 2015, Boyack commented:

This was an exciting time for the new Parliament. Being able to set an agenda for new railway developments was one of the big opportunities that came from devolution. We didn't inherit a series of railway projects – though the Tories had plenty of road schemes. The concept of the railway originated in the Borders, not from the rail industry – this, and being located outwith the Central Belt, meant we had to be more creative in handling what was a more challenging project than others. But as Transport Minister I inherited the feasibility study on the route from former UK Minister Gus Macdonald, which was an important starting point.

In light of that decision to pass responsibility for taking the railway forward to other stakeholders, and comments – as we shall see – by others directly involved in the project locally, Boyack's comment can be interpreted as reflecting mixed views about its merits amongst civil servants and Labour MSPs. Of course, for eight years of the period of evaluation and promotion of the railway and its passage through the Scottish Parliament, a Labour / Liberal Democrat coalition administration held power in the Scottish Executive – and with the Lib Dems' strong presence in the Borders (and to be fair, Labour in Midlothian), it seems reasonable to conclude that reinstating the railway was part of the price of coalition.

Taking their cue from Boyack, Scottish Borders Council (SBC), Midlothian Council, City of Edinburgh Council, BTF, Railtrack and ScotRail quickly set up the Borders Rail Working Group, which then bid for £1.9m from the Executive's Public Transport Fund (PTF) to enable the Parliamentary Order to be secured for construction of the line at least as far as Tweedbank. Once PTF funding had been secured (in November 2000), the three local authorities set up a joint committee – the Waverley Railway Joint Committee (part of the Waverley Railway Partnership) – for the purpose of promoting the scheme. Given that the Scott Wilson study had not found a case for re-opening through to Carlisle, Virgin quietly withdrew from the initiative at this stage, as a route only north of Tweedbank would have no obvious fit with its Anglo-Scottish rail portfolio.

By this stage, BTF had also fallen out of the rail project framework, the coup de grace coming from SBC Director of Technical Services, Ian Brown, in his 12th April letter to BTF Chairman Alan Bailey: 'I believe it would be in the best interests of all if BTF were to withdraw from the working group. This will have the immediate joint benefit of removing the conflict of interests and freeing BTF to pursue its own commercial solution and to compete for appropriate work as it becomes available.' Bailey reflected on this in 2014:

> As the letter makes clear, [the Working Group] was a mechanism to put control of the project firmly in local authority hands. The local authorities saw themselves putting our project out to tender, rather than assisting us as developer. We believed that, given the regulatory climate at the time, a new and cheaper approach to regional lines could be taken but the working group saw a fully fledged full cost industry-standard railway, which is what we are [now] being given at enormous cost.
>
> It is ironic to me that our commerciality was considered a conflict of interest given that we were a Borders company that would have kept the benefits within the Borders, who might have expected their council to step up to the plate with them for the Region's benefit. This they had consistently failed to do in terms that would have satisfied the potential backers that we were talking to.
>
> Ian's suggestion that we sit quietly on the working group hoping for an opportunity to market our then-current intellectual property to tenderers at some stage was implausible, as by the time a design was completed and put out to tender, it wouldn't have been our design and our intellectual property would have been out of date.
>
> We did receive an invitation to tender for consultancy work but we were far too short of cash to bring on board the resources and expertise to put us in the running, after 5 years of battling to get the concept to be taken seriously.

In late 2000 the Working Group reported a revised construction timetable for Edinburgh to the Galashiels area to the Borders Rail Forum. The Forum had been set up in November 1999 – in response to an initiative by Petra Biberbach on behalf of CBR – to secure cross-party support and a co-ordinated approach to rail re-opening. It comprised MPs, MSPs, Councillors, Scottish Borders Enterprise, Community Council representatives, CBR and BTF. The construction timetable – with the line scheduled to open in 2008 – probably looked like a lengthy wait for the railway at that time, but it makes salutary reading from a 2015 perspective.

The Minister's statement on the PTF award emphasised that 'my award towards the development costs does not mean that any future public funding for the development of the project beyond this stage will be granted.' Another imponderable – how the Borders railway could be restored legally – was however about to be clarified, Murray Tosh MSP (Chair of the Scottish Parliament's Procedures Committee) announcing in mid-December that the promoters would

Two key players in the promotion of the new railway project in the early years of the 21st century – (*l*)Drew Tully, Convenor of Scottish Borders Council, and (*r*) Ian Brown, Director of Technical Services – arriving at the Volunteer Hall in Galashiels on 27th March 2000 for the historic meeting of the Scottish Parliament's Public Petitions Committee.

Alastair Watson, courtesy of the Southern Reporter

have to bring forward a 'private' bill. The promoters would have to make a case to be given powers to acquire land and planning permission to go ahead with their proposed development, and the Bill would go before a special committee of MSPs. Unlike the House of Commons, where decisions could be referred to commissioners appointed by the Secretary of State, the process in Scotland would be handled by MSPs and final decisions taken by the Parliament.

As rail powers had not yet been fully devolved to the then Scottish Executive at the early phase of project development, the local authorities had planned to promote a Bill through the UK Parliament, but were persuaded to delay moving to this stage until all rail powers were transferred. This strategy had its merits, but as Midlothian Council transport planner Douglas Muir reflected in 2011:

> Perhaps because it was one of the first transport bills to go before the Scottish Parliament, the Borders Railway became a test bed for subsequent rail re-openings through Holyrood, and it ended up – partly because a number of civil servants and politicians were privately sceptical about the merits of going south of Gorebridge – being subject to a degree of scrutiny which didn't appear to apply to other projects.

Amongst the hurdles which the Borders Railway had to clear – with inevitable time and cost implications – was having to serve notice on not just the parties located on the land to be taken up by the planned railway (the Westminster model), but also all affected parties on adjacent land, which more than tripled the number of notices to be served. Unlike new road schemes, where the promoter has the right to go onto other parties' land for survey purposes, the railway project had no such rights. The physical 'Limits of Deviation' of the Borders Railway corridor would be specified down to the millimetre on the horizontal plane, but until the Bill was approved – and the promoter then had full access to the land involved for ground investigation and topographical survey work – a detailed design could not be produced.

CBR intensifies its campaigning – and Stow comes on to the agenda

CBR's main publicity effort over the summer of 2000 had involved building a steam locomotive with straw bales on the trackbed adjacent to the A7 just south of Stow. This attracted valuable coverage from the local papers and Border TV, even more so when it was destroyed in a subsequent arson attack! By this time CBR's membership was well over 450 and still growing.

While CBR had welcomed the Scott Wilson report – with some caveats about the lack of attention to wider social and environmental considerations, which would have helped the case for Hawick and a South Borders freight line for timber – there were real concerns about the absence of a station at Stow in Scott Wilson's highlighted options. With a perhaps inevitable decline in bus provision along the valley of the Gala Water after rail re-opening, Stow without a rail stop would be in an unenviable position, unable to share in the economic and social benefits which the railway would bring. CBR also challenged the revenue forecast by consultants Halcrow which (with their assumed fare income per passenger-km) equated to a bizarre projection of only five return passenger journeys per day from Stow to Edinburgh. Bill Jamieson – then and now a resident of Stow – recollected in 2011:

> There followed a short correspondence between Stow Community Council and Peter Fuller, the Public Transport Officer at SBC. It was abundantly clear that there was no interest at SBC in pursuing a station at Stow – we even offered to assist in carrying out a proper official survey, but this offer was not taken up. There was a classic line in one of the letters from SBC to the effect that 'a stop at Stow would be a profound discouragement to through passengers from Galashiels when no-one got on or off!'

Looking back at the Stow saga in early 2015, Councillor David Parker reflected that 'we were entirely dependent on external rail expertise, but David Hume [Chief Executive of SBC] and I were always quite relaxed about including a station at Stow. However, it was only later that it became apparent to us – prompted in part by Bill Jamieson and the other Stow campaigners – that the original analysis had not been thought through properly.'

To take its case forward CBR eventually decided to commission its own study, in cooperation with Stow Community Council, and in summer 2001 appointed the TR&IN consultancy, led by Paul Salveson who had pioneered the concept of

'Community Rail Partnerships' in England. The TR&IN report on Stow was published in Spring 2002, having received completed survey forms from 653 individuals (a very high response rate) in Stow and nearby Lauder, Clovenfords and Fountainhall. Its key findings were that even with a cautious interpretation of the survey results, it was possible to envisage some 100 daily journeys originating at Stow station, with potential for a smaller number of incoming trips (people visiting friends and relatives, tourists etc).

The first phase of CBR's history – and certainly one of its most active – drew to a close in early 2002 when Petra Biberbach resigned as Chair, following her move of home from the Borders to Edinburgh. David Roemmele from Selkirk took over in a caretaker capacity for a year, and was followed by the Hawick-based Councillor, Anne Borthwick, for a period of six years. Biberbach's enthusiasm and drive were not however lost to the Borders' railway cause, as she was to play a critical role in the creation of a new group which arguably had some impact on the final shape of the Borders Railway scheme – although much less than it had hoped for.

The Waverley Route Trust – and some gentle rocking of the boat

Ever since the Borders Rail Forum had been set up, CBR – alive to new thinking in England and in mainland Europe – had been advocating alternatives to the conventional model of railway procurement and ownership. This thinking came to fruition when the first meeting of the new Waverley Route Trust (WRT) was held at Edinburgh City Chambers on 3rd April 2002.

For most of its nine-year life WRT comprised ten trustees – Petra Biberbach as Chair; Andrew Boyd (a campaigner against the closure of the Waverley Route in 1969, and by profession a solicitor); David Fasken (by profession a business manager in the food industry) – later replaced by Lorne Anton (a CBR activist and career railwayman); Professor Chris Harvie (President of the Scottish Association for Public Transport, and a campaigner against closure); Bill Jamieson; Lawrence Marshall (by profession a railway operator, and a Councillor on the City of Edinburgh Council); Catherine Maxwell Stuart (owner of Traquair House, and a leading light in Borders tourism); Paul Salveson; the author; and Colin Strang-Steel (by profession a chartered surveyor and farmer in the Borders, with family connections with the London & North Eastern Railway).

Biberbach had trailed the trust concept past a meeting of the Borders Rail Forum in March 2002 and encountered early scepticism which would prove to be a harbinger of the opposition WRT would later encounter from the establishment during its peak period of activity between 2002 and 2006. Under the slogan 'promoting a community railway to and through the Scottish Borders', WRT was publicly launched in the run-up to the Scottish elections on 16th April 2002 in Edinburgh City Chambers, with the aim of providing a platform for new ideas on ownership and management of the railway and opening up funding opportunities beyond the scope of governmental organisations.

The rail network inches south and the Waverley Railway goes out to consultation

The train service which was ultimately intended to provide the framework for the Borders railway timetable was launched on 3rd June 2002 when ScotRail's Edinburgh CrossRail service began operation to Brunstane and Newcraighall stations on the surviving (freight-only) section of the Waverley Route between Portobello Junction and Millerhill. Psychologically, this was an important boost for the Borders rail campaign, and soon proved to be a successful addition to the passenger rail network.

In anticipation of the publication of the Waverley Railway Joint Committee's consultation document on 'Stage 1' of the new Borders railway in July 2002, CBR's June newsletter included a briefing on the anticipated scheme, warning members:

> we are very concerned that the favoured option will be entirely focussed on shuttling commuters in and out of Edinburgh, on an infrastructure tailored around a specific timetable, with no scope for handling freight and tourist trains. As one of the speakers [the author] at our recent freight conference said, this would be like building a new road which could take cars and minibuses but excluded lorries and coaches!

The forecast proved to be correct. In July 2002, the Waverley Railway Joint Committee published its consultation document, with the scheme essentially being that highlighted by the Scott Wilson report – a single-track railway to Tweedbank with long ('dynamic') passing loops south of Newcraighall, between Fushiebridge and Tynehead, and between Stow and Bowland. The only substantive change was a route diversion west of Millerhill Yard to serve a new station at Shawfair, a proposed large housing development on the site of the former Monktonhall Colliery.

The latest railway specification also came with an increased price tag – yet again – of £129 million, and a projected journey time of 61 minutes from Tweedbank to Edinburgh Waverley. At this point, its fears confirmed, the Waverley Route Trust began promoting its objective of 'adding value' to the

Waverley Railway, its new publicity brochure highlighting the concept of an express train service to Edinburgh, taking 50 minutes or less from Tweedbank.

Stow starts campaigning and the Bill is lodged in Parliament

Stow Station Supporters Group (comprised predominantly but not exclusively of CBR members) was set up in response to the official consultation document's failure to include a local station. At the suggestion of Christine Grahame MSP, a longstanding advocate of rail re-opening, the Group decided to petition the Scottish Parliament, and forms were distributed throughout the parish and more widely in the Borders, attracting a rash of publicity from local and national press, radio and TV. 1,330 signatures were eventually gathered, and a group of supporters travelled to Edinburgh in December when the Petitions Committee considered the submission. The Committee recognised the Stow case and agreed to write to the Waverley Railway Partnership asking why Stow had been omitted.

The Waverley Railway (Scotland) Bill was eventually published by the Scottish Parliament in September 2003 – three months later than expected. This was not the first delay to the hoped-for timetable, and it would be far from the last. The Bill was widely welcomed, but some concerns were raised by politicians and the media about the rail specification and the remaining hurdles to be overcome – these included Christine Grahame who commented:

> I think we require to consider a railway that will allow an express through from the Borders, stopping in the first instance at Gala and Stow, and a separate service serving Midlothian . . . As for funding there is no equivocal commitment to this, instead the ominous words 'business case' haunt the project.

The period for objecting to the new railway ended in November 2003. In early 2004 the composition of the Waverley Railway Bill Committee was announced, comprising five MSPs: Ted Brocklebank, Conservative; Gordon Jackson, Labour; Tricia Marwick, SNP (Convenor); Christine May, Labour; and Mike Pringle, Liberal Democrat,(later replaced by Margaret Smith, Liberal Democrat).

Meanwhile CBR was rehearsing some key strategic arguments for rail re-opening which would be presented to the Committee, with its February 2004 newsletter featuring a report by Bill Jamieson drawing attention to the fact that 32% of households in Galashiels and 37% in Hawick did not own a car. He also provided a list of the 12 largest freestanding towns in Scotland which 'demonstrates how almost uniquely disadvantaged Hawick [population 14,573] and Galashiels [14,361] are' – due to the combination of their size and long distance from the rail network, the same points that Frank Spaven had been making at the Scottish Office back in the mid-1960s. Jamieson set this in the context of global oil production peaking within the next ten years:

> This surely points conclusively in the direction of a core transport network for Scotland which either uses available oil as efficiently as possible, can utilise crop based fuels, eg biodiesel, or can be powered by renewable generated electricity. Only rail fits the bill, but extending the network will not be achieved through the mechanisms of STAG appraisals [Scottish Transport Appraisal Guidance] and business cases (which almost seem designed to achieve the exact opposite) – as has been stated often enough in the past it will need political will based on the recognition that a problem exists.

The full Business Case for the line – based on forecasting techniques which later seriously underestimated the actual level of demand generated by Scotland's newly re-opened railways – was published in summer 2004, projecting a very modest base benefit to cost ratio of just 1.01 to 1. Reviewing the situation in the August issue of the CBR newsletter, the author (on behalf of WRT) commented:

> The recent problems with the business case can be traced back to 2000 when the Scott Wilson report was published and the [Scottish] Executive subsequently endorsed development of a specification to construct a single-track railway with a half-hourly service, calling at all stations between Tweedbank and Edinburgh. From the moment a price tag of £129 million was announced in 2001 (up from £73m in 2000) it was clear that a railway with no spare capacity for anything other than commuter trains averaging 35mph from Tweedbank to Edinburgh would struggle to attract enough passengers to demonstrate 'value for money.'

An alternative model for the railway – the Corus Report

During 2003 the Waverley Route Trust had in fact concluded that in the absence of any serious movement within the Waverley Railway Partnership, it would need to commission its own study to demonstrate the case for an alternative model for the Edinburgh-Tweedbank railway. A study specification was drawn up, and WRT successfully raised the £30,000 capital needed through grant awards and donations. Scottish Borders Council declined to make a financial contribution.

A team led by Corus Rail Consultancy was appointed to undertake the study of *Delivering an innovative Borders Railway* in January 2004 – the first recorded formalised use of the name that would ultimately be used for the re-opened railway. Around that time WRT – which had deliberately refrained from lodging an objection to the Bill despite some very serious reservations about the scheme specification – concluded that it would be best to build up a relationship with the Parliament's Bill Committee which was not too 'lobbyist', instead providing its experience and perspective as an aid to the Committee, and suggesting other potential witnesses, such as Corus.

To coincide with the completion of the Corus study, WRT hosted the *Innovation on Rural & Regional Railways* conference at Edinburgh City Chambers on 23rd April 2004, with speakers from England, Northern Ireland and Scotland. There was extensive media coverage, and just a few weeks later WRT was delighted to receive a supportive letter from former Python (and President of Transport 2000) Michael Palin. The author had written to seek his support for the Trust's aims, and Palin revealed a personal connection behind his response, which concluded that he 'would love to receive any information about your plans':

> . . . I have always been fascinated by the Waverley Route. I was born and brought up in Sheffield, and spent many wasted hours watching the Thames-Clyde Express go through (usually several hours late), and names like Galashiels and Melrose seemed to me to epitomise the glamour of railway travel.

Around this time, the Waverley Railway Partnership requested an urgent meeting with the Trust, and this took place in early June at Edinburgh City Chambers, where a basis for working together was agreed, including a mooted seminar for Councillors to present shared findings and discuss the development of community involvement in the railway. However, in a letter received in mid-July the Partnership appeared to retreat from this position. Subsequent correspondence, and meetings with David Hume (Chief Executive at Scottish Borders Council) and Councillor David Parker (SBC Leader) in late August, and seven councillors in mid-September, seemed to have got the process back on track – but there was still no written agreement and no dates for a seminar had been agreed.

Meantime, Corus delivered the Final Report on their study on 10th September 2004. A key conclusion – in line with WRT thinking – was that a 'one-size-fits-all' service was not the right approach, as there were two distinct geographical markets for the train: Midlothian and the Borders. A half-hourly frequency service from Gorebridge to Edinburgh should call at all intermediate stations, while an hourly limited-stop 'inter-regional express' from Tweedbank or Melrose would take under 45 minutes to Edinburgh, including stops at Galashiels and Stow. Additional services would be provided during peak hours. This improved service package would bring more leisure visitors to the Borders and generate a wide range of economic, social and environmental benefits from Day 1 of the new railway.

In contrast, the business case for the official scheme, which was having such difficulties generating sufficient benefits to justify the costs involved, depended to some extent on projected housing developments as far away as 2038. Into the bargain, the linkage of the railway to housing development was sowing the seeds of an anti-rail backlash, which would eventually be articulated by the new 'Borders Party' in local elections. In practice the number of houses explicitly linked to the railway in a developer levy or 'roof tax' capped at £30m – 700 in Midlothian and 1,100 in the Borders – was relatively modest compared to the underlying housing expansion planned in the regional Structure Plans (over 9,000 in Midlothian and some 8,000 in the Borders). With this level of new housing planned it was clear that the regional transport infrastructure would struggle to accommodate the growth without the new railway, but the mere fact of the low-level linkage – and the difficulties with the railway's business case – was enough to allow anti-rail elements to attack the very principle of the railway.

As the promoter's infrastructure specification provided no spare capacity for any trains other than the normal timetabled service (except at night and on Sundays), Corus recommended that from Portobello Junction (east of Edinburgh) to Gorebridge a conventional double-track railway should be provided to support a reliable half-hourly service. South of Gorebridge, a single track with conventional crossing loops at Stow and Tweedbank (or Melrose) and a simpler signalling system would reduce costs without compromising reliability – and still provide enough capacity for regular express services as well as charter tourist trains from England and possible future freight requirements such as waste and timber. The key conclusion of the study was that significantly greater revenues and benefits were likely to be secured by a better railway costing broadly the same as the official scheme.

The Bill Committee takes written evidence – and the Partnership closes ranks

The Waverley Railway (Scotland) Bill committee began taking evidence in mid-2004, and WRT made a detailed submission in early September, supporting the general principles of the Bill but suggesting that the enhanced service and infrastructure package recommended in the Corus study should be incorporated in the specification for the railway.

Around this time it became apparent that the Bill promoters had failed to notify all parties entitled to be consulted on the proposals, and there would therefore be an additional three-month delay in the Parliamentary process, pushing the projected start of construction back from 2005 to 2006 – the second of many delays which were to dog the project over the first decade of the new century.

Meantime, the long-planned joint workshop of the Trust, Corus and the WRP consultants finally took place in Edinburgh in early December. No evident 'showstoppers' were raised by the WRP consultants, other than the potentially key issue of upgrading Portobello Junction from a 'single lead' configuration to a conventional double track layout, but Corus were confident this would cost under £5 million – and that wider network benefits would accrue to the scheme. The author and the Corus consultant, the late Clive Roberts, were however somewhat taken aback – despite their long-held concern about slow journey times – to hear that the latest traffic projections for the promoter's scheme had forecast (for Year 1) just 150 passengers a day from Tweedbank to Edinburgh and 80 per day from Galashiels, equating to only five and three passengers respectively per train!

At the conclusion of the meeting, the WRP consultants suggested they could have a further meeting with WRT/Corus to discuss Bill flexibility and a possible joint statement to the Committee referring to the scope for enhancements to be incorporated within the Bill powers at the detailed stage. In the meantime they would put to the WRP Working Group that the Corus proposals should be costed in detail using common methodology and that the revenue forecasters should get together to make sense of the very different prognoses for traffic levels.

Overall, this seemed like further progress, but any such illusions were severely dashed just weeks later when Scottish Borders Council (SBC) belatedly responded – in a submission to the Bill Committee – to the Corus report which it had been sent four months earlier. SBC's 75-page January 2005 response was to prove to be a turning point in the relationship between the promoters and the Waverley Route Trust. In the latter's non-technical (March 2005) commentary on SBC's response, the Trust noted that the tone of the SBC response was 'overwhelmingly adversarial [and] peppered with emotive and unhelpfully negative language':

> In its evident determination to do a 'hatchet job' on the CORUS report – rather than building constructively on the ideas therein – the promoter has however strayed into territory which betrays some serious deficiencies in the quality, rigour and professionalism of its own analysis.

Amongst the deficiencies were:

- suggesting that an hourly express service from the Borders to Edinburgh would not offer any additional benefits, despite providing a 36% faster journey time, at an average speed of 55mph rather than the 35mph of the promoter's scheme
- claiming that an hourly express service would not be attractive, on the basis that passengers using an hourly frequency would have to precisely

time their arrival at the station, whereas those using a half-hourly frequency allegedly would not

- alleging that the official scheme timings (eg 61 minutes from Tweedbank to Edinburgh) would be 'significantly faster than the competition (road)', when in fact they were referring to bus travel, and not the main competition, the car.

WRT did not pull its punches, concluding that the promoter had 'insufficient grasp of the key issue of markets for rail travel, preferring a top-down mechanistic modelling approach to a genuine understanding of local opportunities based on practical experience of developing rail business away from core inter-city corridors', and had 'insufficient confidence or vision to challenge conventional wisdoms and think imaginatively about innovative provision of rail services, building on international best practice'.

However, in discussion with the author in 2011, Scott Wilson's Project Manager for the Borders Railway, Keith Wallace, defended their approach (and that of the Waverley Railway Partnership) during this unhappy period for the Trust:

At the time of the parliamentary hearings, our team felt that some of the material presented by the Trust was in danger of derailing our case, in terms of sowing doubt in the MSPs as to whether our work was robust, which we firmly believed it was, and that this might delay the decision or send us back for more work as a stalling technique – remember cross-party support was pretty elusive.

It was a regular feature of discussions over the period 2002–2005 between the Partnership and the Trust for the latter to be told there just wasn't time to make changes to the railway specification in line with the ideas in the Corus report – but in practice there was significant delay to the project for other reasons which could have been used as an opportunity to introduce improvements.

It is now clear that the Partnership was leant on very heavily in late 2004 / early 2005 by the Scottish Executive, which presumably was unwilling to break the link with CrossRail and/or took the view that the Trust's changes would require a new Bill – hence the relatively sudden and unexpected change of attitude of the Partnership. At least some key players in the Partnership were unhappy about having to wheel out sometimes crude and ill-conceived criticisms of the Corus/Trust analyses in order to satisfy the Executive's objectives, but they were effectively faced with a *fait accompli*.

Recollecting this period in discussion with the author in early 2015, Councillor David Parker was at pains to emphasise how little room for manoeuvre was available to the Waverley Railway Partnership:

Although Scottish Borders Council was the Promoter of the railway, the Scottish Executive called all the shots, releasing funds for our feasibility and promotional work only in discrete chunks. Civil servants on the finance side had real question marks about the railway, as – predictably – did their roads colleagues. Within the transport directorate there were mixed views and that was also true of Labour MSPs. So we had to tread very carefully to keep the railway on track.

The Bill Committee takes oral evidence – and rail funding is announced

In early 2005 the timetable for the Bill Committee to take oral evidence from supporters, objectors, the promoter and other interested parties was announced – with four separate sessions to be held in February and March at Galashiels and Newtongrange.

At the 28th February Bill Committee meeting in Galashiels, Bill Jamieson was quizzed extensively, not least over the scope for bus services to be improved as an alternative to an expensive new railway. His robust responses – as recorded in edited form in the April 2005 CBR newsletter – placed bus and train firmly in practical context:

> At the moment, the X95, which is not an express service despite its 'X' prefix, takes 75 minutes. There is no way to improve that, especially now that congestion charging in Edinburgh is out of the picture . . . About 200–250 people a day use the bus service on the A7 corridor. If you compare that with what could be achieved were a railway to be built, it is peanuts. At the moment, about 5,000 vehicles a day use the A7 and A68. The penetration of the bus service into the travel market is pretty low. It is a hard job to get people out of their cars and on to buses.

To some observers, the key intervention of the day came from CBR Chair Anne Borthwick, who in response to the Convenor's suggestion that support for rail re-opening was 'based on emotional as opposed to economic and social grounds', responded with a robust and impassioned plea which appeared to impress the Committee considerably:

> You make a strong point. The Borders relied heavily on the railway 36 years ago and before. I recognise the argument about facts versus emotion and there is no harm in being emotional about needing the railway back again . . . We have a new Parliament and we want to be part of the new Scotland, but unless we have proper transport links, we cannot be . . . There are an awful lot of inequalities in the world and there is nothing wrong with being emotional about that. Emotion starts the ball rolling; after that, the facts come thick and fast. Members have had all the facts today.

Shortly after appearing as a WRT witness at the 7th March Bill Committee meeting in Newtongrange – together with Petra Biberbach, the Chair, and Robert Samson, Director of the Rail Passengers Committee Scotland, which had helped to fund the Corus report – the author received a telephone call from a key civil servant during which the latter indicated that he was open to ideas about who should own the infrastructure south of Newcraighall, and that he intended to use his own staff to test out more of the assumptions made to date by the promoter. This evident willingness to think innovatively was seen by the author at the time as vindication of his effort – during the course of answering 17 different questions from Committee members – to flag up the potential for a different approach to the ownership and management of the railway.

Pressed by a Committee member on the likely attractiveness of a service which, as Corus and WRT had flagged up, would average 35mph end-to-end, Robert Samson noted that the proposed 57 minute journey time from Galashiels to Edinburgh would be slower than the fastest British Railways' timing in 1954 with steam haulage, and commented, 'We want people primarily to get out of their cars and to use public transport, but I do not see a journey time of 61 minutes [from Tweedbank to Edinburgh] as particularly attractive to car users.'

A bone of contention amongst witnesses – and perhaps particularly the Waverley Route Trust, which had spent hundreds of (unpaid) hours over the previous three years compiling and submitting evidence, meeting with key parties, and co-ordinating the Corus report – was that at all four sessions the promoter was timetabled to respond at the very end of the day's evidence, thus ensuring that they always had 'the last word'. WRT moved quickly – in a brief response submitted to the Bill Committee on 15th March – to highlight seven examples of what it saw as misrepresentations or failures to compare like-with-like by consultants representing the promoter at the 7th March meeting. One of the more laughable and misleading was:

> The promoter suggested that the difference between the CORUS hourly and promoter half-hourly frequencies was that people would need to turn up 15-20 minutes before the hourly train to 'make sure they catch it' and 'to buy a ticket'. As previously intimated by the Trust it is entirely unclear as to why turning up very early should be a requirement of the hourly service but not the half-hourly service. As to buying a ticket, the promoter is evidently unaware that Tweedbank station is intended to be unstaffed.

WRT also noted that Keith Wallace, speaking on behalf of the promoter, had said that the case for not going beyond Tweedbank was one of the clearest he had come across in any rail re-opening scheme – but the Trust pointed out that the costs and benefits of a short extension to Melrose only had never been independently appraised by the promoter. This was a significant omission.

The official reports of these four meetings total 152 pages and 128,900 words, reflecting the large variety and quantity of questions posed by the Committee and answers given by witnesses. But before all the questions had been answered – and after something like 18 months of the railway's business case shuttling in ping-pong fashion between Newtown St Boswells (SBC HQ) and Victoria Quay (the Minister's base in Edinburgh) – the Bill process was to be temporarily overshadowed by the long-awaited announcement of Scottish Executive funding. Transport Minister Nicol Stephen appeared to give evidence at the 14th March Bill Committee meeting in Galashiels, and while he had been somewhat upstaged by a leak a few days earlier – this swelling the public attendance, including the author, in anticipation of hearing the historic announcement 'live' – the audience was elated when Stephen said:

> I am pleased to confirm the Executive's commitment in principle to provide £115 million at 2002 prices towards the project, as requested in the business case . . . This railway is a real sign that times are changing, that the Borders and Midlothian will play their full part in the strong, confident Scotland that our transport investment will help build.

There were inevitably strings attached to this 85% funding contribution towards the cost of the Waverley Railway Project – Parliamentary approval for the Bill; the business case must hold, including 'housing growth projections that are achievable and based on identified market demand'; delivery of 'a clear and comprehensive risk management strategy'; and integration of the railway with local bus services.

Nevertheless there was a widespread welcome for the announcement, not least from the Chairman of the Waverley Railway Partnership, Councillor Jim Dunsmuir – who was not to know just how much the project timescale was to slip in later years when he commented: 'Our aim now is to ensure that the Bill secures a safe passage through Parliament with a view to Royal Assent being granted next year and the first trains running from 2008.'

The Stow station battle continues

In its response to the 7th March hearing, WRT noted that the promoter stated that there was a 'very, very weak case' for Stow station without clarifying if it had ever looked at the actual situation on the ground or had modelled potential leisure demand from Edinburgh. This failing was taken up in some detail in an article by Bill Jamieson in the April 2005 CBR newsletter, but not before he had set the scene by reminding readers that the promoter had over the previous five years flagged up a whole variety of reasons why a station could not be provided:

> Perhaps the nadir of credibility was reached with a statement in the business case that building a station posed 'extreme technical difficulties'. Although it was not specific, this was presumably a reference to the HMRI [Her Majesty's Railway Inspectorate] guidance (not requirement) that station platforms should be straight, a problem which the Corus Rail Consultancy, in its work for the WRT, has suggested is far from insuperable. The provision of 'Mind the Gap' signs is one possibility – some technical difficulty!

Stow Station Supporters Group had petitioned the Parliament back in 2002 – and had objected to the Bill – and at the 7th March Bill Committee meeting, according to Jamieson, 'got an extremely sympathetic hearing'.

The promoter had evidently ignored the 2002 TR&IN study which had projected 'some 100 daily return journeys originating at Stow station' and appeared to have done the same for the most recent piece of work undertaken for Corus (on behalf of WRT) by Rita O'Neill, an associate member of the rail industry's Passenger Demand Forecasting Council. O'Neill had come up with a likely patronage of just over 50 people a day from Stow. Her analysis, reviewing patronage forecasts in the Corus report against the Waverley Railway Partnership's Outline Business Case, also projected an eye-catching 25% increase in rail passenger demand at Galashiels and Tweedbank as a result of the much faster timetable modelled by Corus.

As we shall see below, the Bill Committee recommended *inter alia* in its 21st July report that a station should be provided at Stow, but it was not until late summer that a key reason for the promoter's low passenger projections became apparent. In the absence of Bill Jamieson on holiday, the author (on behalf of WRT) attended the first meeting at Stow of community representatives and the Waverley Railway Partnership following the Bill Committee's recommendation. He was amazed to see the Partnership's representatives table plans for a station located by the sewage works well to the south of the village, and even more amazed to find that they thought this was the preferred community option.

They were soon disabused of this bizarre assumption by all the community representatives present – and the farcical projection of five passengers a day now began to make some sense, having being based on a station ¾ mile away from the village centre, down a narrow unclassified road, with only a handful of houses within easy walking distance!

The Bill Committee reports – another major hurdle is cleared at last

The lengthy 'Preliminary Stage' process of the Bill finally moved towards a close when the Bill Committee published its report on 21st July 2005. Four out of the five MSPs (with one dissenting) recommended to the Parliament that the Bill should proceed as a Private Bill and that the 'general principles' should be agreed to. Two specific recommendations in particular stood out for rail campaigners:

- The Committee, principally on social inclusion grounds, was persuaded that a Borders Railway should have a stop at Stow
- The Committee called upon the promoter to enter into regular dialogue with the Waverley Route Trust.

The Trust was also pleased to find that the Committee shared its concerns about the Waverley Railway Partnership's quality of delivery, not just the 21 months taken to get to that stage, but also, 'the promoter's lack of effective dialogue and communication with key parties'. The Committee went as far as to call on the Scottish Executive, 'to consider whether this project is being competently managed and to reflect on what action is required to improve the performance of the promoter and its advisers and consultants in advance of the Consideration Stage.'

Looking back in early 2015, Councillor David Parker admitted that this was the only point throughout the whole re-opening process during which he had sleepless nights about the ultimate delivery of the railway:

> We had engaged a private sector company from down south to undertake the specialist 'land referencing' task, and they missed a lot of the plots which were relevant to the railway. The Committee could easily have kicked out the Bill, but Tricia Marwick MSP managed to persuade her colleagues that the whole project shouldn't be written off by a technical detail and that we should be a given a fair crack of the whip.

MSPs subsequently debated this stage of the Bill in September, and the vote was 102 for the motion, none against and one abstention. The first meeting between the Partnership and the Trust – as part of the 'regular dialogue' recommended by the Bill Committee – took place on 22nd September but it did not augur well for continuing dialogue. As Petra Biberbach wrote in her subsequent letter to Bruce Rutherford, the Project Manager for the scheme at Scottish Borders Council:

> We were taken aback to be advised at the last meeting that the Partnership had spent £50,000 on an analysis of the Corus Report without involving Corus or the

Trust collaboratively in the associated deliberations. You indicated that your analysis did not support the Corus conclusions, but we have no basis for assessing the validity of your analysis without sight of the document. It will not be possible to take the substantive elements of our intended dialogue significantly forward until such time as we and Corus have had the opportunity to read and review your analysis.

Biberbach noted that over the three years since the Trust had been launched it had made considerable efforts to secure a constructive dialogue with the Partnership, and in a spirit of co-operation had made a number of significant compromises, including not making a formal objection to the Bill – but 'the Partnership has only demonstrated an evident willingness to enter a regular and constructive dialogue with us when recommended to do so by the Bill Committee.'

WRT was clearly reaching the limits of its patience – the author remembers vividly how close he came to walking out of a meeting at Holyrood with the Partnership around this time – and Biberbach's letter was blunt and to the point: 'We are not interested in devoting yet more time to any agenda which the Partnership determines will only deal with very modest tinkering at the margins of the scheme.'

Biberbach made one last effort to find common ground, focussing more on 'outputs' than 'inputs': 'While these would not provide the step-change enhancement which we would ideally like to see, they would provide a significant improvement on what is currently on offer from the Partnership.' They included:

- a train journey time significantly faster than the planned 61 minutes from Tweedbank to Edinburgh – including a stop at Stow
- route infrastructure and/or scheduled timetable changes to provide two or three day-time paths daily in each direction for passenger charter and/or freight traffic
- infrastructure at Tweedbank to accommodate locomotive-hauled charter passenger and freight trains
- 'Community Rail' type designation south of Gorebridge, to lower costs of construction, maintenance and operation.

Biberbach concluded that the Trust would be happy to attend the next planned meeting, to discuss taking such an agenda forward 'in an open and collaborative spirit', but only on the understanding that clear deadlines for progress would be agreed at the meeting and that the Trust would have early sight of the Partnership's analysis of the Corus Report.

The Waverley Route Trust is driven out of the 'dialogue'

Getting increasingly disillusioned with the prospects of making any real progress with the Partnership – and in the light of growing unrest amongst MSPs about the costs and benefits of the scheme – the Trust decided to launch a media initiative jointly with the Capital Rail Action Group and Transform Scotland (the sustainable transport campaign, of which the author was then Chair). A press release under the headline 'Call for scheme revision to save Borders rail project' went out on 30th January 2006, with Biberbach's comment that:

> We have been pointing the promoter towards better and more realistic ways of building and operating the railway since we set up in 2002, but they have failed to look seriously at practical alternatives. As we predicted, the chickens are now coming home to roost, and a vicious anti-railway campaign is taking root.

The release secured coverage by radio stations in the Borders, and the *Edinburgh Evening News* ran a prominent illustrated article on 1st February, headlined 'Borders rail link campaigners express the need for speed', with the strap line, 'Plans for a one-hour journey dismissed as a slow train to failure'. Biberbach was quoted:

> The specification for the railway has been wrong from the word go – that's why the business case is pretty poor and the line will require significant subsidy. An uninspiring 'one size fits all' timetable with a 61 minute journey from Tweedbank, and no spare capacity for freight and passenger charter trains, is a recipe for failure.

This release, and its press coverage, was the beginning of the end of the relationship and the 'dialogue', such as it had been, between the Waverley Route Trust and the Waverley Railway Partnership. Subsequent correspondence failed to take matters meaningfully forward, and within a nine-page briefing to the Bill Committee on 15th March, WRT raised the fundamental question of which of the key stakeholders in the six-year plus history of the development of the scheme should have been taking responsibility for articulating a wider strategic perspective for the Waverley Railway:

> a recurring aspect of discussions we have had with the promoter and the Scottish Executive has been evidently contradictory assertions about the other party's role and responsibilities in the development of the railway.

The Trust then quoted a number of examples, including the case it had been making for separate express and local services – in response to which, 'the promoter and the Executive have each said this is an issue for the other party', and as a consequence nothing had happened to develop this potentially crucial improvement.

On 15th March WRT issued a press release confirming that it had pulled out of talks. It stated that since dialogue had begun in 2003 the Waverley Railway Partnership had 'demonstrated no intention of taking on board any of the Trust's key ideas to improve the business case for the line', and that 'the recent talks between the two groups have been nothing more than a "smokescreen" by the promoter to try to satisfy the Waverley Railway (Scotland) Bill Committee of the Scottish Parliament.' The release attached Biberbach's letter of 20th February to the Partnership and highlighted her comment:

> If the Partnership is unwilling or unable to treat seriously our key ideas first advanced more than three years ago, there is simply no point in having any further meetings.

The Waverley Railway Act is passed

Before the Bill Committee published its final report confirming its recommendation of a station at Stow, the promoter and the Scottish Executive – in the words of Bill Jamieson in the July 2006 CBR newsletter – 'pulled out the big guns – a senior civil servant and the Transport Minister, Tavish Scott, no less – to try and shoot it down.' Jamieson reported that it had been asserted that including a stop at Stow would make the timetable completely unreliable and could even jeopardise punctuality on GNER's Edinburgh to London service, and wryly commented that:

> One can only be thankful that the when the Channel Tunnel Rail Link opens next year, it will terminate at St Pancras rather than Kings Cross, otherwise the knock on effects would be felt on mainland Europe as well!

It therefore came as a great relief to campaigners when the Committee published its final report on 9th May – this went far beyond just including a station at Stow and made the whole project conditional on it. From a strategic perspective, the most crucial recommendation was that the Waverley Railway Project had to be completed as a whole, right through to Tweedbank, avoiding the danger of a scheme truncated at Gorebridge.

The final debate on the Waverley Railway Bill was held at Holyrood on 14th June 2006. Parliament accepted – with just one MSP dissenting – the Bill Committee's recommendations, including a station at Stow.

Contributing an insider's view to the same CBR newsletter, Tricia Marwick MSP (the Convener of the Bill Committee) commented, 'Well, that's it. After three full Parliamentary years, 29 Committee meetings, 108 witnesses and a 4-ft high stack of paper, the Waverley Railway (Scotland) Act completed its Parliamentary passage.' Noting the Committee's frustration with the promoter and

On the occasion of a press conference on 24th March 2003 promoting the rail re-opening project, Councillor John 'JR' Scott – Convenor of Scottish Borders Council and a long-time rail advocate – poses at Edinburgh Waverley beside a Class 170 diesel unit with mocked-up 'Tweedbank' destination.

One of the Campaign for Borders Rail's best publicity stunts. CBR approached the late Malcolm Stirling, the farmer at Bow Farm, with the idea of building a straw loco on part of the trackbed which he owned adjacent to the A7 two miles south of Stow. CBR members and farm staff built the loco in August 2000, and it thereafter secured even greater publicity for the rail campaign when it became the victim of an arson attack.

Local activists celebrate the announcement that the new railway would have a station at Stow – from left, Bill Jamieson, Alan Buchan, Bob Rowles and Heather Johnston.
Photos: Alastair Watson, courtesy of the Southern Reporter

the tortuous procedure with the Private Bill process (which was to be replaced by a Transport and Works Bill process to streamline future new railways), Marwick reiterated the conclusion of her speech in the Parliamentary debate: 'This is a historic day. The Waverley line, which was butchered by the Beeching cuts, will at least be partly restored. This is a good day for the Parliament and a good day for the Borders.'

Although the Scottish Parliamentary process – at nearly three years – had taken much longer than forecast, it could be argued that it had in some ways performed its function well. Reflecting on the process in 2011, Keith Wallace of Scott Wilson commented:

> The then parliamentary process, ironically now changed because of pressures on MSPs' time caused by the then flood of bills, was a very good and fair process. The promoter's team was in fact able to promote the bill, I like to think in the manner of the Victorian railway engineers 'marching with their plans to parliament', whereas in other formats often the promoters are defending, ie seeking only to prevent QCs from unpicking arguments, rightly or wrongly. The system also allowed the public to have their say in a friendly and unhostile manner, for example the individuals promoting a station at Stow were able to present their case without fear of attack from, say, a sharp QC.

A crucial stage in the project to re-open a key section of the Waverley Route had been passed – but the original momentum had slowed. In the June 2006 CBR newsletter Bill Jamieson reported that the Bill to re-open the Airdrie-Bathgate line had been introduced a few weeks earlier. This would involve 15 miles of new electrified double-track route and a 15-minute service frequency – and had only been identified by the Central Scotland Transport Corridor Studies as recently as 2002. The Borders Railway was now clearly falling behind other rail re-opening projects.

CHAPTER 10

Towards the finishing line
2006–15

IF the Campaign for Borders Rail felt it was entitled to sit back and reflect on its achievements for a while, following the successful passage of the Bill, that was not unreasonable after more than seven years of hard campaigning. Little did activists realise, however, that they would in fact need to regain their strength for a difficult period ahead, during which it became increasingly hard to maintain public enthusiasm for the railway in the face of ever more delays to the project.

Of course the railway had been identified in 1998 as a key agent of economic regeneration, but how did this square with the state of the Borders economy by 2006?

While John Hibbs had been proved right to say back in 1968 that there was no evidence from closures elsewhere to support the argument that shutting the Waverley Route 'would have a disastrous effect upon the economic and social life of the Borders', Hawick in particular has ever since been paying the penalty for becoming the town most isolated from Britain's rail network, with its population in continuing decline and 'enjoying' a poor standard of inter-regional public transport.

Reflecting on the changes in 2011, Bill Jamieson of CBR observed that while Galashiels had flourished overall – on the back of the 'Edinburgh effect' housing boom – during the first decade of the twenty first century, 'then to an outsider, Hawick seemed to have languished over the same period.' The population trend in Galashiels was upwards, but Hawick's long-term decline from being the largest town in the Scottish Borders continued and its rival gained the ascendancy at some point after the 2001 census.

In hindsight, as noted by Jamieson, the start of the development trend in Galashiels predated the railway being on the official agenda – a key example being the ASDA store proposal of the mid-1990s, which as we have seen threatened to block the path of the railway. In addition, the early 21st century housing boom in and around Galashiels was shared by the whole of the northern Borders.

The public transport situation had actually improved by 2006, despite the continuing lack of a railway. In February of that year, the X95 bus service

Simon Longland – whose vision got the modern rail re-opening movement under way – inspects a concrete and steel survivor from the steam age on 2nd April 2010. This pedestrian bridge in eastern Galashiels – crossing both the railway and the Gala Water, and linking the Langlee housing estate with an industrial estate and now the Heriot-Watt University campus – was built in the early to mid 1960s with smoke deflectors to protect pedestrians. Longland is standing on the 'Black Path' which – other than on its viaduct crossing of the Tweed where it shares the solum with the Borders Railway – has been diverted to give walkers and cyclists a replacement route through Galashiels to Tweedbank.
David Spaven

frequency to Edinburgh was increased to half-hourly during the day north of Hawick. The overall bus package nevertheless left much to be desired, with standard journey times still nearly double the fastest train services in 1968; fares continuing to rise above the rate of inflation (at a time when motoring costs had been static in real terms for many years); and patchy quality of service all too often a reminder that passengers were generally regarded by bus management and staff as 'no choice' customers who did not have the alternative of a car.

If the railway was still at least eight years away, physical signs of its impending arrival were soon to 'grace' the Borders landscape. As described in the February 2006 CBR newsletter by 'Captain Cuttle' (a thinly-disguised Bill Jamieson, protecting his Council employee identity), after the imminent demolition of the Station Brae bridge in central Galashiels its £1m+ replacement would allow the railway to pass under the B6374 road, which was being altered as part of the infrastructure changes being undertaken to accommodate the large new ASDA supermarket on former railway lands.

The anti-rail backlash

Not long after the Act passed through Parliament, the railway was to attract its first concerted opposition within the Borders.

Launched in Galashiels in October 2006, the Borders Party had (to quote its web site), 'grown from a combination of campaign groups, business people, community councillors and many others angered by Scottish Borders Council's plans for the region, and its management of local services such as education and transport.' Its attitude to the railway – and not least the 1,100 new houses in the Borders explicitly linked to the project – was clear:

> Everyone was sad to lose the real Waverley line, but the railway to Tweedbank now proposed is slow, cannot carry freight and can only serve a tiny part of the region, and the cost to all Borderers will be enormous . . . The prospect of the railway has already driven up house prices and increased demand for executive housing, a blow against those trying to get onto the housing ladder.

Some of the leading players in the Borders Party had been actively rail-sceptic for some time before the party was set up. In the *Southern Reporter* of 13th October 2005, Christopher Harvie (campaigner against closure, prolific author, and German-based academic, with parents living in Melrose) had responded with his usual eloquence to criticism of the railway by Nicholas Watson, who was eventually to become a local councillor for the party (one of just two successes in the 2007 and 2012 Council elections):

> We are told that more housing will devastate an earthly paradise, but no-one reading Nicholas Watson can be prepared for the industrial dereliction of lower Selkirk, or the car park and big-tin-shed subtopia of west Galashiels . . . The railway will – very quickly – open the prospect of two- way communications, and it will be a dim employer who doesn't see his or her chance in schlepping their factory or office to plentiful brownfield sites down here.

Despite legitimate concerns about the future of the region, at heart the Borders Party seemed to be using the *future* railway as a scapegoat for problems that *already* existed, far in advance of the time when delivery of the line became guaranteed. In Watson's 21st December 2006 letter to the *Southern Reporter* he commented, 'The heart of Gala is already being ripped out . . . What damage is done to our local economy by the attendant superstores? . . . Will Hawick and Jedburgh benefit from more of their residents shopping in Galashiels?'

His long-term vision of the Borders as, 'a place where people choose to live and where investors locate because of our unrivalled heritage and our strong, supporting communities' would no doubt have struck a chord with most rail supporters, but the assertion that, 'we want a fast, flexible bus service which would knock the spots off the proposed railway, both economically and environ-mentally' was a naive view of public transport policy and provision – and of the underwhelming realities of the X95 bus from Hawick and Galashiels to Edinburgh. The Borders Party's rosy view of buses was unlikely to have been informed by much experience of actually using them, nor by any intention of patronising them in the future.

Away from the hothouse atmosphere of local politics, more concrete developments were taking place. The first advance works on the railway were marked by Nicol Stephen, Deputy First Minister, in Galashiels on 27th March 2007 – when the official view was still that the railway would open in 2011. The initial contract was for a 24-week ground investigation programme over the entire length of the route. Within days, however, fresh concerns about the cost of the project emerged in the public domain. On 19th April the *Southern Reporter*, under the headline, 'Rail costs to hit "at least £200m",' followed up an earlier *Scotland on Sunday* story that there had been a further 'shock cost hike' in a technical assessment report prepared by Network Rail for Transport Scotland (a new Scottish Government agency), who were preparing to take over responsibility for delivery of the project from the Waverley Railway Partnership. This cost increase was said to be a key factor in Network Rail's later displacement from the project.

The *Scotsman* of 4th December 2007 revealed the first evidence that the new railway might not be part of Network Rail's national system – an idea that the Waverley Route Trust had pioneered, but not in the form in which it emerged. A report by Alastair Dalton, Transport Correspondent, stated:

> The planned Borders line could be the first in Britain to be run separately from the rest of the network, under radical plans to bridge its funding gap, the *Scotsman* has learned. The Scottish Government is considering whether the Edinburgh-Tweedbank route should be built, financed and maintained by a single company – rather than handed over to Network Rail when it is completed.

Dalton also reported that Stewart Stevenson, the Transport Minister, had said in June 2007 that the funding package 'will not be sufficient to deliver the project' and that the planned opening date of December 2011 'is not achievable'. The revised date for opening was 2012.

More evidence on the ground – and a new political dimension

While the financing of the railway continued to be discussed behind closed doors and debated in the media, further physical evidence was emerging that the Borders Railway (as it had now become officially known) was really coming. The new Station Brae bridge in Galashiels was completed in April 2007, scour protection work was undertaken on four railway bridges in the Gala Water valley, and Scott Wilson on behalf of Transport Scotland were refining a specimen engineering design which would form the benchmark for tendering for construction of the line.

The May 2007 Scottish Parliament election produced a minority SNP Government – the Borders Railway was still supported, but had to await 'due diligence' and the outcome of the Comprehensive Spending Review in October. Once again, delay was being added to the railway timetable.

Following its withdrawal from talks with the Partnership and the successful passage of the Act, the Waverley Route Trust had largely wound down its activities, taking the view that the principal window of opportunity had probably passed. At the Trust's January 2008 meeting it was noted that: 'Due to rail-housing linkage there were increasing amounts of anti-rail feeling, and it was difficult for CBR to maintain campaigning enthusiasm as further time elapsed.'

However, to the surprise of the Trustees – who had been considering winding up the organisation – the Trust soon found itself at the centre of an unexpected burst of renewed activity. Transport Scotland invited the Trust (represented by the author) and Howard Pack of Corus for a discussion meeting in Glasgow on 11th March 2008.

The minutes of the subsequent Trust meeting recorded that, 'The meeting had been very positive overall, with TS indicating support for a number of ideas first raised by the Trust a number of years ago' – these included greater community input; the need for more competitive journey times and for the railway to be constructed with ultimate doubling and electrification as far as Gorebridge in mind; creating a lower-cost double-track junction at Portobello; and provision of a rounding loop and train crew depot at Tweedbank. This was an impressive list – although the WRT minutes did record that, 'the status of these issues varies from commitment to aspiration' – and the Trustees concluded that this meeting reinforced the case for continuing Trust activity.

Meantime, the Transport Minister had made an important statement to Parliament on the project, in which it was announced that instead of Network Rail being charged with construction and maintenance of the new railway, a new 'Non-Profit Distributing' (NPD) model would be used in which conventional

The first significant sign of the coming railway was the April 2007 completion of the new Station Brae bridge over the railway in Galashiels, carrying the Galashiels-Melrose 'B' road – a gigantic structure built by Scottish Borders Council to replace the previous graceful bridge, yet with room for only a single rail track.
David Spaven

construction companies would bid for the right to design, build, finance and maintain (DBFM) the line. The estimated costs had risen yet again, to between £235m and £295m. For a railway that in 1995 consultants Oscar Faber had costed at £18m (albeit only to Galashiels), this was an extraordinary escalation of costs – a topic that is explored in some detail later in this chapter. Jamieson reflected that after his initial shock:

> It became clear that the price range quoted by the Transport Minister had been adjusted forward to 2012, which obviously makes a huge difference with construction industry inflation currently running at around 5% . . . Astounding as the £295m may seem . . . I think there are grounds for optimism in that this number is out in the open and seems to be acceptable to the Scottish government.

Political and media reaction was not so sanguine however. Alastair Dalton's report on the 5th March debate in the *Scotsman* the next day was headlined, 'Fears grow for Borders railway as "untried" funding plan questioned', and opened:

> Ministers' commitment to re-opening the Borders rail line has been called into question after they opted for a funding method untested for such projects . . . In a further blow it was confirmed the start of the work on the line would be delayed at least a year until 2010, and it would not be finished until 2013 – two years later than expected.

Borders Lib Dem MSP Jeremy Purvis had commented, 'I doubt the validity of the funding model and there is no plan B. That is too risky', while Labour's transport spokesman Des McNulty had said that it had become clear that, 'the Government will spend the next three years in the attempt to cobble together a deal with the banks, who will be understandably cautious about investing in an unproven delivery vehicle.' The Borders Railway was to be a test-bed yet again, and the whole DBFM process was to add difficulty, time and cost to the already long-delayed process of delivering the railway to Tweedbank.

The NPD model would, according to Stevenson, 'avoid the high-interest rates of PFI and leave ownership of the asset in public hands' – with project capital sought from the financial markets, and re-paid over part of the asset life by annual service charges met from Transport Scotland budgets – but the paper reported that, 'finance experts said the incentives for private sector involvement remained unclear'.

Transport Scotland takes over – and the Borders Railway goes out to tender

The transfer of responsibility as 'statutory undertaker' to Transport Scotland – which had first been proposed in early 2006 – was finally completed on 6th

August 2008, the *Southern Reporter* the next day reporting that Transport Minister Stewart Stevenson had described this as 'a defining moment in the evolution of the project', removing the burden of risks from the three local authorities, and giving the Government agency full responsibility for the procurement stage.

Campaigners welcomed the switch to Transport Scotland (which had been established in 2006), as the latter was emerging as an organisation of the scale and sufficient rail expertise to drive the rail project forward with greater competence than the previous incumbents. That is not to tar everyone in the Waverley Railway Partnership with the same brush – in the experience of the author (and rail industry insiders) some individuals in the Partnership played skilful, well-informed and unstinting roles in the delivery of the rail project. Keith Wallace, of Scott Wilson, reflecting in 2011 on key reasons why the project was driven through to Parliamentary approval and beyond, commented to the author:

> At the time we were greatly helped in selling this as the best chance of success by the late Ian Brown [Director of Technical Services at Scottish Borders Council], who was experienced in handling politicians, indeed he was often helping the Scottish Executive team with their new experience of having MSPs to deal with. Ian managed to facilitate a council meeting whereby councillors were briefed in advance that the common good would be served by accepting the scheme as preferred and getting wholeheartedly behind it. This was achieved with a strong lead from Drew Tully [then Convenor of SBC] and some well aimed work by Ian and other supporters.

Campaigners would concur with this and other names on Wallace's list – Councillor David Parker, Leader of Scottish Borders Council, who was (and continues to be) a very effective champion of the railway, and Douglas Muir at Midlothian Council who dedicated over 15 years to the project, were key examples. Other individuals also worked with dedication on the project – but overall the promoter was 'not competent' to deal with a rail project, and had to depend, not unreasonably, on specialist consultants who in the case of rail options were evidently not exhaustive in their examination of what might or might not have been feasible. A further suspicion amongst campaigners was that somewhat sceptical Scottish Executive civil servants had been 'pulling the strings' over a number of years, but could readily leave Scottish Borders Council and Midlothian Council to be the scapegoats if the project foundered.

CBR's 2009 AGM was held on 6th January – 40 years to the day since the line closed – and Anne Borthwick relinquished the position of Chair, handing on to Richard Crockett from Galashiels, who had a background in mining and government science. Guest speaker Bill Reeve, Head of Rail Delivery at Transport Scotland, delivered an upbeat address in which he indicated that the benefit to cost ratio now stood at 1.44:1 – although how this had been achieved was not clarified.

The CBR February newsletter also carried an article by Bill Jamieson, exploring how the planned infrastructure provision had improved under Transport Scotland's control of the project. The 'Parliamentary Baseline Design' provided for three 'dynamic' loops (ie crossing loops of sufficient length for trains to cross at speed, rather than requiring at least one train to come to a halt) totalling 15.4 kms out of the 49kms from Newcraighall to Tweedbank. However, the new outline design to be presented to contractors bidding to design (in detail), build, finance and maintain the railway, provided for a total 25kms of loop length, enabling the promoter and campaigners to make the important perceptual (and practical) point that 'more than 50% of the railway will be double-track', allowing enhanced reliability and – given the greater time buffer – the possibility of faster advertised journey times (although still precluding charter train operation for most of the week).

There were further delays in the project during 2009, with the tendering process stalled – as reported by the *Southern Reporter* on 29th October – 'pending discussions between Holyrood and the Treasury over new regulations which require public/private finance projects to be declared public expenditure.' The 'official' tendering timetable was announced by Finance Minister John Swinney at the inaugural meeting of the South of Scotland Forum at Newtown St Boswells on 4th November 2009. Swinney's statement was confirmation that construction would not begin within the lifetime of the current Parliament as promised by Stewart Stevenson, but he had insisted that procurement had been delayed for good reasons: 'The recent unprecedented changes in the economic climate have meant it was not prudent to launch procurement until further market testing had taken place to ensure the project can deliver the best value for public money.'

The formal procurement process began with the publication of a Contract Notice in the *Offical Journal of the European Union* on 16th December 2009. The associated *Prequalification Document for the Borders Railway* seemed at first sight to embody encouragingly visionary thinking about the ultimate role of the railway, and as such was beyond the expectations of most rail campaigners. As well as upfront requirements which met or moved towards key campaign objectives – such as a maximum Tweedbank-Edinburgh journey time of 55 minutes – there was now a stronger strategic perspective underpinning the project, a notable example being the requirement that the final configuration of infrastructure and services should facilitate future improvements such as doubling of the line between Millerhill and Gorebridge, electrification, and extension of the railway from Tweedbank to the south. CBR and the Waverley Route Trust were also delighted to see that 'the DBFM [Design, Build, Finance & Maintain] Contractor will be encouraged and may be entitled to generate certain types of secondary revenue' such as passenger charter train services, freight train operation, and developing station infrastructure for retail and advertising.

The unveiling of this crucial document attracted additional headlines when Transport Minister Stewart Stevenson was asked about the feasibility of ultimately extending the railway back to Carlisle, and responded, 'That's a perfectly reasonable ambition . . . As traffic builds up on this new railway line, I think we will see a case that is much stronger than it currently is for looking at further expansion.' The Campaign for Borders Rail reacted enthusiastically to this unexpected observation, the *Southern Reporter* of 24th December reporting its comments that re-opening the south end of the line would release, 'the huge potential of timber traffic by rail'.

Ironically, in 2009 the only place on the former Waverley Route (other than Millerhill Yard and the Harker stub in Carlisle) where you could see rolling stock on a railway was between Hawick and Riccarton – a stretch effectively devoid of intermediate traffic potential. By 2002 the voluntary Waverley Route Heritage Association had re-laid a first short section of track at Whitrope and operated its first rolling stock movement as part of a long-term plan to create a 'heritage railway' between Whitrope and Riccarton Junction, mainly aimed at the tourist market. However, to some outsiders, Whitrope – far from any established tourist base – seemed a bleak and relatively inaccessible spot to start developing a railway attraction, when by contrast pushing north from Hawick would have been much more visible and accessible, as well as being a useful psychological boost to the idea of re-establishing a conventional railway between Tweedbank and Hawick.

Dialogue develops with campaigners

Buoyed up by encouraging noises in the Prequalification Document – and in anticipation of commissioning Corus to undertake further analysis – the Waverley Route Trust set about preparing a briefing paper on the passenger charter and freight markets. The paper submitted to Transport Scotland in February 2010 took a side-swipe at some of the more questionable outputs that had been generated in earlier feasibility work on the Borders Railway, remarking:

> We do not believe that these relatively niche markets in this very localised corridor
> are fully assessable through standard modelling techniques; at least as important

is an appreciation of the local/regional market, including a qualitative understanding of supply and demand issues.

Other than for timber traffic on the southern section of the Waverley Route, the original Scott Wilson study in 2000 had dealt with potential rail freight demand over the whole route in the briefest manner – just five pages of text in a report of 309 pages. Scott Wilson restricted consideration of freight on a re-opened northern section of the Waverley Route to a market it described quaintly as 'general merchandise', an antiquated term which perhaps reflected a lack of familiarity with the modern freight railway.

The WRT paper highlighted widespread recognition that rail's much greater energy-efficiency than road haulage would lead to 'transformational changes' in the relative economics of road haulage and rail freight, as policies are introduced in response to climate change concerns, and as the energy market responded to 'Peak Oil' (the peaking of global oil production):

> Timescales for these changes remain uncertain, but there is no doubt that they will happen within the timescale of the 30-year franchise for the Borders Railway. It is important therefore that the initial design of the Borders Railway should make as much passive provision as possible for freight traffic, to avoid needlessly inflated costs at a later stage of the franchise.

The paper's analysis of the passenger charter market involved bespoke research into both demand and supply issues (by the author), unearthing the surprising fact that in 2009 there were more than 80 charter train arrivals at Scottish destinations (excluding football/rugby specials and the luxury *Royal Scotsman*). The single most popular destination was Edinburgh, with more than 25 train arrivals, and two thirds of the trains came from English cities. The Trust also explored the arrival day of the week at Scottish destinations, since this was crucial in the context of the Borders Railway, as it was understood that the 'Specimen Design' provided to line bidders only had spare day-time train paths on Sundays. The research results pinpointed how poorly such a specification would meet the arrival patterns of the Scottish charter market, as no less than 51% were on Saturdays, 21% on Fridays and just 18% on Sundays.

The research also encompassed the luxury land cruise train, the *Royal Scotsman*, which operated a variety of 2, 3 and 4 night excursions from Edinburgh to the Highlands and other Scottish destinations. The *Royal Scotsman* had some 160 overnight stays in 2009, with the day of the week of departure being critical in terms of Borders Railway capacity – and again the latter's specification looked decidedly unsuitable for the market, with just 12% of departures being on a Sunday, 11% on Saturdays and 76% on Mondays to Fridays.

The paper made an initial assessment of the likely usage of the Borders Railway by charter trains, based on discussions with charter operators and the *Royal Scotsman*, which revealed a clear interest in sending trains to this new destination and its ready access to the River Tweed, Borders abbeys, Melrose and Sir Walter Scott's home at Abbotsford (where a new visitor centre was planned), plus the scenic attraction of the line itself on its route along the Gala Water. This equated to some 80 trains per annum, the overwhelming majority operated in the months May to October. Subsequent research by the author for the Trust and CBR suggested that if the projected charter train potential could be accommodated in the railway specification, then it could bring £500,000 of new spend into the Borders economy every year.

On the supply side, the paper concluded that, 'the current Specimen Design for the railway could exclude at least 85% of the potential demand', since spare paths would not be available during the day on Mondays to Saturdays, and the Tweedbank terminus could not accommodate the trains (in addition to the normal service trains) or provide a locomotive run-round facility.

On 10th February, Bill Jamieson and the author met key members of Transport Scotland's Borders Railway team in Glasgow, Jamieson reporting back to the other Trustees later that:

> The whole tenor of the meeting was very open, in complete contrast to what we experienced with the Waverley Railway Project people some years back . . . Encouragingly, they are not averse to making changes where this can be done without a significant adverse cost implication and there appears to be a particular willingness to examine what can be done at Tweedbank, as a major redesign is now necessary there anyway.

Another major milestone – the 'Mastermind' clause is triggered

On 3rd March 2010, Galashiels was the scene of an event as crucial as the previous major milestones since Scott Wilson's 2000 report. As the *Southern Reporter* of 4th March stated:

> Against a backdrop of an unprecedented squeeze on public spending, any misgivings about the reinstatement of the Borders railway were quashed yesterday by Scottish transport minister Stewart Stevenson . . . By announcing the commencement of 'advanced ancillary works', worth £5million and including the provision of utilities along the 35-mile route, Mr Stevenson has irrevocably locked his government into the project.

Stevenson had symbolically cut the first sod, accompanied by a piper and veteran campaigner Madge Elliot, thereby triggering the clause of the 2006 Act which stated that once work had begun, the Government was committed to, 'construct the whole of the railway' through to Tweedbank and beginning construction work within five years – unless of course a contrary amendment to the Act were to be passed by Parliament.

The *Southern Reporter* noted the continuing opposition of Councillor Nicholas Watson of the Borders Party, while the industry journal *Rail News* reported on its web site on 4th March that Watson had described the scheme for a line south of Midlothian as 'a colossal waste of money' and that, 'he believes the Glasgow Airport Rail Link, which was recently axed on cost grounds, should have been built instead.' This must surely have been the first instance of a Borders councillor arguing for money earmarked for the Borders to be spent elsewhere! That day's editorial in The *Southern Reporter* was in no doubt however:

> It's time to draw a line under the constant rowing over the Waverley Line once and for all. Whatever people's views on the development, it's coming . . . let's stop kidding ourselves that if the money were not being spent on the railway it would still be spent in the Borders. It wouldn't.

In late June – evidently up to three months *ahead* of schedule – Transport Scotland announced the names of the three consortia (out of five which had submitted formal expressions of interest) which would be invited to participate in 'competitive dialogue' (providing detailed solutions):

- BAM (BAM UK Ltd)
- IMCD (Sir Robert McAlpine Ltd, Iridium Concesiones de Infra-structuras SA, Carillion Construction Ltd)
- New Borders Railway (Fluor Ltd, Miller Construction (UK) Ltd, Uberior Infrastructure Investments).

However, critics of the project would soon have new ammunition. On 26th June – under the banner headline '£300m rail link "offers poor value for money"' – the *Herald* reported:

> Calls are growing for the biggest rail project in Scotland to be urgently revised after a report said the economic benefits of the scheme had diminished significantly. Business groups, politicians and transport experts reacted after the *Herald* learned that the benefit-to-cost ratio of the £300 million Borders railway scheme had slipped over the past three years as estimates for housebuilding in the Borders and passenger forecasts on the 35-mile route had been revised downwards.

The credibility of yet another set of benefit-to-cost ratio figures was perhaps debatable, not least when these were being calculated over a 60-year period, with the *Herald* reporting that the ratio 'had slipped from between 1.55 and 1.75 to 1.2'. A distinct feeling of West of Scotland scepticism came from the report, with Labour transport spokesman, Charlie Gordon MSP, lining up with his Tory opposite number, Jackson Carlaw MSP, to query the railway's justification. Carlaw added that a survey of Borders residents, conducted by John Lamont, Tory MSP for Roxburghshire and Berwickshire, had revealed 'widespread indifference' to the project. Neither Carlaw nor Lamont went out of their way to point out that residents of Berwickshire, far to the east of the Tweedbank terminus, had *never* been a target market for the Borders Railway – and their indifference was largely irrelevant, other than from a crudely party political perspective.

Unfortunately the *Herald* – perhaps still smarting from the Scottish Government's September 2009 abandonment of the Glasgow Airport Rail Link – now had the bit between its teeth. On 9th July, Transport Correspondent Damien Henderson cobbled together a story under the banner headline 'Green case for £300m rail link to Borders "is overstated".' With by now predictable hyperbole, Henderson reported:

> The environmental benefits of one of the Scottish government's biggest rail projects have been dramatically overstated by ignoring the impact on housing growth in the Borders, transport experts have claimed. In a further blow to the £300 million Borders Rail Project, academics and consultants [it was actually one academic and one consultant] accused officials of conducting a flawed appraisal of its ability to cut greenhouse gases.

Professor David Gray of Robert Gordon University was quoted as commenting: 'What is likely to happen is that people's carbon footprint for the journey to work might diminish but it will increase for all other journeys: shopping, recreation and possibly even journeys to school.' But, as the author wrote in a subsequent message to Gray, it was unfair to highlight the Borders Railway in isolation:

> Most rail and road schemes serving 'rural' catchments of the cities will generate the kind of car-based lifestyle problems which you rightly describe, as will virtually every rural housing development – but we don't see the *Herald* or Chambers of Commerce getting up in arms about these!

Despite all the hot air being generated by the media, the rail project continued to make progress on the ground. In summer 2010 Midlothian Council and Scottish Borders Council jointly appointed a transport economist, Jonathan Hepton, to the post of Community Liaison Manager for the Borders Railway –

charged with facilitating the efficient exchange of information between the local authorities (as planning authorities) and Transport Scotland (as the 'statutory undertaker'), and with ensuring that community views are heard during the construction process. Bill Reeve, Transport Scotland's Director, Rail Delivery, noted in *Rail Business Intelligence* of 25th November 2010 that there was a wider strategic argument for not using Britain's monopoly rail infrastructure provider – the evidence that Network Rail (NR) costs were much higher than mainland European counterparts, and the need to see how far an alternative model could deliver valuable efficiency savings, with lessons for other parts of the rail network. What is less well known is that in late 2007 or early 2008 Iain Coucher, Network Rail's Chief Executive, evidently offered Transport Scotland a fixed price contract of £189m to build the Borders Railway. It is difficult to compare this figure with Transport Scotland's £235m–£295m budget, as the latter is a total price including purchase of land etc, which the NR price did not – but NR would potentially have delivered an operational railway by 2011, in contrast to the actual 2015 re-opening.

Corus are brought in again

In August 2010 Transport Scotland released the full Specimen Design for the railway to WRT, who were then able to commission Corus to investigate infrastructure changes to accommodate charter trains and freight. The Corus work identified the scope for commercially viable charter trains to be accommodated – over and above the half-hourly Scotrail service – through the provision of eight additional intermediate signals, but with no extra track requirement other than at Tweedbank, where significant extensions to the terminus tracks and platforms would be required.

Just days after the Corus report had been delivered in November, the Trust's representatives had another productive meeting with the Transport Scotland team, who indicated that it would pass the report on to the line bidders and would examine the scope for 'passive provision' of space for a future small intermodal freight railhead at the Tweedbank terminus, which had to be relocated slightly westwards anyway to avoid a high-voltage electricity cable.

This looked like a very positive outcome from the Trust's perspective, and at its 9th December meeting the Trustees agreed that it should be wound up. Despite the difficult relationship with the Waverley Railway Partnership, the Trust could reflect that over its nine-year life it had appeared to partially or wholly fulfil a number of important objectives in the specification of the railway, including:

- a reduction in the planned rail journey time (albeit still significantly slower than an express service from the Borders)
- a well-located Stow station as part of the core rail specification
- an innovative model for construction and maintenance of the railway
- last but not least, official acknowledgement of the potential role of charter and freight traffic.

The remaining Trust funds were voted to CBR for charitable purposes, principally that of continuing and intensifying the campaign for a 'community' dimension to the railway, including the potential for establishing a 'Community Rail Partnership' such as had been so successful on dozens of lines south of the Border.

Hiccups in the tendering process – and campaigning re-intensifies

The evidently smooth progress of the tendering process received an unwelcome jolt in mid-November 2010 when it was announced that the American firm Fluor had pulled out of the New Borders Railway consortium, and that the latter had as a result withdrawn from tendering, leaving just two consortia bidding. The *Border Telegraph* of 16th November reported that Transport Scotland had nevertheless 'claimed it was not unusual for a consortium member to pull out and works were still expected to start in 2011'.

After something of a lull in campaigning, CBR – which now had an impressive new website, with the topical slogan 'the best possible Borders Railway by 2014' (dreamt up by the author) – redoubled its activities under the new chairmanship of Lorne Anton, who had retired from the rail industry by the November 2010 AGM. Anton continued to bombard the letters pages of the *Southern Reporter*, refuting the anti-rail arguments of the Borders Party, but more quietly CBR also met representatives of the two consortia, seeking to promote a 'community' dimension for the railway, as well as pushing the case for an enhanced infrastructure specification to allow the passenger charter and freight markets to be fully tapped by the new railway.

In late 2010 CBR member Sarah Nelson – a former journalist – wrote two new campaigning booklets for CBR in support of reopening. *20 Reasons to Keep the Borders Railway on Track in 2011* and *Great Ideas and Initiatives for the Borders Railway* were distributed widely to steel support for the Borders Railway among politicians, media, businesses, local communities and tourism agencies in the run-up to the 2011 Scottish Parliament elections.

The concept of partnership to bring the community and the railway together lay behind an imaginative and opportune initiative to save the original Stow station building – one of the few surviving buildings from the original railway – from the threat of demolition to provide additional car parking spaces. In early 2010 Bill Jamieson had been contacted by Nick Bethune, a London-based architect and son of CBR member Andrew Bethune, who was appalled at the potential loss of a perfectly serviceable building dating back to the opening of the North British Railway's Hawick branch in 1849. A site meeting was hastily arranged involving the Bethunes, local SBC councillor Sandy Aitchison and Jamieson. Nick Bethune then designed a new car-park layout, fitting in the required number of spaces without touching the building, and submitted a paper on potential community uses to Transport Scotland. This got a sympathetic reception and a commitment to look at ways of saving the building, and by mid-July 2011 Transport Scotland was able to confirm 'that one of the contract requirements will be to retain the former station building at Stow'.

While who will own and operate the building remains to be seen, there must be a good chance that it will end up in community ownership. A Borders railway museum has been mooted, as has cycle hire and other leisure-related services on the back of its unique location at the station, with adjacent car parking. As rail campaigners – not least Jamieson – had long argued with the Waverley Railway Partnership, until the Borders Railway opens the nearest railway station offering immediate access to hill walking and cycling from the massive Edinburgh market was Dunkeld & Birnam, more than 90 minutes distant. Stow, with a journey time of under 45 minutes from the heart of Edinburgh, would be uniquely well placed to tap a new market, bringing additional custom to the railway and an important boost to the local economy of a village which the railway had threatened to bypass completely.

A bizarre road design saga began in 2010 when Transport Scotland identified an option to put the railway back onto the old Waverley Route trackbed in the vicinity of Falahill (north of Heriot), allegedly saving £4m compared to the alignment west of Falahill Cottages approved by Parliament, which would have involved a very expensive gas main diversion, a long skew crossing of the railway by the A7 and significant disruption to traffic on the A7 during construction. The consequent need for a 'dumb-bell' roundabout, allowing the road to cross the line at right angles, would have the beneficial effect of allowing safe access onto the main road from Falahill Cottages and provide safer overtaking opportunities on the A7.

The plan received support from a majority of local residents, but attracted the ire of some motorists from further down the A7 who objected to increased journey times – averaging around 20 seconds! Transport Scotland got the necessary planning approval, but in a subsequent *volte face* in 2013, the government agency, Network Rail and Scottish Borders Council capitulated to the road lobby and opted for a new alignment with the cottages sandwiched between the new A7 to the west and the railway to the east. It was claimed that this option avoided digging out and disposing of 100,000 cubic metres of peat, but how its cost compares to the previous option remains unclear – and what is certain is that the sheer scale of the new structure and its single-track span width across the railway ensure that there will never again be a double-track railway over Falahill.

Yet more ups and downs

Of all the landmarks marking the coming of the railway which had appeared since the Station Brae bridge in Galashiels in 2007, perhaps the most significant piece of preparatory work – and certainly the most symbolic visually – was the realignment of the 'turnback siding' (for Edinburgh CrossRail trains) just south of Newcraighall station to form the connection between Network Rail and the Borders Railway, completed by early June 2011.

Once again, however, an unexpected hiccup brought new worries. On 16th June the *Scotsman* reported that 'construction giant Carillion confirmed it would not be running in the contest to be the company responsible for building and maintaining the route', and Transport Scotland announced:

> Through discussions with IMCD it is clear they now intend to pull out of bidding as a consortium . . . We have successfully delivered single tender projects before – the M74 which is due to open later this month ahead of time and under budget clearly demonstrates our ability to deliver.

The *Scotsman* had been moving through scepticism to outright opposition to the Borders Railway over a number of years, and its coverage the next day provided a typically negative assessment of the situation. Under the headline, 'Borders rail link in doubt as bidder No 2 walks away', Transport Correspondent Alastair Dalton reported:

> Ministers are to review the future of the troubled Borders Railway project after one of the two remaining bidders signalled it would abandon the race for the £230 million contract . . . The Scottish Government's Transport Scotland agency is now faced with a sole bidder for the 30-mile line, with one source close to the project warning it could call the whole process into question.

An alternative view was that with a single bidder, the procurement process could be simplified and costs even cut through a single continuing dialogue.

Meanwhile, the step-change difference that the railway – with a 50-minutes or less timing from Galashiels to Edinburgh – would make to the quality of public transport was becoming even more apparent to bus users. The Galashiels-Edinburgh bus station timing of the X95 service was slow enough in 2006 at 75 minutes, but successive easings at timetable changes in 2010 and May 2011 meant it now took 86 minutes northbound. As regular user Bill Jamieson commented, 'this simply reflects the reality of traffic congestion in Edinburgh and at least punctuality is now rather better', but the contrast with the last rail timetable in 1968–9 was shocking – the slowest train had taken 65 minutes, and the fastest just 42 minutes.

In an early August letter to Lorne Anton, Cllr David Parker, having met Transport Scotland (but without being able to divulge details) was able to give CBR some comfort in relation to his previous worries: 'I am now much more reassured about the project's future and am satisfied with what Transport Scotland outlined to me when we met.' Parker also took the opportunity to thank CBR, 'for all of the outstanding work that you do in supporting the project', and in dealing with rail critics, in particular through, 'your well written and knowledgeable letters that appear in the local press supporting the project.'

By mid-summer the long drawn-out process of legally winding up the Waverley Route Trust was still not completed, and to the surprise of activists yet another last-gasp opportunity arose to try to influence the outcome of the tendering process. Alarmed by a grapevine rumour that cost escalation was forcing re-examination of the length of the dynamic loops, and tipped off by a rail industry insider that Millerhill Yard was being mooted as a potential electric train maintenance depot, WRT's Bill Jamieson wrote to BAM UK on 12th August, flagging up possible linkage with the Corus work in 2004 on the two-tier service concept and doubling of Portobello Junction.

On the day that the Trust finally ceased to exist as a legal entity – 26th August 2011 – and somewhat to the surprise of its Trustees, BAM expressed interest in seeing the Corus work. Jamieson sent on the 156-page *Delivering an Innovative Borders Railway* report, plus the related review of patronage undertaken in 2005 by the O'Neil Consultancy – which had projected that the Corus timetable would generate 25% more passengers at Tweedbank and Galashiels than the slower but more frequent Scott Wilson specification.

On 19th September the *Scotsman* once again cranked up the negative hyperbole about the Borders Railway, with the banner headline: 'New threat of soaring costs over flagship train link'. Alastair Dalton, Transport Correspondent – a by-now-familiar purveyor of bad news stories about the railway – reported:

The Borders Railway has run into major trouble which will delay the start of construction by nearly a year and could see costs rocketing further, the *Scotsman* can reveal . . . It is understood that the delay has arisen after the sole remaining bidder, Dutch firm BAM, said it was seeking more than the expected £230 million for the construction contract, which would push the total project cost above the planned £295m maximum.

The *Scotsman* had another angle, namely that, 'the latest in a series of delays to the project have led experts to doubt whether the line can be still be opened as planned in 2014. One said: "It's impossible".' Conveniently, all the anonymous 'industry sources' quoted by the paper were pessimistic. Labour attacked the Non Profit Distributing model, but First Minister Alex Salmond was in bullish form when he responded to questions on the railway in the Scottish Parliament on 22nd September:

> The timescales referred to in the media earlier this week are consistent with our programme for delivering the Borders railway on budget and by December 2014. We put the construction figure between £235 million and £295 million and we are sticking to that.

This unambiguous retort – and the continuing commitment to the Borders Railway in the Scottish Government's Spending Review announcement the previous day – provided welcome comfort to campaigners, but, predictably, 'Scotland's national newspaper' did not carry the good news story nor letters to the editor which were supportive of the railway. However, yet another twist in the story soon arrived. On 29th September, in a press release entitled 'Way clear for Borders Railway', Transport Scotland announced that the project was now to be delivered by Network Rail in a new rail industry partnership 'aimed at achieving best value for money'.

Despite the evidence of Network Rail's recent successful delivery of the Airdrie-Bathgate re-opening project, *The Scotsman* went to town on this. In case the front page headline 'Borders rail U-turn sparks fear over costs and delays' didn't give a sufficiently negative spin to the story, the paper also waded in with a sub-headline, 'Claim £295m plan has "hit the buffers" as government drafts in Network Rail.' Yet readers who could be bothered to read the small print of the report would perhaps be surprised to find out that in fact, 'Rail experts believe handing the scheme to Network Rail will increase its chance of being completed' and that the 'buffers' claim came not from an acknowledged expert on rail economics, but rather from Jackson Carlaw MSP, transport spokesman of the Scottish Conservatives – the smallest of the four mainstream parties in Parliament, and a party with a modest track record of support for the Borders Railway.

In the author's experience at the time, informed sources within the rail industry were typically upbeat about this turn of events, citing a range of advantages such as: economies of scale in procurement of construction; the avoidance of overheads like insurance, since Network Rail already had nationwide cover; removal of physical interface problems between two different infra-structure providers; and Network Rail's improved reputation compared to the time when the private contractor route was chosen.

An interesting outcome of this planned change of project leadership was yet another shift in the Network Rail (NR) attitude to the long-mooted re-doubling of the key Portobello Junction, where the existing line from Millerhill (and the future Borders Railway) joins the East Coast Main Line. This had always been a concern for campaigners, as the single track configuration – the outcome of a 1971 rationalisation scheme – limited the scope to run an express service to the Borders. After the Scottish Government opted for the DBFM procurement model in 2008, NR had appeared to lose earlier interest – yet once it had re-entered the Borders Railway frame in September 2011 (presumably after some months of discussion with Transport Scotland), the re-doubling of Portobello Junction once again emerged as a planned NR priority (although the estimated cost had risen to £16m–£19m), this time in the September 2011 *Initial Industry Plan Scotland*.

While the due diligence process was progressing in late 2011 and early 2012, further advance works were underway, including attention to Lothianbridge viaduct and devegetation work along various sections of the solum. On 21st February, nevertheless, a *Scotsman* editorial took its opposition to the ultimate conclusion:

> The Borders rail link was agreed in a shameful political deal by Labour and Liberal Democrats in government, carried on by the SNP. Even at this late stage, the Scottish government should abandon its plans to press ahead with this scheme beyond Midlothian.

Around the same time the draft Strategic Development Plan for South East Scotland went out for consultation, incorporating an intriguing action 'for delivery in 2019–2024' – namely 'Deliver reopening of Borders Railway Line Phase 2 Tweedbank to Carlisle'. The seriousness of this intention was thrown into doubt just a few months later when a planning application for the revised Tweedbank station location was lodged with Scottish Borders Council (SBC). Far from taking on board suggestions by CBR and WRT to increase the flexibility of the terminus, the two platforms and associated platform tracks remained far short of the length required for viable charter trains, and a new car park location obliterated the alignment of a potential freight facility and onwards extension of the line towards Hawick. The unwillingness or inability of the promoter to take on board new ideas to increase the economic value of the railway was deeply disappointing to campaigners, who once again felt that they had been duped, and had been unwise to accept at face value Transport Scotland's evident willingness to explore enhancement of the Tweedbank specification.

CBR activists did not however give up – a detailed comment on the station layout's failings was submitted to SBC, and personal contact was made with a number of key charter train companies to alert them to the opportunity to use the planning process to air their concerns about this market being frustrated, and to put public and political pressure on Transport Scotland. By the end of May, the bungalow built on the rail solum at Stow – which had come to symbolise the lack of strategic vision from the 1970s to the 1990s – was just a pile of rubble. Meantime Network Rail and Transport Scotland were deep in the financial, legal and technical process of transferring the Borders Railway 'statutory undertaker' role to the rail company.

At last, the green light – but new concerns emerge

Inspired by a suggestion from Peter Walker, Operations Manager North of West Coast Railways (operator of the popular 'Jacobite' steam train between Fort William and Mallaig), CBR activist Bill Jamieson organised a delegation of Borders tourism interests – and Claudia Beamish MSP, a long-time advocate for the railway – to visit the Settle & Carlisle railway in August 2012, to sample the impact of charter trains. Fired up by the visit, Beamish wrote to request a meeting with Scottish Transport Minister, Keith Brown, and in October Beamish, Jamieson and the author – together with Christine Grahame MSP, who had also been pressing the tourism case, as had Scottish Borders Council – met Brown and representatives from Transport Scotland and Hugh Wark, Network Rail's Project Director for the Borders Railway, at the Scottish Parliament, to discuss the scope for enhancing the Tweedbank terminus to handle charter trains of a commercially-viable length.

CBR (and previously the Waverley Route Trust) had been arguing the commercial and wider economic case for charters for more than 10 years, and confirmation that their dogged lobbying had finally borne fruit came on 6th November. At a ceremony in the Scottish Mining Museum at Newtongrange, Keith Brown and David Simpson, Network Rail's Route Managing Director, Scotland, signed the contract for construction of the Borders Railway, with train services scheduled to begin in 2015 – and Brown confirmed that Tweedbank station would be redesigned to accommodate 12-coach charters.

This was an emotional occasion for key CBR activists – past and present – who attended the signing ceremony. Not only was there final confirmation that the railway would definitely re-open, but also that persistent campaigning had secured a second key enhancement to the rail infrastructure, following the earlier Stow station success. While there remained concerns about the specification of the new line – including the lack of any spare track capacity to handle charters (over and above the ScotRail service) other than in the evenings and on Sundays – the overwhelming feeling was one of relief and delight. In three years' time, the Borders would no longer be the only region of Britain without a train service.

Growing interest in the new railway was not confined to those looking forward to being train passengers. As STV News reported on 7th February 2013, 'ScotRail have been bombarded with applications from people wanting to be train drivers on the new £300m Borders railway', with no less than 2,229 applications received for 18 trainee posts for the planned Tweedbank train crew depot. With a starting salary of £22,281 rising to £39,204 after training and a probationary period, the financial attractions were clear – but ScotRail was also keen to recruit people with local connections. Driver Manager David Campbell revealed in the company's internal magazine *Between the Lines* that, over and above eight current drivers, "we've taken on 10 excellent trainees – all of them hailing from the Borders, with a wide range of experience in different careers."

Just a few weeks later, the Scottish Government released the final business case for the £294m scheme (at 2012 prices, and excluding £50m in earlier preparatory development costs) – and the prognosis did not look good. The 3rd March issue of *Local Transport Today* magazine reacted to the announced benefit to cost ratio of just 0.5:1 with the comment that, 'This makes the scheme one of the worst-performing major transport projects to be funded in recent times.' Transport Scotland were reported as defending the investment on the basis that re-opening would improve access for residents of the Borders and Midlothian to the Edinburgh labour market, remove 530,000 road trips a year, cut carbon dioxide emissions and reduce road accidents. In a letter published in the next issue of *LTT* on 25th March, this author commented:

> What seems to be missing from the current debate about the Borders Railway benefit:cost ratio is whether the modelling that produced the patronage estimates has taken on board the lessons from the Bathgate, Alloa and Larkhall re-openings – all of which vastly exceeded forecasts. Can we really have any confidence in a projection that suggests that Galashiels will generate only 23,431 return rail trips in the first year, equating to around 70 passengers a day – or just three per train!? Even the utterly underwhelming X95 bus from Galashiels to Edinburgh (journey time 85 minutes) does better than that.

There are of course limits to what modelling can do, and I suspect that understanding how the Borders can benefit from rail-based tourism is one number-crunch too far. Even the consultants who undertook the original feasibility study back in 2000 failed to appreciate the subtleties of tourist potential, and I doubt there's any model that can add 'Sir Walter Scott + Abbotsford + just a mile from Tweedbank station + less than an hour from the massive Edinburgh tourist market' and come up with anything meaningful.

The overall projected patronage of 600,000 journeys annually – which First Minister, Alex Salmond, later suggested should rise to one million – included 60,000 peak hour car trips removed from the roads. Of course, the final business case must – presumably – have taken on board the patronage consequences of maximum journey times being increased, as we shall see, from 55 to 60 minutes. Old hands on the railway could pointedly highlight that the traditional 'elasticity of demand' ratio – a 1% reduction in journey time leading to a 1% increase in revenue – also works in reverse . . .

CBR would soon find – yet again – that there was still a pressing need to keep campaigning. In 2011, as we have seen, there had been rumours that a Transport Scotland cost-cutting exercise would reduce the length of dynamic loop provision, but this only came into the public domain in June 2013, as CBR Committee Member Nick Bethune later recounted:

> Studying the detailed engineering drawings, we quickly realised that the dynamic loops had been cut back from 16 to 9½ miles. Our immediate concern was that with the reduced 'buffer' against late-running trains, there would be much more chance of knock-on delays to other services.

To compound the problem, the new specification involved all eight new road bridges across single-track sections of the railway being built only to provide sufficient width for single-track. The absence of future-proofing – given noises that had been made in the past by Transport Scotland about 'passive provision' for double-tracking – shocked CBR. Of particular concern were the five bridges on the extended single-track section from Tynehead to Stow (see map on final page of colour photo section) where there were few other barriers to future extension of double track. It was clear that any requirement to extend doubling after the 2015 opening of the railway would now involve massively greater costs for bridge widening than if the bridge specifications were amended while the railway was still under construction. Nick Bethune recalled:

> The most obvious candidate for future proofing was Overbridge 41, a farm access road at Cowbraehill, which was to have been double track under the long-loop

On 2nd April 2010, the author samples one of the refuges for permanent way men set into the brick retaining wall opposite Ladhope Vale in Galashiels. This imposing piece of infrastructure was built by the North British Railway following a major landslip in 1916, and is one of the author's abiding memories from his last journey on the Waverley Route on 2nd January 1969.
Simon Longland

scheme. Retaining the option to lengthen the nearby loop by incorporating a longer bridge span from the outset would have offered a prudent safeguard against the possible reliability problems – our own research indicating that the cost would be just a tenth of that for wholesale reconstruction over a live railway.

This short-termism was also being compounded by the construction of key underbridges (over roads) to just single-track rail width on the 'inner suburban' section of the railway as far south as Gorebridge – notably Bridge 16a and Bridge 24a (both over the A7) at Hardengreen and Gore Glen respectively. The cost of ever building second independent rail bridges at these locations would be astronomical.

CBR also found that, by contrast to the skimping on rail infrastructure, the new roads over the railway were to be built to the highest standards, often becoming the widest section of a local road (and all paid for by the rail project). Even more perversely, for the A701 Edinburgh City Bypass a longer structure than required under the bypass was being constructed – to cater for possible future extra road lanes to accommodate growth. Statistics subsequently released by principal contractor BAM Nuttall included the nugget that the rail project was actually paying for no less than 10 kms of new road in addition to the 49 kms of railway. The Borders Railway project has been funded via Network Rail's 'Regulated Asset Base' – sometimes wryly described within the industry as 'the Network Rail credit card' – by means of which NR borrows the money to fund the work up-front and is then compensated by Scottish Government for the funding costs through the agreed regime over a period of some 30 years. By contrast, Scottish road projects are generally funded through conventional public expenditure grant funding whereby the capital costs are paid in the year in which the money is spent.

As soon as it discovered the specification cut-backs, CBR quickly wrote to Transport Minister Keith Brown, but the attempt to communicate the urgency of the situation to him was rebuffed by Transport Scotland. A CBR meeting with the latter and the Network Rail project team on 22nd August yielded 'assurances', but (in Nick Bethune's words) 'no substantive evidence to show that matters of performance resilience, contingency planning and capacity had been adequately allowed for.' As we shall see, there ensued a flurry of correspondence and then meetings in late 2013 and early 2014, before CBR, in the interests of promoting the railway unreservedly in the run-up to re-opening, decided to draw a line under the issue, having made a marker for future reference with Transport Scotland. But with every passing month, Transport Scotland's inflexible specification was becoming increasingly – and literally – set in concrete.

In discussion with the author in early 2015, Councillor David Parker reflected that Network Rail had insisted that the cutbacks were essential if the project was to stay on budget and on time, and that the additional capital expenditure 'could have tipped the business case'. Campaigners might conclude, however, that a slight worsening of the 0.5:1 benefit-to-cost ratio would be a small price to pay for a much more resilient and future-proofed railway.

Good news and bad news for campaigners

Meantime, following a Scottish Cabinet meeting in Hawick, rail campaigners were pleased to read in *The Border Telegraph* of 21st August, under the headline 'Iconic trains to maximise tourism on Borders Rail', that First Minister Alex Salmond had extolled the 'stunning scenery' of the new railway and was 'delighted to announce that talks are now underway with charter train firms to ensure that people have an unforgettable experience travelling along this incredible rail route on some iconic rail engines.' Perhaps predictably, there was not a mention that none of this would be happening without the persistent efforts of CBR and latterly Claudia Beamish MSP. And the contrast with Scott Wilson's unimaginative assessment of tourist potential in its 2000 feasibility study report was marked:

> Apart from Midlothian's mining museum at Newtongrange, existing tourist attractions are not likely to benefit from the proposed rail service, primarily because the other current major attractions of the Midlothian and the Borders are not in the settlements that would be directly served by the line.

> South of Gorebridge the line runs through moderately attractive scenery, and this could be exploited in promoting the line generally. However, the relatively short distance between Gorebridge and Galashiels and the presence of the A7 (allowing

The first main-line train to reach the solum of the Waverley Route since the last track-lifting train passed through in late 1972. Just after 14.30 on Monday 13th October 2014, GB Railfreight No. 66 736 propels the rail-laying train through Kings Gate Points where the new Borders Railway alignment via Shawfair joins the original route from Millerhill through the trees to the right.
David Spaven

Another prize for lack of vision in the design of the Borders Railway goes to Gorebridge station, seen under construction on 6th November 2014. The original Victorian station which survived here until 1969 had double track and two platforms, yet Transport Scotland and Network Rail have found room for only a single track and one platform – now hemmed in by extensive gabion baskets, guaranteeing that any future need to extend the double track section from Tynehead to Fushiebridge (which terminates just a few hundred metres to the south of this northward view) will be an extremely expensive exercise.
David Spaven

The difference between Victorian and 21st century standards for railway construction is brought home in this view south from Borthwick Bank on a wet and windswept 6th November 2014 – with many hundreds of tonnes of stone replacing the original grassed cutting slope. The basic geometry of the railway is unchanged nevertheless, bringing to mind railway author AJ Mullay's apt description of the Waverley Route's "serpentine succession of curves".
David Spaven

Still a construction site on 24th February 2015, but it's clear that Stow's double track and two platforms will make it one of the biggest stations on the Borders Railway – despite serving the smallest community – located as it is on one of the line's three dynamic loops. Sadly, the rural charm of the original 1849 station building is now challenged by Network Rail's intrusive concrete ramp work. Hopefully a 'Friends of Stow Station' group will be set up to nurture the location with creepers, shrubs and plants – but why should voluntary groups have to make good the damage done by Network Rail's insensitive imposition of rigid centralised design standards?
David Spaven

Gala station's single platform takes shape in this northward view on 24th February 2015, with work also progressing on the adjacent new Transport Interchange for buses. Thanks to lobbying by the Campaign for Borders Rail, the maximum waiting time for signals to allow passengers to cross the intervening A7 road will be just 30 seconds.

David Spaven

Work progresses on the island platform at the Tweedbank terminus – extended to accommodate charter trains as a result of lobbying by the Campaign for Borders Rail and Claudia Beamish MSP – in glorious weather on 24th February 2015. The station's setting, with the distinctive backdrop of the Eildon Hills, is essentially delightful – but gains nothing from Network Rail's 1.8m high urban-industrial metal mesh fencing.

David Spaven

Borders Railway Route Infrastructure

Not all structures are shown. Figures show distance from Waverley Station.

Campaign for Borders Rail 2014

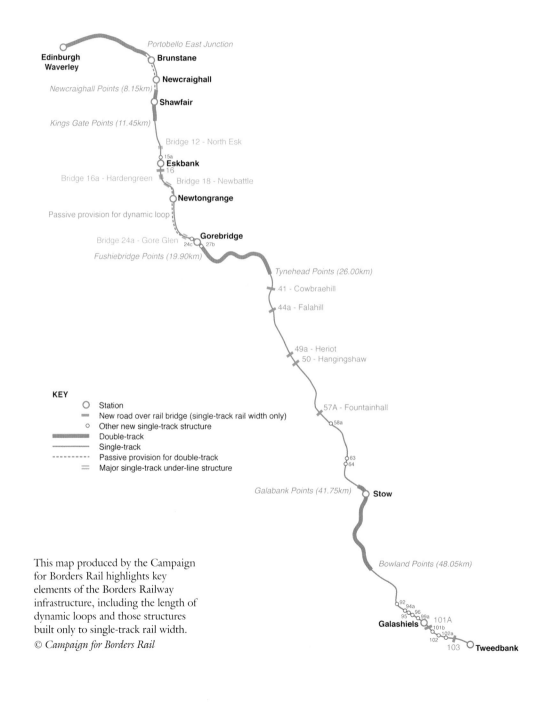

Portobello East Junction

Edinburgh Waverley

Brunstane

Newcraighall

Newcraighall Points (8.15km)

Shawfair

Kings Gate Points (11.45km)

Bridge 12 - North Esk

15a
Eskbank
16

Bridge 16a - Hardengreen   Bridge 18 - Newbattle

Newtongrange

Passive provision for dynamic loop

Bridge 24a - Gore Glen   **Gorebridge**
24c   27b

Fushiebridge Points (19.90km)

Tynehead Points (26.00km)

41 - Cowbraehill

44a - Falahill

49a - Heriot
50 - Hangingshaw

57A - Fountainhall
58a

63
64

Galabank Points (41.75km)   **Stow**

Bowland Points (48.05km)

92
94a
96
95   99a
99b   **101A**
Galashiels   101b
102a
102
103   **Tweedbank**

KEY

○ Station
— New road over rail bridge (single-track rail width only)
○ Other new single-track structure
▬ Double-track
— Single-track
- - - Passive provision for double-track
= Major single-track under-line structure

This map produced by the Campaign for Borders Rail highlights key elements of the Borders Railway infrastructure, including the length of dynamic loops and those structures built only to single-track rail width.
© *Campaign for Borders Rail*

people to make the same trip by coach) is such that it seems unlikely (compared with the Highland routes or the Settle & Carlisle) that many people would travel it simply to see the scenery. Those who do will probably be those who are staying in the Borders anyhow. Some tourists will travel out from Edinburgh 'for the ride' on the line, but there is no reason to believe that they will spend significant amounts of money in the Borders.

CBR's 2013 AGM was held in late November in Hawick, the event acting as a launch pad for its new 'Onwards to Hawick' campaign. At a well-attended event, presentations were made by speakers representing business, tourism, political and campaigning interests, all backing CBR's call for the Borders Railway to be initially extended 17 miles from Tweedbank through Melrose and St Boswells to what until recently had been the biggest town in the region. Speaking to the media ahead of the meeting, CBR Chair Simon Walton argued that Hawick had suffered more than any other town in the Borders from the loss of its railway in 1969 and commented that 'We want the Scottish Government, together with Scottish Borders Council and local authorities from Carlisle and Cumbria to commission a new and broad-based feasibility study, properly taking account of both the strategic and local benefits that reinstatement would bring.'

The same month brought more good news on the campaigning front – Transport Scotland's Draft Invitation to Tender for the new ScotRail franchise commencing in April 2015 revealed that CBR's lobbying for timetable flexibility to allow charters to reach Tweedbank on peak demand day – Saturdays – had been successful. Section 2.6 of the document specified that:

> The Scottish Ministers consider that it is desirable to allow the operation of charter and tourist services by other operators on this route to promote tourism. The Franchisee will be required to facilitate such operation, and cooperate through alterations to its regular timetabled service, at no additional cost.

While it was unfortunate that the limitations of Transport Scotland's infrastructure specification meant that the price of properly tapping the charter market would be dropping the ScotRail frequency to hourly for a few hours on Saturdays (mostly during the summer), at least there might be scope for the hourly trains to be strengthened to give double the number of seats at these times.

Bad news soon followed good. Fears that the reduced length of dynamic loops would lead to 'pathing' time having to be added to journey times – as a consequence of the need to integrate Borders trains into the busy East Coast Main Line in eastern Edinburgh – were realised in November when ScotRail issued its draft Borders Railway timetable for consultation. Transport Scotland's

2009 'maximum' journey time of 55 minutes from Edinburgh to Tweedbank had in fact become the minimum – with 26 out of 33 daily (Monday to Friday) trains scheduled to take longer than 55 minutes. In the reverse direction, journey times would vary from 54 to 60 minutes, with 13 out of 33 trains taking longer than 55 minutes. Given that the RAC Journey Planner advised a door-to-door journey time of 1 hour from Tweedbank to central Edinburgh, it was clear that rail could struggle to attract motorists out of their cars in off-peak hours when city road congestion is less of a problem.

CBR felt certain that the increased journey times were attributable to the cut-back in loop lengths. It decided to focus on tactics which might persuade Transport Scotland to make the symbolic (and practical) concession of building Overbridge 41 to double-track width, as well as flushing out answers on the decision-making process – as a marker to hold Transport Scotland to account post-2015. A further CBR letter to the Transport Minister on 25th November led to a meeting on 15th January 2014, at which CBR Committee members Tom Curry and Stuart Middleton, together with Claudia Beamish MSP, met senior members of the Transport Scotland project team. Transport Scotland agreed to supply copies of the timetable graphs for CBR scrutiny, with this task falling naturally to CBR Vice-Chair Tom Curry, with his 15 years' experience as an operator and business manager in the rail industry. His detailed analysis confirmed that the shortened loops were indeed a problem, but further corres-pondence yielded no concessions from Transport Scotland – and clarity on how and why the specification for the railway had been cut back remained elusive.

In its formal response to the Borders Railway timetable consultation, CBR highlighted a very basic planning error: 'We are surprised to see the consultation document claiming that the first service of the day from Tweedbank is "to connect to the 06:30 Edinburgh-Kings Cross service". There is no 06.30 East Coast service – there is however an 06.25 departure to Kings Cross, but the first train from Tweedbank is scheduled to arrive at Waverley just five minutes earlier, at 06.20. The National Rail Timetable publishes a Minimum Interchange Time of 10 minutes for Waverley – so there will be no guaranteed connection from the 05.25 ex Tweedbank into the 06.25 ex Waverley.' A subsequent iteration of the draft timetable eliminated this embarrassment by programming the first train of the day to run five minutes earlier.

Back on the core issue of the decelerated timetable, CBR had submitted a detailed 'Freedom of Information' request to Transport Scotland Chief Executive, David Middleton, seeking answers to the key outstanding questions on journey times, reliability, loop length reduction and future-proofing. At the January meeting noted earlier, Transport Scotland sought to attribute increased journey times to the busy section of the East Coast Main Line between the east end of Waverley station and Portobello Junction, the slow approaches to which by Newcraighall-bound trains had for many years been a concern of rail campaigners. But of course this section had already been part of the equation when Transport Scotland had set down a maximum 55-minute journey time in 2009.

Transform Scotland – the sustainable transport alliance, and long-time supporters of the railway – had joined the infrastructure debate in November with a letter to David Middleton on future-proofing and reliability concerns, citing the experience of the Bathgate line prior to it being doubled, and leaving Middleton in no doubt as to its worries: ' . . . the success of the railway now appears to us to be seriously compromised by decisions taken to cut back on the scope of the dynamic passing loops and, most recently, to build all overbridges south of Gorebridge to single track only". Transform warned that the railway could open to a wave of criticism, which 'will not be confined to Scotland as the progress of the railway is being keenly followed across the UK and reported in both the railway press and the national media. Under such circumstances criticism surely will be directed not only at the franchise operator but also at Ministers and Transport Scotland.'

Meantime CBR – while keeping correspondence with Transport Scotland 'private' for the time being – sought to keep up the public pressure with a press announcement on the proposed timetable. This reaped dividends with a full-page report in the late January 2014 issue of the widely-read RAIL magazine, headlined '"Significant flaws" in draft Borders Rail timetable', citing CBR's belief that 'most of the flaws "stem from Transport Scotland's decision to reduce the total double track length from 16 miles to 9½ miles".'

To continue the pattern of campaigning success following disappointment, December 2013 had brought news that Scottish Borders Council (SBC) would drastically cut the planned waiting time at traffic lights for passengers crossing the A7 Ladhope Vale from the new bus station to the new rail station in Gala. It had been suggested previously by SBC that waits of up to 90 seconds would be involved, but following CBR lobbying – concerned that long delays would undermine the success of the railway and encourage dangerous crossings of the road during the 'red man' phase – the Council confirmed that the maximum delay would be 30 seconds, in line with Department for Transport national guidelines.

By the spring of 2014, CBR had consciously pulled back from pro-actively criticising in public the sub-optimal elements of the rail specification, but a number of 'arms-length' campaigners – including the author – remained conveniently active on this front; and the press continued to show interest. On 29th April, under the headline 'Borders Railway cuts "could hold back development",' The *Scotsman*'s Alastair Dalton (now being seen in a different light by campaigners frustrated by establishment obfuscation) reported concerns about the shortened loops and revealed that:

> The Scotsman has been told that Network Rail officials raised concerns about the failure to 'optimise' the project to accommodate future growth. This is understood to have happened before Network Rail agreed in 2012 to construct the line, following a failed attempt by ministers to have it built and maintained by the private sector.

As Nick Bethune of CBR commented in a subsequent message to Claudia Beamish MSP and key activists:

> If true, this is somewhat at odds with the sanitised version of events given by TS when we met them, and in their FoI response to us back in January. In the latter they stated that: 'the Network Rail offer to Transport Scotland optimised the balance between infrastructure and cost.' They also insisted that all decisions about the detail of the infrastructure – reduction in amount of double track, lack of future proofing of bridges etc – were made solely by Network Rail in response to the 'output specification' provided by TS and imply that both parties are completely happy with the result.'

Bethune concluded that 'We think it is important to discover <u>exactly</u> what Network Rail's alleged concerns were, by whom the ultimate decision to disregard them was taken, and on what basis (e.g. cost analysis) that decision was made.' Meantime Transport Scotland continued to try to maintain the fiction that there had been no commitment to a 55-minute maximum journey time, despite indisputable evidence to the contrary – and, in the concluding letter of an unsatisfactory correspondence, on 21st July 2014, CBR Chairman Simon Walton once again had to draw their attention to the specific page of the Government body's 2009 Pre-qualification Document for the railway, 'plainly showing that such a commitment was made public at the time.'

At last, rails return to Gala and Tweedbank

While campaigners remained unexpectedly busy on a number of fronts, the construction of the new railway had been proceeding well, aided by generally good weather conditions. A variety of advance works had been undertaken under the auspices of Scottish Borders Council from as early as 2007, with Network Rail taking over in November 2011. Mining remediation works began in Midlothian in October 2012, and the following month Network Rail formally became the "authorised undertaker", with BAM Nuttall (part of the BAM group which had been the last surviving bidder for the ill-fated DBFM initiative) appointed as Network Rail's Principal Contractor in December.

Transport Minister Keith Brown marked the start of construction with an earthworks ceremony at Shawfair in April 2013, followed in June by commencement of a lengthy period of restoration of the mighty viaduct known variously as Dalhousie, Lothianbridge and Newbattle. Visual confirmation that there really would be a new railway terminus in the heart of the Borders came with the start of excavations at Tweedbank the following month. The biggest and most costly single engineering task on the new railway – and one which would have been entirely unnecessary if the Scottish Office's Reporter into the 1986 plan for the Edinburgh City Bypass had required the solum of the Waverley Route to be protected rather than obliterated – began in August 2013 with the creation of a temporary carriageway for the bypass (the A720) to allow construction of a new bridge to carry the road over the new railway.

The failure to make any 'passive provision' for future freight – or onwards extension towards Hawick and Carlisle – at the Tweedbank terminus had underlined the absence of a consistently strategic and imaginative government perspective on the potential role of the railway. At least high-level planning policies were in place to prevent further piece-meal encroachment on the solum, but getting to Hawick – the town which suffered most from the loss of the railway – will be much harder than it should have been, as result of short-sighted decisions made by local and central government from the 1970s to the 1990s. Assiduous research in late 2013 by CBR member Robert Drysdale (a professional planner) revealed – astonishingly – that while in Volume 1 of the new Scottish Borders Local Development Plan for public consultation, Scottish Borders Council confirmed that it wished to see the Borders Railway extended in due course to Hawick and Carlisle, in Volume 2 the individual settlement maps for each of the Borders towns and villages located along the railway contained no reference to its reinstatement, and did not show any safeguarding of its route! Once more, it would take CBR involvement to try to make good the flaws in the establishment's approach to railway development in the Borders.

A major new (single track) rail bridge over the A7 at Gore Glen had been completed in late 2013, and further visual reminders that the railway was coming appeared in early 2014 with the refurbishment of the two tunnels on the line of route at Bowshank and Torwoodlee. The same period saw the installation of the project's longest new (regrettably single-track) rail bridge at Hardengreen – another task which would not have been required had central and local government had the vision to protect the alignment of the railway from the early 1970s until as late as 2000. In June 2014 the A720 Edinburgh City Bypass was returned to its original alignment and, in July, BAM Nuttall began the symbolic task of laying the first solid 'slab track' in Bowshank Tunnel. The progress of the railway was attracting increasing UK-wide attention, and the May issue of Modern Railways magazine featured two articles on the Borders Railway. In the first, Ann Glen, railway historian, covered the construction work, whilst in a 3,000 word piece the author rehearsed the background and story of Transport Scotland's flawed infrastructure specification.

By mid-2014 a new source of regular promotion of the railway story was well established. Stuart Cameron of StuMedia put together *Borders Railway From Start To Finish* – the TV series to record the progress of the Borders Railway from the beginning to the time when passengers would once again travel by train between the Scottish Borders and Edinburgh. Presented by enthusiast and broadcaster Paul Brownlee, the programmes also covered the politics and history as well as providing quirky features and interviews with experts and key figures connected with the project.

Around this time, with some high-level political support, Transport Scotland began privately pushing the idea of a railway-naming competition, but Scottish Borders Council (SBC) was strongly opposed, its Leader Cllr David Parker commenting to the author: 'Although I can understand the nostalgic attraction to the Waverley Line, I think that the current title of Borders Railway, which was arrived at by the Bill Committee during their final hearings on the Bill, is in fact a good strong brand identity and that we shouldn't be seeking to alter it'. Although campaigners views were split, a number concurred with Parker – harking back to the forward-thinking approach behind the CBR title adopted in 1999, and viewing the potential use of 'Waverley Route' or 'Waverley Line' as historically inaccurate since these names only ever applied to the entire 98¼ miles of the Edinburgh–Carlisle railway. CBR Chair, Simon Watton, agreed:

> There is an established brand – and that brand is Borders Railway. It's been posted all over the site, up and down the line, and all over every printed and digital asset issues thus far. It says exactly where the line goes; promotes the best asset of the line. It's a well-known brand, and in the twenty-first century, brands are vital. Do not interfere with it. I can think of very few other railway lines that have a nationally recognisable identity.

SBC maintained its resistance, and the competition idea was then quietly dropped by Transport Scotland, presumably in belated acknowledgement that the Borders Railway had already – well in advance of opening – achieved a level of name recognition which only a handful of lines had secured in nearly two centuries of Scottish railway history.

For several years CBR and others had been promoting the idea of a 'Community Rail Partnership' (CRP) for the railway, based on the encouraging experience of CRPs in England and Wales. CRPs are a bridge between the railway and local communities, bringing together a wide range of interests – including community organisations, lineside businesses, local authorities and the rail industry – along the rail corridor. Their work includes improving bus links to stations, developing walking and cycling routes, bringing station buildings back to life, art and education projects and organising special events which promote the railway and its relevance to the community. Some partnerships have been instrumental in achieving spectacular increases in use of rail through innovative marketing, improved services and better station facilities.

Due to civil service resistance within the Scottish Executive, Scotland did not feature in the first years of CRP development, but in April 2012, Keith Brown, Minister for Transport, had agreed to establish a pilot to which the Scottish Government pledged £150,000 to assist the Association of Community Rail Partnerships (ACoRP) in the creation and operation of CRPs in Scotland, with up to a further £50,000 project funding available to CRPs. After a lengthy gestation period, a formal CRP application for the 'Borders Railway Community Partnership' was finally submitted in September 2014. An impressive range of Borders and Midlothian businesses and organisations had lined up a long and varied programme of proposed activities and initiatives, and there were high hopes that the combination of a CRP and ScotRail's popular 'Adopt a Station' scheme – with station gardens cultivated by volunteers, and appropriate local businesses and services encouraged to develop at and around stations – would maximise the integration of railway and community (to the benefit of both) in a way which the successful but engineering-dominated Airdrie-Bathgate re-opening had not achieved.

In 2014 the personal enthusiasm of First Minister Alex Salmond for the Borders Railway in general, and steam charters in particular, became ever more apparent. In the closing days of his leadership, central and local government, Scottish Enterprise and VisitScotland jointly published A Blueprint for the Future of the railway which announced a pilot 'Steam Train Experience' and market demand analysis working towards developing a regular steam tourist service on the line, partly linked with the planned location of the Great Tapestry of Scotland visitor centre adjacent to Tweedbank station. The presence of this major visitor attraction could in fact prove to be a key factor in boosting railway patronage beyond official forecasts for the Borders stations – with visitors less likely than daily commuters switching from the car to be put off by any service unreliability resulting from the line's constrained infrastructure. Prior to the launch of the blueprint, it had already been revealed that the Gala station platform would be extended to accommodate charters, and that a study would be undertaken into the scope for a rounding loop and turntable to facilitate the handling of charter trains at Tweedbank. This latter-day establishment conversion was an (unacknowledged) tribute to the persistent and well-informed lobbying of CBR and other Borders rail campaigners over a period of more than ten years.

The official Borders Railway web site had long stated that 'There are no immediate plans for the route to carry freight; however, the line will be built to accommodate freight transport in the future'. In late 2014, the author – in his capacity as the Scottish Representative of the Rail Freight Group (the trade association for users and suppliers of rail freight) – was made aware of a potential freight flow to Tweedbank. A Scottish Borders Council (SBC) flood prevention scheme near Selkirk required delivery of 50,000 tonnes of clay in 2015–16, and one of the potential suppliers in west central Scotland was an established rail terminal operator. Despite the constraints of some line structures being restricted to around 20–30 mph maximum speed for standard freight locomotives and wagons – Network Rail were unwilling to release detailed information on axle loads 'not suitable for the public domain', even though this was crucial for the now-acknowledged charter market – the operator concerned saw the opportunity to run trains at night and discharge the clay into lorries at Tweedbank.

Meantime, in parallel, CBR were working up design ideas for 'passive provision' for a modest freight handling facility at Tweedbank (for containerised commodities such as biomass, oil, timber and waste), together with the proposed rounding loop and steam turntable provision. However, initial reactions from Network Rail to the idea of a one-off freight flow were not encouraging, despite this special opportunity to demonstrate a 'can do' approach illustrating the wider commercial and economic potential of the railway. Nevertheless, SBC, with direction from its Leader, Cllr David Parker – and encouragement from CBR – was showing signs of an open-minded and imaginative approach to ensuring passive provision for a permanent freight railhead in the Tweedbank area.

The first of 93,000 individual concrete sleepers – brought in by lorry – had been laid at the north end of the route in September 2014, and on 6th October a specialised rail-laying train brought in from the continent began inching its way south from Newcraighall. Each train carried 24 rails of 108m length (manufactured in Scunthorpe), allowing 1.3 kilometres of track to be completed every day. Early progress was good, with the (modern-day) territory of the Scottish Borders near Cowbraehill reached on 5th November, but when a sleeper broke free from equipment on 25th November and caused serious injury to a construction worker, work was halted, and it soon became clear that the target of completing all track works through to Tweedbank by the end of December would not be achieved.

At this point, those of a more superstitious nature may pause to reflect that the number 6 has a particularly strong relationship with this railway. The Waverley Route closed on 6th January 1969, the Borders Railway contract between the Scottish Government and Network Rail was signed on 6th November 2012, the rail-laying train began operations on 6th October 2014, and ScotRail train services will begin operation to Tweedbank on Sunday 6th September 2015!

In practice, the final rails were laid at Tweedbank station on 5th February 2015, soon followed by the last of the rail-borne 90,000 tonnes of 'top ballast' to complement the earlier road-delivered 130,000 tonnes of 'bottom ballast'. The laden ballast trains – at 2,900 tonnes gross trailing load, 'topped and tailed' with two Class 66 locos – were by far the heaviest freights in Scotland at the time. These were operated at slow speeds due to several bridge weight restrictions, but there was nevertheless some irony in the presence of such giant trains when the railway establishment had – at least initially – set its face against the possibility of accommodating any commercial freight traffic on the re-opened Borders Railway.

Cabinet Secretary Keith Brown himself arrived at Tweedbank on 12th February in the cab of a Freightliner locomotive, for the ceremony to celebrate the completion of tracklaying, in which he clipped the final length of rail into place. Much as campaigners were enthusiastic about the tourist potential of the railway, there were more than a few eyebrows raised when Brown said – echoing remarkably closely the words of Alex Salmond just three months previously – that there would be "few, if any" railway journeys in Europe with such outstanding scenery as the Borders Railway. Had the Minister never been on the West Highland Line, the Settle & Carlisle Line, or travelled by train in Austria, Germany, Norway or Switzerland, to name just a few countries with spectacularly scenic railways? A small point perhaps, but representative of a wider problem – as on too many occasions throughout the history of the project, over-hyped establishment PR trumped robust and rational analysis.

Back at the sharp end, Network Rail's remaining construction programme after completion of tracklaying was based on installing communications and signalling – a GSM (global system for communications) system with 'axle counters' on the track, controlled from the Integrated Electronic Control Centre adjacent to Edinburgh Waverley station – by April 2015. With the seven stations, 600 car parking spaces (including 241 at Tweedbank alone), and access roads and paths constructed in parallel, the aim was to have all construction work completed and the railway handed over to Network Rail operators (and the stations adopted by

ScotRail) by June 2015. Thereafter a three-month period of driver training – to gain Borders Railway 'route knowledge' – would culminate in a three-day opening celebration and festival, commencing on Friday 4th September.

When the official timetable for ScotRail services starting on 6th September was published in mid-April, it quickly became clear that unresolved industry worries about unreliability due to reduced loop lengths had led to a further slowing of the timetable – from Edinburgh, 29 out of 33 Monday-Friday services would now take longer than the maximum 55 minutes to Tweedbank promised in 2009, compared to 26 in the 2013 draft timetable. The slowest train would take 66 minutes (compared to 59 in 2013), and the average end-to-end Edinburgh-Tweedbank journey time of 58 minutes would represent an underwhelming 36 mph. A political decision had evidently been taken to load the additional time buffer to compensate for inadequate infrastructure on to the southbound services, as 'only' 13 out of 33 northbound services would take longer than 55 minutes, the fastest taking 54 minutes. This was making the best of a bad job, the headline outbound journey times for commuters from the Borders being perceptually more important than those for the predominantly leisure / tourist market from Edinburgh. But it was a very far cry from the typical 39-minute journey time for a Tweedbank-Edinburgh express service projected in the 2004 Corus report *Delivering an innovative Borders Railway* for the Waverley Route Trust...

Rail campaigners and historians had hoped that the early September celebrations would feature at least one of the two surviving locomotives from the last days of Waverley Route operations still registered for main-line operation – Deltic No. 55 002 and English Electric Type 3 No. 37 667. However, the 'Borders Railway Opening Celebrations Committee', led by Transport Scotland, was keeping its cards very close to its chest at the time of writing – although it was understood that the Queen would officially open the railway, following the arrival of a steam-hauled train from Edinburgh at Tweedbank conveying 180 guests. Appropriately, special trains operated for the local authorities would convey prize draw winners and community activists on the Saturday – but once again local rail campaigners had been firmly excluded from the rail planning process. From the outside, it appeared that Transport Scotland was too focused on maximising the PR impact for the Scottish Government rather than embracing a wider and more generous perspective on railway history, the role of campaigners and meeting (rather than frustrating) the substantial pent-up demand for charter train access to the railway before the ScotRail service began.

More positively, further evidence that the re-opening to Tweedbank would prove to be an event of UK-wide significance came with the prominent appearance of the Borders Railway in a 17th February report on the nationwide rail revival in the London *Times* – reinforced by a leading article which argued that 'it is welcome news that a section of the famous Waverley line will be reopened this summer.' History was going to be made.

Why did it take so long to deliver the Borders Railway?

By any yardstick, re-opening to Tweedbank will have been a long haul, in particular for those campaigners who were in there at the start of the process. The key trigger for the re-opening campaign was Simon Longland's 1992 report on *A preliminary case for the reinstatement of a Borders Rail Link* – this leading on to the formation of Borders Transport Futures, and then in 1998 to the Scottish Office commissioning feasibility work on rail re-opening. So, by the time the railway re-opens to Tweedbank in 2015, no less than 23 years will have elapsed from the effective birth of the modern re-opening movement to the day the trains start running, and government involvement will have spanned 17 years. How then does this compare with the delivery period for other rail re-opening schemes in Scotland?

The Larkhall line (re-opened in 2005) took 16 years from the first campaigning initiative and 13 years since local government backing began; Alloa (re-opened in 2008) involved no less than 29 years for a similar process (although it was not until 1999 that the complete passenger / freight resumption plan was being promoted by local government); and Airdrie-Bathgate (re-opened in 2010) took 23 years in total, albeit just 10 years since formal local government support. Overall, therefore, the other rail re-opening schemes generally made faster progress than the Borders Railway, but there were important route-specific factors which, at least in part, explain the contrast:

- all three were significantly shorter than the 30½-mile Borders Railway – 4, 13 and 15 miles respectively
- all generated wider 'network benefits' helping the business case
- none had suffered the quantum and severity of solum breaches of the Borders Railway
- none had the complexity of highly-fragmented land ownership of the long-sold solum of the Borders Railway.

The physical breaches of the Waverley Route solum and its fragmented ownership added an unwelcome additional dimension to what was a massive enough task reinstating a long-abandoned railway over a route corridor of 30½ miles. Based on Simon Longland's 1992 survey of the line, Borders Transport Futures had estimated in 1994 that the breaches would add a third (later studies would suggest as much as 40%) to what re-opening would have cost, had protection of the alignment not been abandoned by local and central government in the early-1970s. Scott Wilson's detailed 1999 survey found no less than 26 instances where the solum or station sites had been destroyed or blocked between Millerhill and Tweedbank. This bald total in itself does not convey the scale of the individual reconstruction tasks involved – the worst of which would be the need to tunnel under the Edinburgh City Bypass, crassly built without provision for a railway in the late 1980s.

Bearing in mind, therefore, the particular burdens faced by the Borders Railway project, a rather different verdict may be reached compared to a superficial comparison with the other three completed rail re-opening schemes. While the Waverley Railway (Scotland) Bill Committee was critical of the performance of the Waverley Railway Partnership and the associated delays in the Parliamentary timescale, a review of the points at which the official timescale slipped shows that as much delay came *after* the Bill was passed as before:

- early 2005 – line to open in 2008
- mid-2006 – line to open in 2011
- mid-2007 – line to open in 2012
- early 2008 – line to open in 2013
- late 2009 – line to open in 2014
- late 2012 – line to open in 2015.

Seen in this light, it is clear that the post-2007 Scottish Government decision not to fund the building of the railway through conventional public investment has contributed as much, if not more, to the delay than any inadequacies of the Borders Railway's original promoter. It is not easy to say how much of this aspect of the delay can in turn be attributed to the unprecedented global financial disorder which was unleashed in 2008. One can nevertheless conclude that being the Scottish Parliament 'guinea pig' for re-opening a completely abandoned railway – a key insider prefers to express this as 'the many obstacles intentionally and unintentionally put in the way of the railway by the Scottish Executive' – added years to the delivery of the Borders Railway.

Finally, by 2012 there had been no less than seven rounds of studies and designs of the railway since 1999, and each had been competitively tendered, adding more time to the process. Taken together with the abortive 2008–2011 DBFM exercise, one can speculate that these processes have delayed the delivery of the Borders Railway by up to five years.

Why has the cost of the railway escalated so much?

An overview of the costs projected for the Borders Railway does – at least superficially – suggest an incredible escalation between the first serious analyses in the mid-1990s and the final budget range provided by Transport Scotland in 2008. Of course, the early estimates were essentially desk-top studies and some pre-2008 estimates did not include land purchase etc, so a straight comparison is not meaningful – but one can see how such figures (particularly if not adjusted for inflation) could later be used simplistically by the media to underpin accusations of a 'troubled' rail scheme. Adjusted to 2012 prices, the cost range is as follows:

- 1995 (Borders Transport Futures) – circa £75m
- 2000 (Scott Wilson) – circa £130m
- 2002 (Waverley Railway Partnership) – circa £185m–£195m
- 2007 (Network Rail) – circa £200m (excluding land purchase etc)
- 2008 (Transport Scotland) – £235m–295m.

In its August 2004 report for the Waverley Railway Bill Committee, consultant Oscar Faber had commented that a £129m figure quoted in 2002 had made no provision for 'optimism bias' – an allowance for risk and uncertainty in the estimation of both costs and benefits (reflecting the experience of previous schemes where cost forecasts were under-estimated), whereas a range of 3–44% was recommended by the Department for Transport 'Green Book'. As Douglas Muir – Midlothian Council's lead officer for the railway until his retirement at the end of 2014 – commented to the author in early 2015, 'In the early days of scheme when both the costs and the benefits were emerging, it was difficult to achieve a balance that was neither too optimistic nor too pessimistic as either scenario could lead to the project being rejected by Parliament. Given the limited information available to us without the benefit of detailed survey and design work, we submitted a cost to the Parliament which was, in our opinion, defendable whilst remaining within what might be considered the "affordability" envelope for the scheme.'

As we have seen, in the May 2008 CBR newsletter campaigning stalwart Bill Jamieson penned a review of the financial circumstances, prompted by the rise in estimated costs to between £235m and £295m. He concluded by reflecting on the widespread escalation in road building costs (including the controversial M74 Northern Extension in Glasgow), demonstrating that 'spiralling railway construction costs are not occurring in a vacuum.' Reviewing the situation in 2011, he cited a range of factors which explain at least part of the substantial cost increase – optimism bias, above-inflation rises in the costs of key materials like steel, the diversion via Shawfair, difficulties caused by having to squeeze the railway around the ASDA development in Galashiels, significantly more double track than originally envisaged, and the substantial rise in property acquisition costs resulting from the Edinburgh boom.

Nevertheless, as Jamieson noted, 'the most recent inflationary impacts would go nowhere near accounting for the Transport Scotland top-of-the-range figure, which represents a nearly 50% increase on what Network Rail had come up with.' In fairness to the promoter, certain costs – which could only be identified robustly after detailed ground investigation and survey work had been undertaken – could not be known before the Act had been passed by Parliament and full access to the land corridor permitted. The later cost estimates also include all of the Transport Scotland and parliamentary costs, plus unforeseen costs caused by new environmental and safety legislation. As one informed insider has speculated to the author, the combination of repeated competitive tendering and the abortive DBFM process may have added anything from £25m to £60m to the cost of the railway (including inflation, which is a significant factor over the period of time involved).

Comparisons with the three other rail route reconstruction projects in Scotland (Larkhall, Alloa and Airdrie-Bathgate) are fraught with difficulty, as each had different specifications – but all three suffered from cost escalation, ranging from threefold to sixfold, excluding the effects of inflation. By way of comparison, the projected Borders Railway saw a three to fourfold increase in eight years, again excluding inflation. Major road schemes during the same period suffered similar cost rises, so in practice the evidence suggests that it is unfair to single out the Borders Railway.

In terms of public expenditure, one of the great ironies – given the financial imperatives which drove the 1969 closure – is that overall it would have been much cheaper for central government to keep a skeleton service going between Edinburgh and Hawick over the last 43 years than to rebuild the railway as far south as Tweedbank in the 21st century. Using the Bank of England's inflation indices, campaigning veteran Bruce McCartney calculated that BR's 1968 'Basic Railway' service proposal (five to six trains daily), at an estimated £220,000 subsidy pa, would have cost the taxpayer – with all costs uprated to 2010 values – roughly £267m subsidy from 1969 to 2010. Of course, as we saw in Chapter 4, the BR grant estimates were almost certainly based on excessive costs and highly conservative revenue projections, so the net loss to the public purse has probably been even greater. Richard Marsh may be turning in his grave.

Are we getting 'the best possible Borders Railway'?

Superlatives abound when describing the new Borders Railway. At 30½ miles length, it will be the longest rail route re-opening in Britain – 1½ miles longer than the 'Robin Hood' line from Nottingham via Mansfield to Worksop re-opened in the 1990s, and one mile longer than the Bletchley-Bicester/Aylesbury line due to re-open in 2017. It will be the longest railway of any description to have been built in Scotland since the Fort William-Mallaig line was completed in 1901, and – as the Borders Railway web site (www.bordersrailway.co.uk) notes – it will be 'the longest new domestic railway to be constructed in Britain for over 100 years.'

Little-remarked railway facts are that the 'new' Falahill Summit – at 880' – becomes the tenth highest standard-gauge railway summit in Britain, just 35 feet lower than the renowned Shap Summit on the West Coast Main Line; and that the almost continuous climb at a 1 in 70 gradient over eight and a half miles from Hardengreen (south of Eskbank) towards the summit will be one of the most arduous in Scotland – both important aspects of the scenic attractions of the railway for discerning enthusiasts and leisure travellers alike.

The political significance of the new railway will be profound – partially righting the wrong of arguably the worst closure of the Beeching era, and ending the Borders' unenviable 46-year record as the only region of Britain without a rail service. That is no mean feat, and a tribute to the work of politicians, promoters, consultants, legislators and construction companies – and to the often unsung and always unpaid efforts of hundreds of campaigners, backed by many years of support from the public.

This is a timely opportunity to reflect on whether central and local government and their contractors – the key agencies of reinstatement – will have delivered, in the words of CBR, 'the best possible Borders Railway' in 2015. Enthralling as it would have been to see the whole Waverley Route re-opened, it is hard to envisage circumstances in which this could have been a realistic objective in the late 20th and early 21st centuries. However, recognising that circumstances were not ideal to achieve the most ambitious outcome, how far will the railway delivered in 2015 actually go towards meeting the legitimate aspirations of Borders residents and rail campaigners?

The line's **terminus** at Tweedbank has much to recommend it, being close to significant housing and business development, and crucially – with its ready access to the A68, A7 and other important roads – being a very good location for a park-and-ride station and also an interchange with local bus services (the main rail-bus interchange being in Galashiels). As Keith Wallace, Scott Wilson's Project Manager for the original study, commented to the author in 2011:

> At the time of the 1999 study it was crystal clear that the 'Central Borders Option' with a park and ride station at Tweedbank was an ideal optimisation of capital costs, operational costs and demand generation, and hence would have the best

benefit to cost ratio. It should be noted that both capital costs and operating costs rose steeply after Tweedbank, without any dramatic increase in demand. It would therefore be the best option to get a first step approved, the key objective of the early works.

As we have seen, however, Scott Wilson's report did not evaluate the costs and benefits of a short extension to Melrose only, beyond which lay the overwhelming majority of the breaches between Tweedbank and Hawick. Operating costs would have risen steeply through extension to Melrose only as a result of the all-stations stopping service (requiring an additional train set) and Scott Wilson's failure to evaluate an express timetable from Tweedbank or Melrose, overlaid on a stopping service from Gorebridge to Edinburgh.

In the absence of evidence to the contrary, and given the town's central role in Borders tourism, there is therefore a strong argument that Melrose should have been the terminus of the Borders Railway, but with the park-and-ride function retained at the key Tweedbank interchange.

As we have seen, the **train service** to be provided on the Borders Railway has been one of the major bones of contention between the promoters and campaigners. In terms of the net impact on the market, the main determining factors will be service frequency and journey times. The planned half-hourly frequency for most of the day will clearly be very attractive to potential users, both motorists and bus travellers. Arguably, however, it comes at a big price – in the sense that this generous frequency (stopping at all stations, other than Stow which will 'only' be served by 23 trains daily to Edinburgh) utilises train resources which could have been more optimally deployed in a two-tier service package, with half-hourly services north of Gorebridge and an hourly express (with extra trains at the peak) from the Borders calling at just one or two intermediate stops in Midlothian / Edinburgh.

Despite sections of the route being designed for speeds up to 90mph, the anticipated journey time from Tweedbank to Edinburgh is one of the less satisfactory features of the new railway. While 50–56 minutes from Galashiels will be very attractive compared to the X95 bus now scheduled to take typically 83 minutes to get to the centre of Edinburgh, 54–60 minutes from Tweedbank (an average of 35–39mph) will – in off-peak hours, when there is less road congestion – offer less clear-cut advantages to the motorist, the key modal switch objective from an economic and environmental policy perspective.

Integration of rail and local bus services was a key condition of the Scottish Executive's funding commitment to the Borders Railway in 2005, and Scottish Borders Council (SBC) is providing a strong infrastructure underpinning for this objective with its new Galashiels Transport Interchange, bringing bus and rail stations virtually adjacent to each other. Tweedbank station has also been designed to facilitate interchange with local buses to Borders General Hospital and Melrose. At the time of writing, SBC's detailed plans for integration at Gala had still to be announced, but through ticketing and train departure information in the bus station were anticipated. Likely to be much more problematic are service 'connections', since in the deregulated bus environment SBC has no control over 'commercial' services such as the X95 to Selkirk and Hawick – and the relative fragility of the rail timetable means that train services to Edinburgh are highly unlikely to be held awaiting late-running incoming buses. However, local bus services supported by SBC will be much more amenable to robust connectional arrangements.

The original Transport Scotland specification envisaged use of Class 158 or Class 170 diesel units, the latter being favoured by campaigners because of their spacious feel, with large windows and wide doors and vestibules (the latter features suiting commuter traffic at fairly frequent stops) – but by 2014 it had become apparent that the Borders Railway service would primarily be operated by Class 158s, which have been a familiar sight in Scotland since 1990, and not always a welcome one. Prone to air conditioning failures, and with narrower doors and a relatively cramped interior, they are far from the cutting edge of rail travel, with the *Scotsman*'s Alastair Dalton reporting on 2nd April 2015 on industry experts' fears of service disruption 'when ScotRail's least reliable trains are drafted on to the new Borders Railway'. Units based in the Highlands have however been refurbished, with key improvements being more bike and luggage space and better matching of seats with windows – important aspects of developing tourist and leisure traffic to the Borders. CBR lobbied both Transport Scotland and prospective ScotRail franchisees on this issue, and it was therefore with some relief that the 2014 CBR AGM in Gala on 6th November welcomed the announcement from Abellio's UK Rail Development Director, Mike Kean, that the units operating the Borders Railway would – in line with a Transport Scotland requirement – be upgraded to match the Inverness-based 158s, although timescales remained unclear.

The line's **infrastructure capacity and capability** is perhaps the most disappointing feature of the Borders Railway specification. As we have seen, since the 2000 Scott Wilson report this railway – unusually for British practice – has been designed around a single snapshot timetable of trains.

The cutback in the length of the line's dynamic loops – from a planned 16 miles in total in 2009 to just 9½ miles in 2013 – has contributed to an extension of planned journey times, and is likely to be a source of service unreliability (albeit that timetabled journey times were further lengthened in the official timetable published in April 2015 in an attempt to overcome the reliability issues). Industry insiders are known to be concerned that the 'junction margins' – the passage of time allowed between two trains passing the same point – have been trimmed from the industry norm of three minutes to just two and a half minutes, in order to try to make the timetable work despite the severely pruned loops. Certainly the reduced specification will demand meticulous attention to the management of train operations over the now largely single-track railway. And the strategic error of cutting back on double track provision has been compounded by Transport Scotland's crass decision to build road bridges over the single-track sections of the railway to just single-track railway width. So, instead of cost-effective 'future-proofing' before the railway opens, future extensions of the double-track sections after the railway becomes operational will now be massively more expensive and disruptive.

That this is symptomatic of a wider malaise – although evidently much more prevalent with rail than road schemes – was underlined by the Institute for Government's November 2014 paper on the *Political Economy of Infrastructure*, which concluded that 'government needs to change how it makes decisions about infrastructure policy if these are to be done efficiently . . . poor policy-making processes could lock the economy into inadequate infrastructure systems for many years to come, placing a heavy burden on future prosperity.' Borders rail campaigners could only ruefully agree that 'the UK must better engage local communities, interest groups, experts and politicians in infrastructure decisions.'

Inside sources have indicated that Network Rail did challenge Transport Scotland's cut-back specification before signing the November 2012 contract. However, repeated written requests to Government (including via the statutory Freedom of Information process) in order to get to the bottom of this unsatisfactory story – by, variously, CBR, Claudia Beamish MSP, Alastair Dalton of *The Scotsman*, Transform Scotland and private individuals – had by April 2015 yielded only obfuscation and a complete failure to lay bare how and why the critical infrastructure decisions were taken.

Ironically, some elements of the new railway – far from being skimped – looked 'gold-plated' both to railway observers and some insiders. Any work to do with associated roads fell clearly into this category, but slope stabilisation (such as heavy stone works along cutting banks and extensive use of stone gabion baskets) also looked 'over the top' to many outsiders. Network Rail could reasonably argue that modern engineering and safety standards – also catering for greater extremes of weather, and minimising future maintenance – necessitated a much more rigorous design specification than in the Victorian era, but the contrast with the penny-pinching and short-sighted approach to core capacity issues was stark.

The elegance of many of the surviving Victorian railway structures inevitably contrasts with some highly utilitarian new infrastructure, admittedly with a degree of modern style in the case of some steel bridges – but all too often the outcome has been clunky or brutalist concrete additions to the landscape (usually associated with new roads), reinforced by intrusive installation of 1.8m high metal mesh fencing throughout urban stretches of the railway (and even on the rural side of the Tweedbank terminus). At Stow there was a unique opportunity to create a sensitive modern station to complement the 1849 rural station building, saved from demolition as a result of campaigners' efforts; instead, Network Rail's rigid standards have surrounded the original structure with a sea of unimaginative concrete, the worst of it for large access ramps and retaining walls. There was some irony in the contrast between Network Rail's insensitive imposition of urban-industrial designs on a largely rural railway and Scottish Ministers' eulogies to the scenic qualities of the Borders Railway. However, the prospect that insult would be added to injury was averted when, in mid-April 2015, it emerged that although a projecting gable and window of Stow station building were up to 300mm foul of the current minimum required clearance from the platform edge, Network Rail had undertaken to dismantle the whole gable wall and re-erect it, set back by 300mm, so the appearance of the original building would not change materially. But no-one had seen fit to contact Stow Community Trust, whose interest in the building had long been well known to NR.

One infrastructure omission beyond the Borders Railway, but with a strong bearing on it – which will hopefully be remedied in association with the planned stabling of new Edinburgh-Glasgow electric train sets at Millerhill Yard – is the long-mooted double-tracking of the 'single lead' Portobello Junction and an associated increase in train speeds. This would have wider network benefits as well as helping to minimise knock-on service reliability/journey time impacts of Transport Scotland's cut-back in the Borders Railway specification.

In the earlier years of infrastructure planning within the wider rail project, the complete failure of the Waverley Railway Partnership to recognise the charter market opportunity provided a classic illustration of the difficult position that rail campaigners had been put in. As a consequence of a promoter who did not understand railways (not unreasonably, given the geography and history), and a group of consultants working for the promoter who did not always appreciate the subtleties of the territory they were dealing with – or did not have the freedom to do so, subject, as they were, to the control being exerted by the Scottish Executive – CBR and the Waverley Route Trust had no choice but to criticise the railway being offered.

It was not until the eleventh-hour intervention by Transport Minister Keith

Brown in 2012 that the convincing intelligence on the charter market gathered by unpaid research volunteers for campaigning groups was finally acknowledged. Now we can look forward to connecting coaches (with integrated ticketing) linking Tweedbank station with the nearby Abbotsford home of Sir Walter Scott, and Melrose Abbey – likely to be of great appeal to the massive Edinburgh tourist market, as well as the customers of charter trains from England and Scotland, not to mention the luxury *Royal Scotsman*.

Overall, what is the verdict on the Borders Railway that opens to the public in 2015? Any railway is vastly better than no railway – and the train will certainly transform the quality of public transport between the western end of the Central Borders, Midlothian and Edinburgh – but its ability to compete with the car is less certain. For the author – based on over 45 years as a rail campaigner and over 40 working in and around the rail industry – the current specification now gets 6 marks out of 10, having slipped further in his estimation after the confirmed cut-back in double-track provision and associated failure to fully future-proof the infrastructure. Of course, there is always the prospect of future enhancement (including electrification – which has been allowed for – providing superior acceleration away from station stops and speed restrictions, and up gradients) and even extension, economic and political circumstances permitting. But upgrading an operational railway will be vastly more complex and costly than doing the work before the trains started running.

CHAPTER ELEVEN

Looking back and forward

It does not need the benefit of hindsight to argue that Transport Minister Richard Marsh should have reprieved the Waverley Route north of Hawick in the summer of 1968. But travelling on the dismal X95 bus service from Edinburgh to Galashiels and Hawick 47 years later, the public transport user can have no doubts that a grave regional injustice was inflicted on the Central Borders. Before considering what the new Borders Railway may do for the region, it is a sobering exercise to speculate on what kind of reprieved railway would have emerged if Marsh had made the right decision, and what contribution it might now have been making to the Borders economy and way of life.

What might have been

The 'Basic Railway' option rejected by Marsh would almost certainly have formed the initial template for a new timetable commencing in May 1969, with five or six trains a day – on a regular interval basis – linking just Hawick, St Boswells, Melrose and Galashiels with Edinburgh. With a consistent fast journey time to the heart of the city, even this relatively infrequent timetable would have provided a decent starting point for reviving the railway's fortunes, particularly with proper marketing of its scenic and tourist attractions. The track would have been singled south of Lady Victoria Colliery (and after the closure of the latter, south of Millerhill Yard) – a sensible economy – retaining one or two crossing loops to accommodate the normal timetable, with some flexibility for late running and for a local freight service which would probably have survived into the early 1980s. By the time freight disappeared the remaining spare capacity on the Borders railway would have begun to be taken up by the burgeoning national market for tourist charter trains, with 'Walter Scott country' and Melrose Abbey a natural draw.

Ironically, a reprieve north of Hawick might eventually have allowed a heavily scaled-down version of the Border Union Railway Company (BURCo) initiative to succeed. With an ongoing BR rail connection to the north from Edinburgh (and its major and expanding visitor market) – and proximity to the advancing M6 motorway and the growing tourist 'honeypot' of the Lake District to the south – the 21 route miles through the dramatic country from Hawick to Newcastleton could have been turned into a successful volunteer-led steam railway. And with an eye on future prospects (for through excursion trains from the West Coast Main Line, timber from the vast maturing harvests in the Kershope, Kielder, Newcastleton and Wauchope forests, and aggregates and cement for the construction of the largest reservoir in Britain at Kielder Water), might BR even have been persuaded in 1969 to retain a single mothballed connecting track over the 36 miles from Longtown to Hawick – initially for diversionary use during the 1970–74 electrification, relaying and resignalling of the West Coast Main Line?

Looking at the experience of other railways radiating from Edinburgh, the 1970s and 1980s would certainly have brought expansion and enhancement of a Borders rail service. One can envisage a new Tweedbank station being funded by Borders Regional Council in the mid-1970s to serve the housing and industrial development advocated by the 1968 Central Borders Plan. By the mid-1980s the train service frequency would have increased to hourly (at least north of Galashiels), and – as part of the Lothian Regional Council policy of 'buying' extra train services through grant funding more stations – new calls at Eskbank, Gorebridge and Newtongrange would doubtless have been added to support new housing and associated commuting to an increasingly road-congested Edinburgh.

The introduction of 'second generation' diesel multiple units (or 'Sprinters' as they were originally called) would have enabled a significant speed-up in the late 1980s, with the journey from Hawick to Edinburgh taking just over an hour, half the time taken by the residual bus service labouring up the A7. Track redoubling from Millerhill to Gorebridge – to accommodate the increased frequency of an 'inner suburban' service – might well have been followed by electrification, as an add-on to the 1991 East Coast Main Line scheme.

New trains and increased frequencies to Hawick would undoubtedly have helped British Rail to market leisure and tourist travel to the Borders, with integrated 'Days Out' fares taking rail passengers around the Borders Abbeys by vintage coach from Melrose station. To complement the regular timetabled service, charter trains would have been finding their way with increasing frequency to the Borders. If Hawick to Newcastleton had survived as a heritage railway (with freight south of Riccarton) and Newcastleton to Longtown as a low-cost BR operation, then a classic charter operation to rival the appeal of the Highlands would have been from English cities over the Settle & Carlisle line then via Hawick and Melrose drop-off points to Edinburgh.

As congestion and house prices in Edinburgh continued to grow disproportionately to other areas, it is clear that a rail-connected Central Borders would have become an increasingly attractive location from which to commute to Edinburgh. Initially this might have impacted noticeably on the railway only at re-opened stations in Midlothian and at Galashiels, Tweedbank and Melrose, but with a late 1980s speed-up and increased frequency – in line with experience elsewhere in Scotland – St Boswells (as a railhead for Kelso) and even Hawick would have begun to see significant growth in peak-hour train use.

The presence of the continuing BR rail link to Edinburgh and a BURCo steam operation to Newcastleton would have allowed Hawick to develop a more robust tourist sector, better placed to withstand the calamitous swathe of textile factory closures in the late 1990s. Hawick might well have retained its position as the largest town in the Borders, with a greater concentration of services and facilities than it now has, following the rise of Galashiels. Long-term population decline in Hawick could have been stemmed by the ongoing availability of the railway, and the region's ageing population profile would have benefitted from the wider education, leisure and work opportunities afforded to younger people by a fast and convenient rail service.

For Newcastleton, which arguably suffered the worst from the 1969 closure, the combination of a BURCo tourist passenger operation, a local timber railhead, and eventually the arrival of tourist charter trains from the south, would have helped this small settlement to survive the loss of its regular passenger train service.

But, tantalising as it is to speculate on 'what if ', a much more important consideration is the likely practical impact of the reopening of just over a third of the old Waverley Route, so that the Borders will no longer be the only region of Britain without a rail service.

A new chapter of Borders history begins in 2015

While the transport benefits which the Borders Railway will deliver are clear, its genesis was very much as an economic regeneration project, and the line's promoters have always emphasised the wider benefits which the railway will bring to the region. In a September 2005 public briefing document produced for Scottish Borders Council (SBC), the key message about the Waverley Railway Project (as it was then known) reflected this perspective:

> The reintroduction of the railway will assist in tackling social exclusion in the Scottish Borders and Midlothian, by providing an effective public transport link to enable residents of these areas to access employment, education, health and leisure opportunities. It will allow both areas to maximise their economic development opportunities. It will facilitate new housing, including affordable housing, and help in combating the overheated Edinburgh housing market. It will also tackle congestion and assist in addressing the Lothians' predicted labour market shortfall of 18,500 people by 2015 . . . Once the railway is established, employment is

247

estimated to increase across the three areas by between 207 jobs and 548 jobs, plus construction jobs arising from new housing and from building the railway.

So will the Borders Railway deliver? As seen in Chapter 10, the line – whatever its shortcomings – will certainly transform transport between the Central Borders and Edinburgh. Experience from other Scottish rail re-openings – and the particular opportunities for tourist and leisure traffic on this route – suggests that the trains will be very popular and encourage a significant shift from road to rail. The advantages of the train will be most pronounced for existing bus users, particularly in Galashiels, Stow and Tweedbank, where public transport to Edinburgh has, since 1969, taken longer than it did in 1910. But with purpose-designed bus-rail interchange facilities, people in Hawick, Melrose and Selkirk will also benefit from significantly faster public transport journeys than the current end-to-end bus times. With 20% of Borders households not owning a car, and a significantly higher proportion in the Galashiels and Hawick populations, this will be a step-change in terms of social inclusion.

Park-and-ride at Tweedbank and Stow will give motorists significantly faster peak-hour journeys to Central Edinburgh than using the car throughout – and the train will provide a less stressful travel experience, toilet facilities, and no requirement to find a city centre parking space. The relative advantage of the train for motorists will probably be greater in Midlothian, since the railway will be providing a reliable alternative to journeys predominantly over busier roads. The train will also significantly better journey times to central Edinburgh by bus, which can be chronically affected by city congestion and peak-hour queues at the notorious Sheriffhall roundabout on the city bypass.

But modal shift is only part of the planned outcome – the bigger aspiration is that Borders and Midlothian residents will enjoy new travel opportunities (including younger people who may no longer need to move home to access work and education opportunities), and that more people will be encouraged to move home to these areas. More and/or longer journeys, in some cases switching to entirely new destinations for work, education, leisure and shopping purposes, can be seen as a social and economic benefit – but perhaps not as an environmental gain.

Douglas Muir, formerly of Midlothian Council, pointed out to the author in early 2015:

At present it's extremely difficult to get direct public transport from Midlothian to Queen Margaret University and various retail outlets at Newcraighall – the railway will open up new travel opportunities here, and also for Edinburgh College students between the two campuses at Eskbank and Brunstane.

Such markets – like tourism – have not lent themselves to patronage modelling techniques. It is also arguable that tourists and leisure visitors will be more tolerant of any service unreliability (and/or extended journey times, as in the timetable published in April 2015) resulting from the cutback of the line's infrastructure specification than will core commuting markets. This – and as sound as possible a service in the critical first weeks after re-opening – could make a significant contribution to the success of the Borders Railway, and in turn to the prospects of extending southwards to Hawick.

While most attention has focused on northbound morning commuting to destinations in Midlothian, Edinburgh and beyond, 'reverse' flows will offer an important opportunity to fill up otherwise empty seats on trains. Probably the biggest potential southbound market will be leisure / tourist travel to the Scottish Mining Museum at Newtongrange and a variety of Borders attractions – including Sir Walter Scott's Abbotsford and the Great Tapestry of Scotland – accessible from Tweedbank station by local bus, bike or foot. Given Edinburgh's massive visitor base, plus the significant resident population with ready access to Haymarket, Waverley and other stations, it will be a disappointment if the railway does not attract a substantial number of new visitors to the line's environs, with associated economic benefits. It will be ironic indeed if inbound tourist traffic to the Borders – which was largely dismissed by the original Scott Wilson feasibility study – proves to be a crucial rail traffic generator.

Turning to linkage with the most sustainable forms of transport, the standard ScotRail service – enhanced to form part of the 'Great Scenic Railways of Scotland' initiative announced as part of the new franchise which began on 1st April 2015 – should, in conjunction with the planned Borders Railway Community Partnership, allow walking and cycling to become a valuable source of patronage for the railway. The stations at Stow, Galashiels and Tweedbank will offer ready access to a wide range of hill walking routes, including the Southern Upland Way and St Cuthbert's Way, as well as designated long-distance cycle routes. However, the new railway has obliterated most of the 'Black Path' over four miles of the former railway solum from the north end of Galashiels to Tweedbank. Only over the 'Red Bridge' across the Tweed at Tweedbank will railway and path continue to share the same corridor – a disappointing loss reflecting the risk-averse nature of the modern railway, despite its vastly superior safety record over road transport.

One of the wider lessons of the last 16 years – with implications for future rail re-opening schemes – is that if the line promoter (with its understandable conservatism, wanting to present a robust business case) had been more willing to enter a constructive dialogue with campaigners (with their instinctive optimism about the benefits of scheme enhancements), then an emerging consensus and sense of compromise could well have yielded an improved rail specification, and the project would have attracted significantly less criticism than it has done. Reflecting on CBR's difficult relationship with Transport Scotland over the previous several years, campaigner Nick Bethune commented in early 2015:

> This project has inevitably involved compromises, but the lack of openness has been depressing. If Transport Scotland hadn't worked so hard to cover up the fact that compromises needed to be made to get the thing built, then there would have been a lot more understanding from campaigners – and the possibility of discussion about what those compromises should have been.

However, local rail campaigners – notably CBR, Stow Station Supporters Group and the Waverley Route Trust – can take credit for some important successes, a number of them secured in spite of initially implacable opposition from establishment forces:

- first coining the 'Borders Railway' name
- incorporation of a station stop at Stow
- saving of the original 1849 station building at Stow
- the Tweedbank track layout redesigned to take 12-coach charter trains
- the new ScotRail franchisee required to accommodate paths for charters in the service timetable
- maximum waiting time at the pedestrian crossing of the A7 from the bus to rail stations in Gala cut from 90 to 30 seconds
- the first train of the day to Edinburgh retimed to provide a robust connection into the 06.25 service to London
- Class 158 trains to be refurbished to provide better window/seat matching and enhanced luggage/cycle space.

Two other enhancements, initiated by Midlothian Council, were also warmly welcomed by campaigners – a direct staircase from Lady Brae to the south end of Gorebridge station platform, improving the walk-in catchment from new housing developments, and a direct path from Newtongrange station to the National Mining Museum.

As we have seen, given the very long period since campaigning began, some of the early enthusiasm for the new line inevitably waned between the 2006 Act of Parliament and the 2012 construction contract signing, not helped by regular jibes about the 'ill-fated' or 'troubled' Borders Railway in Scotland's two quality newspapers. Abusing a Borders tradition of inter-town rivalry, Conservative MSP John Lamont even stooped to describing the scheme as 'the Galashiels Railway Project' – ignoring the very real benefits it will bring, through connecting bus services and park-and-ride facilities, to people in Hawick, Melrose, Selkirk, St Boswells and beyond. Might the new railway act in fact as a catalyst for a pan-Borders vision for the future, eschewing the worst aspects of the old local rivalries which arguably undermined the original campaign against closure of the Waverley Route?

The period from 2012 to 2015 saw all the physical evidence of one of the most remarkable rail projects in modern British history. A workforce peaking at 1,100 on any one day transformed 30½ miles of abandoned solum, 137 bridges (95 refurbished and 42 newly constructed) and two tunnels into a civilised, safe and sustainable transport link which will partially put right one of the great wrongs of the old model of London-based transport policy. This is an astonishing achievement for a prospect which was dismissed by all but a handful of rail visionaries 21 years ago.

Bibliography and Sources

Abbott, S and Whitehouse, A *The Line that Refused to Die* (Leading Edge, 1994)

Bort, E and Hart, T (Editors) *The Borders & The Waverley Route: Transport Problems and Solutions for an Excluded Region* (International Social Sciences Institute, 1999)

Bonavia, M, *The History of the LNER, The First Years 1922–33* (George Allen & Unwin 1982)

British Railways Board *The Reshaping of British Railways* (HMSO, 1963)

Brodribb, J *An Illustrated History of the East Suffolk Railway* (Oxford Publishing Company, 2004)

Bytheway, D *Back on track: the story of the Alloa railway network from the early wagon ways to the rebirth of the line* (Clackmannanshire Field Studies Society, 2008)

Campaign for Borders Rail, Briefing/Newsletter, No's 1 (Jan 1999) to 40 (2011)

Caplan, N *The Waverley Route* (Ian Allan 'Railway World Special', 1985)

David Block Associates *Border Union Railway Co. Ltd Feasibility Study* (privately published, 1969)

Fiennes, GF *I tried to run a railway* (Ian Allan, 1967)

Gourvish, T *British Railways 1948–73: A Business History* (Cambridge University Press, 1986)

Hardy, RHN *Beeching: Champion of the Railway?* (Ian Allan, 1989)

Henshaw, D *The Great Railway Conspiracy* (Leading Edge, 1994)

Hibbs, J *Transport in the Borders* (privately published, 1968)

Hillman, M and Whalley, A *The Social Consequences of Rail Closures* (Policy Studies Institute, 1980)

Hodge, J The District Controller's View No.8: *Edinburgh-Hawick-Carlisle (the Waverley Route)*, Xpress Publishing, 2010

Loft, C. *Government, the Railways and the Modernization of Britain: Beeching's Last Trains* (Routledge, 2006)

Mackenzie, RF *A Search for Scotland* (Collins, 1989)

Marsh, R *Off the Rails: An Autobiography* (Weidenfield and Nicolson, 1978)

Mullay, AJ *Rails across the Border* (Patrick Stephens, 1990)

Mullay, AJ *Scottish Region: A History 1948–1973* (Tempus, 2006)

Mullay, A.J. *The Railway Race to Scotland 1901* (Moorfoot Publishing, 1987)

Peacock, B *Border Railway Portfolio* (Cheviot Publications, 1982)

Ransom, PJG *Iron Road: the Railway in Scotland* (Birlinn, 2007)

Robotham, R *The Waverley Route: The Postwar Years* (Ian Allan, 1999)

Scottish Development Department / University of Edinburgh *The Central Borders: A Plan for Expansion* (HMSO, 1968)

Siviter, R *Waverley: Portrait of a famous route* (Runpast, 1996)

Steel, D *Against Goliath: David Steel's Story* (Weidenfeld & Nicolson, 1989)

StuMedia, *Borders Railway From Start To Finish – the TV series*, www.bordersrailway.info

The *Railway Observer* (Railway Correspondence & Travel Society, various 1966) from the
Bill Lynn archive

Thomas, J *A Regional History of the Railways of Great Britain, Volume 6 Scotland: The
Lowlands and the Borders* (David & Charles, 1984 revised edition by Alan JS Paterson)

White, HP *Forgotten Railways* (David & Charles, 1986)

Whittle, G *The Newcastle & Carlisle Railway* (David & Charles, 1979)

Wolmar, C *Fire & Steam* (Atlantic Books, 2007)

Public archive sources:

The undernoted files are held by the **National Records of Scotland** (formerly the National
Archives of Scotland) in Edinburgh (reference BR for British Railways Scottish Region; DD
for the Scottish Office Development Department; GD for the North British Railway Study
Group archive; SEP for the Scottish Economic Planning Council; SOE for the Scottish Office
Home & Health Department).

BR/RSR/4/1412 (1993–68) Management papers including copies of objectors' letters

BR/RSR/4/2087 (1964) Inverness-Kyle objectors' letters

BR/RSR/4/2243 (1964) Inverness-Wick/Thurso objectors' letters

BR/RSR/4/2025 (1968) North Berwick line closure papers

DD12/3464 (1966–79)

DD17/556 (1967–68)

DD17/822 (1966–68)

DD17/1139-40 (1966–67)

DD17/1192 (1966–67)

DD17/1410 (1963–67)

DD17/1476 (1964–66)

DD17/1752 (1966–68)

DD17/1753 (1966-68)

DD17/1478 (1968-70)

DD17/531-2 (1965-66)

GD536/8031 (1937 Galashiels resignalling diagram)

GD536/8035 (Waverley Route closure: folder of BR and other documents)

GD536/8055 (folder of papers re Carlisle railways in BR period)

GD536/8081 (1963 BR Scottish Region paper on trunk freight train haulage costs)

SEP5/2 (1963–67)

SEP16/4 (1967–68)

SEP16/58 (1968–69)

SEP17/168 (1968)

SOE12/207 (1968)

The undernoted files are held by the National Archives in London (Kew)

AN 155/98: TUCC reports from 1966

AN169/108: 1969–70 BR correspondence with Border Union Railway Company.

CAB 134/2765: Meeting No 4 (08/04/1968), Paper 1; Meeting No 7 (21/05/1968),

Papers 24 and 25 – both meetings of the Ministerial Committee on Environmental Planning.

CAB 134/2766: Papers 17, 18, 24 and 25 – memoranda for the meetings of 08/04/68 and 21/05/68.

HC/OF/S5/768: Hansard record of Richard Marsh's statement to the House of Commons on consent to closure, 15/07/68.

PREM 13/2366: 1968 correspondence between Willie Ross and Harold Wilson.

PREM 13/2431: 1968 correspondence between Ministers and Harold Wilson on railway closures.

Private archive sources:

Ian Bell

Andrew Boyd

The late Baroness Elliot of Harwood (courtesy of Alan Bailey)

Ian Holoran

Bill Jamieson

Bill Lynn

Bruce McCartney

Rae Montgomery (now held as part of the North British Railway Study Group archive at the National Records of Scotland in Edinburgh – reference GD536/8035)

Roy Perkins

David and the late Frank Spaven

Index